Introduction to International Human Rights Law

Curtis F.J. Doebbler

CDP
CDPublishing

Introduction to
International Human Rights Law
Curtis F.J. Doebbler

Published and Distributed by
CD PUBLISHING
Washington, DC, USA
Fax: +1-206-984-4734
Email: cdpublishing@publicist.com
http://cdpublishing.filetap.com

© CD Publishing
First Edition 2006
Revised Reprinting 2007

ISBN: 978-0-9743570-2-7 (pbk)
Stock number: HRCBK0012 (ebook)

Printed in the United States of America, Palestine, Uzbekistan, and India on acid free paper meeting ANSI/NISO Z39.48-1992 paper quality standards.

Generic Cataloguing Data:
Doebbler, Curtis, F.J. 1961-
    i-xv/253 pp, 12.7 cm X 17.78 cm
    Introduction to International Human Rights Law/ by C.F.J. Doebbler
    Includes index, glossary, models.
    Library of Congress Classification: K3240 .D6 2004
    Dewey Decimal Classification: 341.48 — dc22
    Keywords: 1. international human rights law, 2. law, 3. human rights,
    4. international relations, 5. politics, I. Title

Library of Congress Control Number: 2006920739

Introduction to International Human Rights Law

Curtis F.J. Doebbler
Professor of Law
An-Najah National University

CD Publishing

Summary Table of Contents

Table of Contents

Abbreviations

ACHR	American Convention on Human Rights
ADRDM	American Declaration of the Rights and Duties of Man
ACHPR	African Charter on Human and Peoples' Rights
ACommHPR	African Commission on Human and Peoples' Rights
Art.	article
Artt.	articles
CAT	Convention against Torture and Other Cruel, Inhumane or Degrading Treatment or Punishment
CEDAW	Convention on the Elimination of All Forms of Discrimination Against Women or Committee on the Elimination of All Forms of Discrimination Against Women
CERD	Convention on the Elimination of All Forms of Discrimination
CESCR	UN Committee on Economic, Social and Cultural Rights
CHR of the CIS	Convention on Human Rights and Fundamental Freedoms of the Commonwealth of Independent States
Comm.	Communication
CRC	Convention on the Rights of the Child or Committee on the Rights of the Child
ECHR	European Convention for the Protection of Human Rights and Fundamental Freedoms
ECtHR	European Court of Human Rights
ESC	European Social Charter (revised)
IACommHR	Inter-American Commission on Human Rights
IACtHR	Inter-American Court of Human Rights
ICCPR	International Covenant on Civil and Political Rights
ICESCR	International Covenant on Economic, Social and Cultural Rights
ICJ	International Court of Justice
ICRC	International Committee of the Red Cross
IHL	international humanitarian law
IHRL	international human rights law
MWC	International Convention on the Protection of the Rights of All Migrant Workers and Member of Their Families

ILO	International Labour Organization
No.	Number
P.C.I.J.	Permanent Court of International Justice
RC	Convention relating to the Status of Refugees
SC	Convention relating to the Status of Stateless Persons
UDHR	Universal Declaration of Human Rights
UK	United Kingdom
UN	United Nations
UNDP	United Nations Development Programme
UN HRC	United Nations Human Rights Committee
UNTS	United Nations Treaty Series
US	United States

Acknowledgements

This book is based on the much longer coursebook entitled International Human Rights Law: Cases and Materials that was published by CD Publishing in 2004. In that book numerous people were thanked for their contribution especially everyone connected with CD Publishing as well as all those who assisted on the much longer coursebook. Those expressions of appreciation are reiterated here.

In addition a special thanks goes out to the following people who have assisted in the editing and preparation of the text of this book especially, Ms Kamila Nishanova and Mr. Mohammed Ghannam, and Dr. Gerald Doebbler. Their research and proofreading has been invaluable.

Without the assistance of all these people, and many more, this book could not have been written. My sincere appreciation to all who contributed in any way.

CFJD
November 2005

Introduction to
Studying International Human Rights Law

This book is a revised and substantially abridged version of the course book International Human Rights Law: Cases and Materials by the same author (cdpublishing.filetap.com or www.lulu.com/cdpublishng). This book provides a short introduction for individuals new to the study of international human rights law, but it is strongly suggested that it be complimented by additional materials from the Internet, libraries, and/or the aforementioned course book. Thus it is hoped that this book introduces you to international human rights law and encourages you to take your study of this law further.

I.1 Studying International Human Rights Law

The techniques used to study international law are surprisingly similar to those used to study domestic law. This is because the study of international human rights law begins, like that of its domestic counterpart, by reading the texts of laws and the cases of tribunals. An international human rights lawyer must be able to do research into what states do and think over different periods of time.

Studying international human rights law requires that you read materials relevant to the much broader field of international or public international law as well as materials specific to human rights. The difference in these materials is usually quite clear in the title or because the bodies from which the materials (especially cases and comments) emanate.

Here are some suggestions of the type of materials you should read and use as you study international human rights law:

1. Books on International Human Rights Law: Although writers are only subsidiary sources of the law, they provide a good starting point because they often explain the law clearly and point you in the direction you need to go. You will find textbooks that explain the law, course books or casebooks that include original materials and/or excerpts of others writings, and treatises that are intended to explain the law in detail, usually for practitioners or experts of the subject.

2. Books on General International Law: These will help you to understand general principles of international law. Like human rights books you will find textbooks, course books, casebooks, and treatises.

3. Cases on International Human Rights Law: Judicial or quasi-judicial international human rights bodies decide many cases which are eventually published both in printed form and electronically. The most important judicial bodies are the European Court of Human Rights and the Inter-American Court of Human Rights. Another judicial body of importance to international law more broadly, is the International Court of Justice. Among the many quasi-judicial bodies are the Inter-American Commission on Human Rights, the African Commission on Human and Peoples' Rights and the seven United Nations treaty bodies, all of which you will learn about later on in this book. Cases relate to a specific set of facts and usually one or more individuals, but sometimes also large groups.

4. General Comments on International Human Rights Law: General comments are given by the quasi-judicial international human rights bodies just mentioned, but do not relate to a specific case. Instead they concern a broader problem that might occur in different cases. Often they are related to a specific article in a treaty and explain that article. They are very useful for interpreting a treaty because they are based on authority given a specific treaty body to comment on a specific treaty.

5. Government Statements in International Organizations or Otherwise: These are probably the hardest to find, although more and more governments are putting their official public documents on their websites. These may include statements made at the UN or in another international forum by any individual entitled to represent a government. They may also be anonymous statements or reports issued on behalf of a government.

6. Contemporary Newspapers and Magazine: Finally, these may be your specific local papers or national or international magazines. Magazines

or newspapers like Al Ahram Weekly in Egypt, The Nation in Kenya, The Economist or the Christian Science Monitor in the United States, and many more, are often valuable sources for information.

I.2 Case Briefs and Legal Memorandum

Case briefs are summaries of cases. The object is to provide yourself a one or two page summary of a case that identifies the important parts of a case and which you can use to study the case and thus the law. Often you will want to work case briefs into an outline of the topic you are studying. An "outline" is a summary of a larger topic, such as one human right, like torture. An outline is something you should be familiar with so here the concentration is on describing a case brief.

The case brief should be written in clear concise language. You may wish to use abbreviations, but this is up to you. The goal of a case brief is to explain the case and determine the *ratio decidendi* of the case—that is the main legal reasoning. The main parts of a case brief, which always appear, are: (1) your name, (2) the date, (3) the full and complete name of the case, (4) the full and complete citation of the case, (5) the facts of the case, (6) the issue(s) at stake in the case, (7) the decision of the court or tribunal, and (8) the reason for the decision. You may also want to include: (9) the arguments of each party and (10) your own comments on the case. A case brief relates to a single case and should be short and easy to read. You also want to use facts and other markers that are memorable because a case brief is a study tool.

A legal memorandum is different from a case brief because it is not about one case, but it is about a legal issue or issues. In other words, you may use many case briefs to write a legal memorandum. You might also have to read and research treaties, government statements, newspapers, legal writings such as books and law review articles, etc. The goal of the legal memorandum is to explain a legal issue in a clear and concise manner taking into account all the relevant legal sources. You may be writing a legal memorandum for yourself, but almost always you are writing it for someone else. The main parts of a legal memorandum are: (1) your name, (2) the date, (3) to whom the legal memorandum is directed, (4) a statement of the issue you have been asked to write about, (5) the statement of the legal problem, (6) a discussion of the legal problem, including how courts or tribunals have dealt with it and the important legal principles they have used, (7) a conclusion expressing your findings about the legal problem. You will want to adapt your conclusion to the task you have been given. For example, if you have been asked to describe the law applying to the termination of human rights treaties for a specific case at a law office where you are working, you will want to conclude your legal memorandum by stating clearly when a human rights treaty can be terminated under the law you have discussed.

I.3 Drafting Legal Documents

The drafting of international legal documents is a very specialized expertise that requires special training. Nevertheless, just like domestic law, the object of drafting any international legal document should be to provide a clear exposition of its meaning and intention.

There are many kinds of legal documents ranging from treaties to petitions to briefs or memoranda of points of authorities in specific cases. Treaties are usually drafted under the auspices of an international organization or a government with a significantly staffed drafting department whose only task is to draft treaties. Sometimes a treaty may also be drafted at a conference convened for that purpose. For example, the Rome Statute of the International Criminal Court was drafted during a conference convened in Rome, Italy in the summer of 1998. But even when a treaty is drafted at a conference, much work will have been done on the text prior to the conference. At the conference the state parties will consider different versions of text and discuss different principles they might want to put into or remove from the treaty. Ultimately, it will still usually be a working group especially skilled in drafting that will draft the treaty text for adoption by the plenary gathering of states.

Finally, one other form of legal document that almost every international human rights lawyer will have to draft at some point in his or her career is a 'legal pleading'. This term refers to a wide category of documents among which are: a legal memorandum (for a tribunal), a case brief (for a tribunal), a petition, and a memorandum of authorities and points of law (and/or facts).

The following list of elements for a legal pleading is general, but should always be included in any substantive argument you are making to a court or quasi-judicial tribunal:

1. Title Page
    i.   Body to whom the petition is directed
    ii.   Parties to the action
    iii. Description of pleading
    iv.   Name of person submitting and contact address
2. Table of Contents
3. Table of Authorities
4. Statement of Jurisdiction
5. Statement of Facts
6. Summary of Arguments
7. Arguments
8. Prayer for Relief
9. Your Signature

In each case, however, you are well advised to consult the body for which the pleading is being written to see if there are specific requirements to which you must adhere. Often these requirements can be found in the rules of the body or, increasingly, in models posted at the website of the body or models posted by other lawyers.

CHAPTER ONE
Human Rights in Domestic Contexts

Human rights are protected first and foremost in their domestic context by the legislature, the executive and the courts. The legislature enacts laws, especially a country's Constitution, in which individuals' rights are established. The executive executes these laws and provides protection of the human rights of all persons under its jurisdiction. And the courts interpret and apply the laws often acting as a check on the executive's power to implement the laws and the legislature's power to enact the laws.

Internationally protected human rights are part of the laws that national institutions should implement. The legislature should pass legislation making internationally protected human rights applicable in the domestic sphere. This is in fact an obligation under many human rights treaties. Article 2 in both the International Covenant on Civil and Political Rights as well as the International Covenant on Economic, Social and Cultural Rights make this an international legal obligation. The executive, which includes the police and the armed forces as well as other government officials, must respect these rights. And finally, the national courts must provide individuals with meaningful and effective remedies when their internationally protected human rights have been violated. Because all of these national mechanisms are meant to protect human rights, a common requirement for bringing a case before an international human rights tribunal is that a petitioner has exhausted his or her domestic remedies.

In this Chapter we will examine some manifestations of human rights in domestic law. First, we will examine the differences and similarities between domestic and international law. Second, we will see some examples of how domestic law treats international law. Third, we will examine how domestic law protects human rights in written instruments or laws, namely in Constitutions. Fourth, we will briefly review some ways in which domestic courts have protected human rights by applying both domestic and international law.

1.1 Some Comparisons between National and International Law

International human rights law is like domestic law in that it is based on the texts of legal instruments and the decisions of judicial or other authoritative decision makers. However, because international law does not create a strong hierarchical relationship between its primary actors, which are states, it often lacks a functioning and effective enforcement mechanism. This does not mean that the mechanism does not exist in theory, but merely that states are sometimes unwilling to implement for political, not legal, reasons. A comparison to domestic law helps illustrate this. For example, in most domestic legal systems if you are wronged by an act of the government you can go to a court that can issue a judicial decree that can, and often must, be enforced by the police or another governmental authority. Under international law if a country violates the law there is not always a means by which a victim—whether a state or an individual—can seek redress. Having said this, in many countries the independent and impartial recourse to legal redress is also less than perfect and in some cases non-existent. One need only look at the United States government's denial of due process to the individuals it detained at Guantánamo Bay under the guise of its war on terrorism and in violation of both domestic and international law. These individuals were denied any opportunity to protect their rights under domestic law for years. Nevertheless, their lawyers have been able to use international law and international human rights mechanisms to provide some minimum attention for their situation.

Another important difference from most, but not all systems of domestic law, is the importance of customary international human rights law. While some indigenous African and Asian societies still use customary law, many societies have now codified their laws and no longer apply traditional or customary law. In the field of international law there has been increasing codification of the law, but customary law continues to have a parallel. This is especially true because not all states have ratified some of the most widely ratified human rights treaties. For example, the protections provided for civilians in international armed conflict are best expressed in the 1977 First Protocol to the Four Geneva Conventions, yet many states have not ratified this Protocol. Because of this situation, the duty upon states to ensure that their troops distinguish between combatants and civilians — one of the most essential rules in this Protocol and one which is considered as having achieved the status of customary international law — is the basis for this important duty for many states.

The value of *stare decisis* or the binding precedent of judicial decisions is also a difference between domestic and international law. The Anglo-American legal tradition, and other legal systems adopting this tradition such as those of India and Nigeria, put emphasis on the precedent value of the decisions of courts. Under international law, the decisions of international tribunals are never binding on precedents of the tribunal itself or other tribunals. Having made this point, however, the degree to which an international tribunal itself or other tribunals will follow a decision depends very much on the tribunal, but it would appear that many international human rights tribunals do try to follow their own jurisprudence as well as that of other relevant human rights bodies.

International lawyers often argue about the meaning of the law. This is in part because there is no authoritative body to determine its meaning and states — the ultimate authorities — often have different meanings. It is also because determining what is customary international law or a state's understanding of its treaty obligations requires careful study of state practice and the opinion (*opinio juris*) of states. This means not merely looking at a treaty or judicial decision, but painstakingly researching hundreds of statements and sometimes hard to find documents that might indicate a state's intention and researching the history of how states act. These are talents of political scientists and international historians, which must be learned by the international human rights lawyer.

1.2 International Law in Domestic Contexts

Because international human rights law is part of general international law, it is important to understand the different ways that states deal with general international law. Traditionally, academics have divided the ways that states deal with international law into categories of "monists" and "dualist" approaches.

A monist views both international and domestic law as part of a single unified legal system. But in a monist state either international or national law must be superior, and usually it is the latter. The English international legal scholar Hersch Lauterpacht, however, advocated a monist view of international law that recognized the superiority of international law. His arguments were based in large part on his belief that the human rights of individuals are best protected when international human rights law is considered superior to domestic law. While there is surely something to be said for the benefit of protecting individual rights when domestic law does not, Lauterpacht's assumption that international human rights law always provides a greater protection of human rights than domestic law is flawed. Sometimes domestic law, particularly in the case of recently drafted constitutions will provide greater protection for individual rights. Article 64 of the Kenyan Constitution, for example, protects consumers' rights, which are not protected in any human rights treaty to which Kenya is a party. This problem is resolved, however, in most human rights treaties by a provision stating that both domestic and international law must be interpreted to provide the greatest protection to the individual possible.

A dualist views the two systems of law as distinct and separate. In dualist states, the national courts may decide a case based on national law without any concern for international law and an international court may decide cases concerning this state on the international plane without any concern for domestic law. A strict dualist approach, however, whereby international law is completely ignored by domestic courts was not considered satisfactory by many states because it completely fails to consider the relevance of the international obligations that are undertaken by a state and encourages other states to ignore their obligations as well. The dualist approach has been popular among civil jurists such as the Italian jurist Dionisio Anzilotti who argued that the state is the supreme actor in international law and therefore the laws enacted by its institutions must be accorded the highest degree of respect. It is also the basis of the common law rule applied in both English and American courts whereby neither treaties nor customary international law will be applied unless the legislature has passed a law that explicitly refers to or restates the rule in the treaty or under customary international law. This rule has been mitigated to some extent by several legal developments. First, the courts in these countries will generally interpret domestic law to be consistent with international law. Second, American courts have applied a doctrine of self-executing treaty provisions whereby treaty provisions viewed as intending to create individual rights will be applied by the courts. And third, in the United Kingdom, the government's consent to the jurisdiction and binding nature of the judgments of the European Court of Human Rights is an additional check on the government's ability to infringe upon human rights.

Most states today apply modified versions of a monist approach. In the United States, Article III of the Constitution makes international law part of the law of the land. Nevertheless, the American Courts have held that only treaties that are self-executing or that have been incorporated by the legislature should be considered by domestic courts. In the Netherlands, articles 94 and 95 of the Dutch Constitution states that international law is not only part of Dutch law, but it is superior to any domestic law. Article 95 of the Dutch Constitution instructs judges to not apply domestic law that is inconsistent with an international obligation of the Netherlands. Both treaties and the decisions of international bodies to whose jurisdiction the Dutch government has consented are binding in the Dutch courts. Article 15(4) of the Russian Constitution provides expressly that international law is superior to domestic law and must be applied by the courts whenever there is a conflict between the two. In Namibia, the somewhat general statement about international law in article 144 of its constitution as been interpreted as requiring the application of international law above domestic law. And paragraph 3(3) of article VI of the Constitution of Bosnia and Hercegovina gives its Constitutional Court the ability to review a domestic law for its consistency with the European Convention on Human Rights. Many states, while commanding their courts to take international law into consideration remain ambiguous about how the law should apply. Countries such as Italy and Uzbekistan, for example, either make international law part of their domestic law or empower their courts to interpret international law without clearly specifying what has to be done when international law has been identified.

Some states have resisted the influence of international law. For example, in the United Kingdom, treaties are only applied when they have been enacted by Parliament. This may occur by an act of Parliament directly making a treaty part of English law or indirectly by the incorporation of provisions of international law into a new law passed by Parliament. The Human Rights Act that was enacted in the United Kingdom in 1998 allows its courts to take into account the European Convention on Human Rights, but it does not require the courts to do so nor specify how this must be done. In 2004, despite article VI of the constitution that states that all treaties — together with domestic law — shall be the supreme law of the land, the United States Senate and the House of Representatives proposed resolutions criticizing the courts for even considering international or foreign law in their judgments. Such trends towards isolationism are not the norm and display a serious disrespect for international law that has already gained these governments the ere of their neighbours.

An important principle of domestic law that has often been in opposition to the application of international human rights law is the doctrine of sovereign immunity. This doctrine derives from the traditional concentration on state sovereignty. It was considered in the *McElhinney v. Ireland* (Application 31253/96 decided on 21 November 2001) by the European Court of Human Rights. The Court held that the state could hide behind sovereign immunity when a private individual claimed that the state's invocation of this doctrine to prevent a suit against a soldier for assault violated the individual's right to a remedy for violations for his human rights (Articles 6 and 13 of the ECHR). The ECtHR did recognize that the doctrine of sovereign immunity was gradually being eroded, but refused to find it not applicable in this case. This reasoning was followed in *Al-Adsani v. UK* to uphold the English courts' dismissal of a case against Saudi Arabia for torturing a British citizen. Again the ECtHR held that a state could not be forced to provide a remedy when general rules of international law protect the state.

Finally, whatever the view taken by their government or their courts, it is important for international lawyers to always remember the basic rule of international law: domestic law can never be an excuse for the violation of international law. When domestic courts or other government entities refuse to apply international law they therefore become the instrument of the government that is contributing to a violation of international law.

1.3 Individual Rights and National Constitutions

There are several ways in which individual rights are protected in nations' constitutions. In older instruments, like the English Bill of Rights or the French Declaration of the Rights of Man, individual rights were merely declared. Little thought was given to a mechanism for ensuring them. This concern was left to the realm of politics. The rights are therefore often stated in general form.

Similar declaratory statements about human rights appear in the preambles of many modern constitutions. The Preamble of the Indonesian Constitution states that the welfare of the people and social justice shall be secured by the state. An even longer, but just as vague duty to protect individual rights appears in the Constitution of the Islamic Republic of Pakistan. The Preamble of the Constitution of East Timor refers to human rights expressly stating that the Constitutive Assembly drafting the Constitution reaffirms its obligation to respect and protect human rights. And the Preamble of the Constitution of Madagascar states that the government will protect both individual and collective rights.

Some constitutions also mention human rights in principles that lie somewhere between the preamble and operative Bills of Rights. These principles are referred to as directive principles. In the Indian Constitution the directive principles follow — not precede — the articles on fundamental human rights. The directive principles in the Indian constitution include such human rights as the right to work, to social welfare and to education (all in article 41) and have sometimes been given direct effect by the Indian Supreme Court.

Finally, most modern constitutions contain a written Bill of Rights. This practice is perhaps most significantly supported by the British government that in the mid-twentieth century required all its former colonies to have written Bills of Rights before they became independent — and despite the fact that Great Britain had no written Constitution or Bill of Rights. In the United States Constitution individual rights are found in amendments, some of which were adopted at the same time as the United States

Constitution entered into force. In the French Constitution individual rights can be found in several documents which are incorporated into the current Constitution, including the French Declaration of the Rights and Duties of Man from 1789. In the next two sections of this Chapter you will explore some examples of Bills of Rights in modern Constitutions.

CHAPTER TWO
The Theory and History of Human Rights

2.1 Different Understandings About Human Rights

There are different theoretical understandings about human rights. These different understandings have emanated from the fields of law, philosophy, morality, ethics, economics, health, politics, international relations, etc. The following descriptions reflect but a few of the theoretical approaches. The descriptions are limited to theories espoused by western European and American writers. Although there are very valuable theories from writers of many other cultures, they are often not accessible in English. It is therefore strongly suggested that one seek out other theories and perspectives of international law and human rights and compare them to those described here.

The oldest theory is perhaps that of the natural law of human rights. These theories can be traced back to the works of Francisco de Vittoria and Francisco Suárez, both of which identified God as the ultimate source of the individual's rights. Later Hugo Grotius expanded this understanding to be more inclusive by claiming that such rights could be derived from reason. In other words, rational human beings would agree on human rights. Both these theories of human rights base the grant of human rights upon phenomena that are beyond the individual. Although this does not absolve human beings of their responsibility for protecting human rights, it removes these rights from the realm of compromise and discussion among human beings. Human rights then become truly inalienable, at least in a theoretical sense. In contemporary times, the natural law theory of human rights has gained importance in the work of writers who have strongly argued for the unchallenged universality of human rights.

A theory of human rights as entitlements and capabilities has been advocated by Nobel Prize winning economist Amartya Sen. Professor Sen argues that human rights are the consequence of individuals being able to realize their potential in society. To achieve this level society must provide an open forum for expression, the result of which will be claims by individuals that will ensure the conditions for the fulfillment of entitlements or basic social and economic rights. This theory prioritizes civil and political rights over economic and social rights. Sen has illustrated this consequence by comparing India to China. He argues that India was better able to fend off famine in the middle of the 20th century because it allowed greater freedom of speech, which consequently led to people complaining about famine and forcing the government to act to prevent it. In contrast, China, which experienced famine at the same time, tried to cover up the situation and this caused more people to die. Ironically, however, as it entered the 21st century, China appears to have succeeded in encouraging more rapid and consistent social and economic development than India, in part because of its policies of social control, including its 'one baby policy'. Despite this apparent contradiction, the 'entitlements and capabilities' arguments of Amartya Sen and his frequent co-author, Jean Drèze, nevertheless, call upon states to take urgent public action to ensure basic economic and social human rights.

John Rawls and Ronald Dworkin are two American neo-liberal legal philosophers who viewed human rights as the inalienable rights of human beings based on law. Although similar to the natural law approach, these writers conceded that there might be a popular basis for human rights in the will of the people. However, once the people had decided upon the rights that were endowed with the status of 'human rights' then these rights became sacrosanct and immune from challenge, except through special *modus operendi*. In addition, these rights, in the famous words of Ronald Dworkin, became 'trumps' over other types of rights. These views reflected the American constitutional system of individual rights requiring significant respect for a central authoritative decision maker.

The policy approach to authoritative decision making in relation to international human rights law was coined by Myres S. McDougal, Harold Lasswell and Lung-Chu Chen who viewed individual's rights through a policy-oriented perspective: human rights as the claims, demands and expectations of individuals. This view is based on the premise that individuals can and will claim their due from their governments. This theory acknowledges the supremacy of state-based authoritative decision-making processes as well as the influence of individuals' claims and demands. A policy-oriented perspective on human rights thus provides actors, whether they are individuals attempting to influence the process or the authoritative decision makers, some basic tools by which they can develop international human rights law. The view of law as a process underpins the policy-oriented perspective.

Conceptions of human rights based on community were prominent among socialist writers. For these writers, human rights were the expression of the individual in community with others. Often, therefore, individual human rights were accompanied by responsibilities. Although socialist theories of law have dwindled with the demise of the USSR, in the 21st century the communal basis of human rights can still be seen in international human rights law in Africa. The African Charter of Human and Peoples' Rights and the jurisprudence of the African Commission, for example, reflect the communal nature of human rights by including both group rights and individual responsibilities towards one's community.

This book espouses the simple, but perhaps dogmatic approach of human rights as international law, relying on the rules of law that have been agreed to by the international community. It is suggested that such a legalistic approach has the value of providing the student with the best elementary framework for understanding international human rights law. This approach does not exclude the development of the law, or *lege feranda*, but it does recognize that a distinction must be made between attempts to develop the law and *lex lata*, the law as it has been agreed upon by consensus (customary international law) or express consent (treaties).

International human rights law expresses the idea that individuals have basic rights that reflect their most important values and that these rights are protected by laws. International human rights law may thus be viewed as a process by which prescriptive statements and authoritative decisions are made concerning the conduct of human beings. The prescriptions include the claims, demands, and expectations of individuals and groups of individuals, including states and non-governmental organizations. Traditionally, the most authoritative of these claims, those applicable to the entire international community, have been international agreements between states. These agreements are treaties, although they are frequently titled charters, covenants, or the products of conventions. International agreements, which carry these designations, are considered to be binding on states and to create obligations for states. Whenever a state does not fulfill its obligations, it violates international law. This is the case even if national law does not recognise the violation, or even justifies it.

For example, an individual who is fleeing from persecution retains all his or her human rights. As a result, if this individual enters another country that has ratified the Convention Relating to the Status of Refugees this host country violates its international legal obligation if it returns the individual to his country. Such action is prohibited by article 33 of the Refugee Convention. Even if the decision to return the individual has been taken by a court of law or the executive branch of government it will not be justified. It is certainly not justified merely by the practice of some states that violate the law by sending individuals back to countries in which they are not safe from persecution. Unless a state party to the Refugee Convention withdraws from the treaty, it is bound by it regardless of what its national laws say or its national courts decide. This legal condemnation forms the essential character of international human rights law. This does not mean that practical implementation is not important, but that a thorough understanding of the norms is necessary in order to implement them.

2.2 History of International Human Rights Law

Modern international human rights law found part of its inspiration in national law, but it also found inspiration in western pronunciations of international norms. This is not to say that there were not normative pronunciations that preceded those of western states. Indeed our first laws do not emanate from Europe or the Americas. It was, however, through the development of these norms in Europe that our modern international human rights law was born.

It is primarily in the norms of international humanitarian law — the laws of war — that one can see the development of the principles of international human rights law. International humanitarian law was a response to a concern about respect for minimum standards in the most barbaric of all human occupations, the waging of war. The initial rules in this area of law arose while war was still a legitimate means of conducting foreign policy. Some of these rules are as old as the practice of war itself and can be found in societies from around the world. In western society some of the most cited expressions of the *temperamenta in bello* were articulated by Hugo Grotius in his famous treatise, *De jure belli ac pacis*, written in 1625 during the Thirty-Years War (1618-1648) between the kings of France and the Habsburg rulers of the Holy Roman Empire and Spain. Grotius expressed the belief that limits on warfare were necessary for a civilised society.

The history of modern international human rights law emanates from more recent times. An appropriate starting point is the concern for humanitarian principles relating to the protection of individuals that was espoused by Geneva businessman J. Henry Dunant. His emotional book *Un souvenir de Solferino* in 1862 gave rise to the Red Cross Movement and the first rules of international humanitarian law to be codified in a modern treaty. Dunant and several other citizens of Geneva founded this movement by creating the "International Committee for Aid to the Wounded," which later became the International Committee of the Red Cross. The first treaty concluded because of the momentum generated by this movement was the Convention on the Amelioration of the Condition of the Wounded in Armies in the

Field. As the title implies, this treaty dealt with the protection of soldiers or combatants. As most of the casualties of war were soldiers at that time, making them the primary concern of protection was natural.

In 1899 and 1907, the development of humanitarian principles continued in the context of war with the negotiation and adoption of several Hague Conventions. The Hague Conventions, an initiative of the Russian monarch Czar Nicholas III, limited in more detail the means by which states might conduct hostilities.

After the first world war the Versailles Treaty adopted in 1919, creating the League of Nations, encouraged states to protect the rights of minorities and even provided a mechanism for resolving disputes between states or between members of minority groups and states where states had made agreements providing for minority rights. Around the same time, in 1928, the major military powers of the world agreed to renounce the use of force as a means of conducting their foreign policy. But shortly thereafter another world war broke out and protections of individual's basic rights were made subservient to elites' political interests. The consequence was another bloody war that saw Nazi Germany's leader attempt to annihilate certain groups of people and the United States bomb several cities to rubble, including with the world's only recorded use of nuclear weapons. The acts of brutality that were carried out by all parties to the armed conflict shocked the public conscience.

The immediate result was a movement to draft a more comprehensive set of rules for the waging of war. These were the four Geneva Conventions of 1949, which were later complemented by 1977 Protocols. The fourth Geneva Convention Relative to the Protection of Civilian Persons in Time of War provides for protections of individuals' human rights and article 3 common to all four Geneva Conventions provides some basic protections that apply at all times.

At about the same time, the United Nations was created as a body that would impose more effective restrictions on states' ability to wage war and do more to promote and protect human rights.

Most modern international human rights instruments are from the period following the Second World War. Many were created and administered directly under the auspices of the United Nations and all have been influenced by this organization. Although attempts to introduce detailed human rights provisions directly into the Charter of the United Nations failed, it was agreed unanimously that such provisions would be forthcoming shortly after the United Nations was formed. Because of this, the Charter does not contain detailed human rights provisions--these were left for the Universal Declaration and the two Covenants--but it does contain references to human rights. Articles 55 and 56, for example, contain general references to the obligations of states for ensuring human rights. Articles 1 and 2 also include human rights among the general purposes and principles to which all the United Nations organs and member states must adhere.

Almost at the same time as the United Nations was being created as an international organization, its Commission on Human Rights (CHR) began work on a universal international human rights instrument. Among the leading proposals were the United States' draft, which concentrated almost exclusively on the right to freedom of expression, and drafts from Panama and Cuba, which more closely resembled the Universal Declaration of Human Rights that was finally adopted. Also of interest was a report by UNESCO, the international organization for culture and education, based on a survey of national traditions. The survey concluded that there were fifteen rights upon which a consensus could be reached. Among these rights were the right to life, the right to education, the right to property, the right to work, the right to health, the right to receive information, the right to freedom of thought, the right to take political action, the right to justice, the right to citizenship, the right to speech, assembly and association, and surprisingly, the right to "rebellion or revolution ... [i]n the event that the government of his nation operates contrary to the fundamental principles of justice and the basic human rights in such fashion that no redress is permitted by peaceful means ..." Additional input came from NGOs and private experts, usually academics. Ultimately, however, state representatives were the authoritative decision makers who adopted the first instrument of what became known as the International Bill of Human Rights, or, more correctly, the Bill of International Human Rights.

The Bill of International Human Rights is comprised of three instruments: the Universal Declaration of Human Rights (UDHR) adopted in 1948, and the International Covenant on Civil and Political Rights (ICCPR) and the International Covenant on Economic, Social and Cultural Rights (ICESCR) both adopted and opened for signature and ratification in 1966. The first of these instruments, the UDHR, is not legally binding. The other instruments, the ICCPR and ICESCR, are treaties that have been ratified by approximately 150 states each. Although initially only one instrument was intended, differences among states about the relative equality between civil and political rights on the one hand and economic social and cultural rights on the other lead to one non-binding instrument being drafted followed by two legally-binding treaties, one of each set of rights.

At its inception the UDHR was not considered to reflect legally binding obligations, but merely aspirations. Today this view has changed. Many countries have incorporated the UDHR into their Constitutions in one way or another and many judicial bodies—both international and domestic— have referred to several of the human rights therein as reflecting customary international law.

Since the adoption of the three core UN human rights instruments, there have been many more human rights instruments adopted. Even while the

United Nations was working on universal instruments, regional instruments were being adopted. For example, in 1948 the Organization of American States adopted its own Declaration of the Rights and Duties of Man. In 1950, several European states did even better by adopting a legally binding human rights treaty, the European Convention for the Protection of Human Rights and Fundamental Freedoms, that also contained a mechanism to enforce the rights with legally binding decisions. The Americans in 1978 followed Europe's example and in 1981 African nations adopted one of the most progressive human rights instruments.

These developments have continued up until today with the adoption of new instruments and the strengthening of the already existing instruments. Among the new instruments adopted have been European and American conventions on torture, American conventions on women and disappearances, an African protocol creating a court, and treaties that are open for universal ratification concerning torture, prohibited forms of discrimination, women's rights, children's rights, refugees rights, and an international criminal court to punish individuals committing acts that are violations of internationally protected human rights often found in these treaties. These legally binding instruments have been joined by many aspirational instruments that often ultimately reflect customary international law. One such example is the Declaration and Programme of Action of the Second World Conference on Human Rights, last held in 1993.

Some Achievements in International Human Rights

1862	Swiss Philanthropist Henri Dunant's *Un Souvenir de Solférino* spawns the Red Cross Movement that tries to limit inhumanity in time of war.
1919	The League of Nations is formed with the Versailles Treaty with a procedure for the protection of minority rights guaranteed in other treaties.
1929	The Kellogg-Briand Pact (or Pact of Paris) enters into force prohibiting states from using force in their foreign policy.
1945	The United Nations is formed and begins work on human rights starting with the drafting of the Universal Declaration of Human Rights.
1948	The Universal Declaration of Human Rights (UN) and the American Declaration of the Rights and Duties of Man (OAS) are adopted.
1949	The four Geneva Conventions on the Laws of War are adopted, the fourth which protects civilians in time of war and during occupation.
1950	The Council of Europe adopts the European Convention for the Protection of Human Rights and Fundamental Freedoms.
1966	The other two instruments of the International Bill of Human Rights—the International Covenant on Civil and Political Rights and the International Covenant on Economic, Social and Cultural Rights—are adopted and opened for signature and ratification by states.
1968	The First World Conference on Human Rights in Teheran, Iran adopts a Declaration confirming that all states must respect human rights.
1978	The American Convention on Human Rights enters into force.

1981	The African Charter on Human and Peoples' Rights enters into force.
1989	The Convention on the Rights of the Child is adopted and becomes the world's most widely ratified human rights treaty with all states but the United States and Somalia becoming a party.
1993	The World Conference on Human Rights takes place in Vienna, Austria and adopts a Declaration and Plan of Action confirming the necessity of all states to respect human rights and the universality of human rights.
1993 and 1994	The United Nation's Security Council creates two special International Criminal Tribunals to try crimes committed during a specific period of time in the former Yugoslavia and Rwanda.
1994	The United Nations High Commissioner for Human Rights is created.
2002	The International Criminal Court is created (July 2003 opens).
2003	African states adopt a protocol creating an African Court of Human and Peoples' Rights

The creation of the International Criminal Court and the African Court are not the last developments in the protection of human rights, but merely further steps that will hopefully move us closer towards achieving real respect for human rights.

History, however, has taught that states are often more willing to create international human rights norms, than they are to implement these norms, especially in cases that may not serve their political interests. Recently United States officials have even suggested that the United States might use the four Geneva Conventions as essentially weapons against other countries. As this unfortunate expression of opinion (and perhaps policy) suggests, the development of human rights does not always move forward.

2.3 The State as the Protector of Individuals

Human rights have existed since individuals began to think that they were owed certain duties by the organizations they created. Initially these claims to "human rights" were moral or human claims. When the main means of organizing cooperation between individuals became states, then states also became the natural center of attention for the duties that were owed to individuals. Thus, since the advent of the state as the main actor in international society, the protection of the basic human rights of individuals has traditionally relied on the responsibility of the state. It is therefore the state in modern society that either protects human rights or violates them.

The nation-state, and its predecessor the sovereign, were expected to provide for the rights of its people. However, there was often a contradiction between protecting individual subjects' rights and the sovereign's own interests. The basis of this contradiction and the manner in which the state initially acquired its importance can be seen in a quick sketch of the history of the state as the primary actor in international affairs. The concept of the state may be said to have emerged as soon as people required an administrative structure to organise themselves. Although no one has precisely identified this point with any degree of reliability, it is certainly well before the western European concept of the state emerged. However, the early concept of a state was not as developed as the definition that is used today. The contemporary 'state' is defined, at a minimum, to include the constituent elements of a state as outlined by the 1933 Montevideo Convention on the Rights and Duties of States. These are (1) a defined territory, (2) a population, (3) the ability to enter into foreign relations with other states, and (4) an authoritative and representative government. Since 1933, other requirements have been introduced, such as the requirement that the state respects human rights. This provision was included in the European Union report on recognition of states after the break-up of the former state of Yugoslavia. It is now the regular practice of the European Union states and the African states to require that a state is able to ensure respect for the human rights of individuals under its jurisdiction before it is recognized. Today, respect for human rights can be said to be a necessary element of legitimate government.

Most international legal analyses of the state are based on the concept of the state that is reflected by a combination of the Montevideo Convention criteria and the human rights criteria reflected by the European Union statement. This concept has developed largely in Europe, Latin American and North American contexts, which makes its validity to other countries problematic. It is nevertheless valuable to indicate some important points in the historical development of the modern state.

One starting point is the emergence of the concept of 'the sovereign' or 'sovereignty' in the sixteenth century. In 1532, Niccolò di Bernardo dei Machiavelli published the first edition of *Il Principe* (The Prince). This book was intended as advice to reigning or aspiring princes. The central theme of the advice was that the maintenance of power over a community of people required the exercise of power. Machiavelli's prince was as benevolent as his subjects permitted him to be and the failure of his subjects to show allegiance justified the full wrath of the prince's power. There was little room for the rights of individual subjects as only the prince had rights. The prince's subjects had only duties. Subsequently in 1576, Jean Bodin, in his *Six livres de la Republique,* constructed a broader definition of authority in the term *"souveraineté"* or its English equivalent "sovereignty". Sovereignty was defined as the inalienable and absolute power of a ruler to represent the ruled. It was the prerogative of any central authority and it was necessary to provide security and order to society. It was Bodin's concept of sovereignty that inspired the sixteenth century rulers of Europe. However, during this time much of the rest of the world remained organized in more de-centralised institutions such as fiefdoms, tribes, clans, kingdoms, and decentralised empires.

It was in the shadow of Bodin's theory of absolute sovereignty that Dutch jurist Hugo Grotius (Hugo de Groot, 1583-1645) developed what is commonly referred to as the first theory of international law. Grotius used the term *ius gentium* to describe public international law, a term that in its original Roman meaning was used to describe a much wider field of law. At times, Grotius also expands his theory of public international law to extend not only to states, but also to individuals. He constructs a system of basic rules for world public order recognizing that it is not enough to provide for rules for states' action, but that these rules must encompass the acts of individuals within states as well, if they are to provide a successful world public order. Before Grotius, the natural law theories of Francisco de Vittoria (1486-1546) and Francisco Suárez (1548-1617), with their Catholic foundations, also included rules that applied to the individual as the servant of God endowed with the responsibility for his or her own life. Again, it is worth reiterating that Grotius, like Bodin and many of their predecessors, was writing in the midst of a Europe in transition, where wealth and power were becoming increasingly concentrated.

Elsewhere in the world, concepts of social organization were developing through more decentralised means. In the Ottoman Empire, for example, the decentralised social and administrative system called millet was employed by the Sublime Porte to maintain control over far-flung territories and populations that over-extended the resources of the rulers in Istanbul. The outposts of the Ottoman Empire thus had a degree of autonomy. At the same time, Emperors were employing similar systems in China, as were the colonial rulers of overseas empires. Often, however, these administrations depended as much on brutal force as on the enticements of co-operation. A review of forms of government during the sixteenth century would lead one to agree with Adamantia Polis who reminds us that "[t]he modern state is a product of modern Europe ... [i]t existed neither in the Europe of earlier centuries, nor in any other continent; absolute monarchies, feudalism, theocracies, and empires were among the varying forms of rule in the world order."

It was not the theory of international law that led to the emergence of the state as the centre of attention in international relations and law, but the practice of individuals recognizing the state as the legitimate centre of authority that contributed to the profound effect of the modern state on world society. Moreover, it is in the context of a Europe recovering from a disastrous war that this practice took place. In addition, it was through the acceptance of this practice by rulers all over the world that it became globalized. Like the European process, the process that took place in many other parts of the world was based on the belief that the state was the best means of ensuring security and stability and thus ensuring the respect for the most basic human values that individuals hold. However, in other regions contrary to the European experience, the movement away from a fragmented social organization was more gradual. Part of this, as is still reflected in social attitudes today, was the prominence that 'society' occupied in many cultures. Society in many African and Asian cultures did not mean the separation of the individual from the state, but often the reconciliation of the two identities. Even today, this assimilation of individual and society continues in most societies outside of Europe and North America.

The European concept of the state, however, gained increasing prominence in national vocabularies all over the world after the Peace of Westphalia, which ended more than eighty years of intermittent war in Europe. The state envisioned these treaties as a technique for centralizing power and authority in the state to make these more manageable. The central element of the Westphalian state is the idea of fixed territorial boundaries, the principle of *uti possidetis*. This is the principle that traditional state borders deserve to be respected. It is a principle that remains of vital importance to international law, and especially to the principle of self-determination under international human rights law. *Uti possidetis* legitimizes authority over a population by entities defined by their territorial boundaries and reflects a concentration on the property of territory more than the individuals who make-up the population. In many respects, this stretched a formality of Roman law to new lengths. As Dr. A.V. Eyffinger points out, *uti possidetis* was traditionally a mere legal formality applied in Roman times by interdict of the Praetor to ensure that the possessors of land did not change their possession into ownership and thereby avoid legal challenges to their possession (*rei vindicatio*) because writs could not be served against owners. The Westphalian concept of the state was intended as a similar fiction that could provide order to a world that was in the midst of turmoil. But just as the Roman construction only made sense in light of the legal restriction on the service of writs on owners, so the Westphalian state only makes sense as long as the state is the main actor in world society. In the years after Westphalia, states consolidated their authority and strengthened their legitimacy by recognizing transactions and dealings between themselves. In areas of the world where no concept of the sovereign state had existed, states now began to emerge. This was due in part to the colonial power that European states exercised. Because of this power, European states became examples to rulers throughout the world who aspired to such extremes of power.

The continued emphasis on the state and its role as the protector of human rights was confirmed by the primary judicial organ of the United Nations, the International Court of Justice (ICJ), in one of its first decisions. In the *Nottebohm Case*, the ICJ was called upon to decide the extent to which a state could exercise its authority to protect its nationals against violations of their rights by other states. It confirmed this right; but also held that an individual must have real and effective contacts to a state for that state to be able to exercise protection as against other states. The Court also considered the connections between Liechtenstein and Nottebohm and found them to be lacking genuineness.

In the Barcelona Traction Case the ICJ was again asked to decide upon some of the rules regarding the protection of individuals' rights to property. This time the Court decided that only a country where a company was incorporated could protect the rights of that country's shareholders. However perhaps more importantly for human rights, in its *obiter dicta*, the Court stated that there are some basic rights of the individual that may have achieved a status whereby every country would have an interest in protecting them. These rights were referred to as creating obligations *erga omnes*. Note that the ICJ says Canada could exercise diplomatic protection. Indeed, Canada did start to intervene but stopped. The ICJ seemed to ignore the relevance of this cessation of the exercise of diplomatic protection by Canada mainly for reasons of avoiding confusion that might be caused by duplication. The Court appears to believe that Canada could reassert its right of protection arguing that—"right of protection ... cannot be regarded as extinguished because it is not exercised." As in the Nottebohm Case, property rights were among the rights concerned. The right to property is a controversial human right and its protection allows broad exceptions, but what if the right to life, the prohibition of torture or procedural rights had been at stake? In a case concerning Sudan the African Commission on Human and Peoples' Rights did consider the *erga omnes* character of human rights provisions concluding in very general terms that "[t]he African Commission feels that the [human rights] obligations of States are of an *erga omnes* nature."

The broad nature of human rights obligations can be contrasted with the general principle of international law that no state or international organization may interfere with the internal affairs of another sovereign state. This general principle is stated in article 2, paragraph 7 of the Charter of the United Nations. The key phrase in paragraph 7 is "matters which are essentially within the domestic jurisdiction of any state." What such matters are and who decides what they are is not clearly defined. One may argue that such matters are limited to areas over which the Security Council exercises its Chapter VII powers. The Security Council can undoubtedly restrict the area reserved to state discretion in the name of international peace and security. Such a restriction might be adequate for action by the Security Council, especially in light of the serious consequences that flow from the use of armed force or even economic coercion. The Security Council has used its power to exert coercion to protect international peace and security in instances of gross violations of human rights in Rwanda, Liberia, and other areas. But sometimes states have also acted to protect human rights in other countries. The NATO bombing of Serbia and Montenegro to protect persons in Kosova is an example of such humanitarian intervention, but it is perhaps the lone example.

Today it is increasingly accepted that state sovereignty may be limited by human rights law. The recognition of these limits through enforcement measures by the United Nations Security Council is very rare. The more common manifestation of these limits is human rights treaties. When a state signs a human rights treaty, it takes the first step in limiting its sovereignty, by obliging itself not to take positive steps that might violate the treaty or make compliance with its terms impossible. This rule of customary international law is codified in Article 18 of the Vienna Convention on the Law of Treaties. When a state ultimately ratifies a human rights treaty it agrees to the international legal obligation to protect the human rights enshrined in that treaty under the principle of *pacta sunt servanda*. This principle means that states are legally bound to observe their treaty obligations in good faith. Again, this reflects a limitation on state sovereignty.

Finally, when a rule of customary international law comes into force, it binds a state even if that state has not expressly consented to it. Some individuals and states, however, argue that a state that constantly objects to a rule may not be bound by it when it ultimately becomes customary international law because they have been a "persistent objector." One might argue against the application of this rule to international human rights law because of the fundamental nature of the rights involved.

2.4 International Human Rights Law as Public International Law

International human rights law is a special part of public international law. The specialty lies in the protection of the individual and the creation of rights for individuals and not merely states. Because international human rights law deals with individuals' rights it may be necessary to interpret its rules differently than those of general public international law. Nevertheless, both areas of law focus on the obligations of states. International law deals with the rights of states and the obligations of states, although occasionally inter-governmental organizations are the subjects of international law. International human rights law deals with the rights of individuals and the obligations of states.

In both cases, the obligations may flow from either treaties or customary international law, or occasionally from general principles of international law. The identification, application and interpretation of legal obligations in treaties and under customary international law are discussed in detail in the chapter on the obligations of states.

Areas of public international law other than international human rights law include the law of the sea, the law of state responsibility, diplomatic law, international trade law, treaty law, *et cetera*. These various areas of the law are not exclusive. They overlap each other, sometimes to a great extent. For example, treaty law is generally applicable to the interpretation of human rights treaties. This is just one of many examples in which state responsibility under international human rights law relies on the general principles of public international law. The various categories of law have been developed by lawyers to help them understand their field. Creative human rights lawyers should consider how these categories may be inadequate and what aspects of them might be valuable for developing contemporary human rights law.

Like international law, human rights law is part of public international law and includes sub-areas of international human rights law. These areas include refugee law, international humanitarian law, minority rights law, children's human rights, women's human rights, human rights in developing countries, human rights in emerging democracies, *et cetera*. Again, these areas of international human rights law are categories created by lawyers to describe their work.

It is common for books on international human rights law to begin by outlining the rules of public international law. In this Course book, the rules of public international law are discussed integrally with the areas of human rights law to which they are relevant. Thus, for example, the law of treaties and state responsibility are discussed in the Chapter on Government Responsibilities and Institutions for Protecting Human Rights. In this Chapter, several general issues that are common to international law and specifically to international human rights law are discussed. The first of these is the status of the individual.

2.5 The Norms of International Human Rights Law

The legal expression of human rights is what is commonly referred to as international human rights law. This law is a part of public international law. International human rights law is thus the part of public international law that reflects the most basic common shared values of world society. Often the instruments in which these values are expressed are vaguely worded. This does not mean that these instruments have lesser or no meaning, but it instead indicates that the level of agreement achieved--the lowest common denominator--is not as specific as it could be. It is the obligation of the international human rights lawyer to understand this and to strive to ensure as broad a protection of individuals as possible, but to do so in accordance with the expectations that world society shares.

The task of the international human rights lawyer might be described as one of interpreting social concerns and acting to influence policy. Unlike her or his counterpart in national legal systems, the international human rights lawyer cannot represent a single client at all costs, but must strive to uphold the integrity of the system of protection of human rights and the values that they represent. It is in this critical perspective that this Course book examines the promotion of human rights in emerging democracies. In light of this, important questions to remember when reading the various prescriptive instruments of international human rights law are:

Who is deciding what human rights are protected?
How are they deciding?
What is influencing their decisions?
What values are reflected in the international instruments?
Whose values are they?

The last question asks us to consider whether there are universally recognized human rights. If there are, what rights are they? To answer this question it is perhaps necessary to make the somewhat shaky assumption that the consensus of governments' representatives at international conferences is a legitimate form of decision-making and really represents the various interests and values that individual citizens hold. If we accept this we can look to the claims governments have made in international human rights instruments to determine the content of international human rights law.

The consensus of participants on some fundamental human rights is reflected in the leading human rights treaties. This consensus includes the following human rights.

Human Rights Agreed to by a Large Consensus of States include:
◊ the right to life;
◊ the right to liberty and security of person;
◊ the right to due process or fair trial in the determination of one's rights;
◊ the right to work;
◊ including the right to fair and equal remuneration for work of equal value at a rate that provides a decent living for the worker and his/her family;
◊ as well as safe and healthy working conditions, equal promotion opportunities based on seniority and competence with conditions of adequate rest, leisure, reasonable working hours, periodic holidays and remuneration for public holidays;
◊ the right to housing;
◊ the right to education;
◊ the right to social security;
◊ the right to vote;
◊ the right to participate in one's government;
◊ the right to freedom of expression;

◊ the right to freedom of assembly;
◊ the right to freedom of association;
◊ the right to freedom of thought and religion;
◊ the prohibition against slavery;
◊ the prohibition against torture, cruel, inhuman or degrading treatment;
◊ the prohibition of discrimination on grounds of race, colour, sex, language, religion, political or other opinion, national or social origin, property, birth, or other status;
◊ the prohibition of genocide;
◊ the prohibition of apartheid;
◊ the right to development;
◊ the right to self-determination; and
◊ the right to a healthy environment.

These claims are international human rights law, perhaps even customary international human rights law. They are the rights that enjoy the consensus of the world community and the express consent of most governments. Governments that reject these rights can be publicly condemned for violating the trust that their people and the international community have placed in them.

CHAPTER THREE
Government Responsibilities
for Protecting Human Rights

The most efficient and effective means of protecting human rights is through the institutions of a government. The reasons for this are several. First, the government is still an extremely powerful political actor. Second, the state has an interest in the protection of human rights: its own existence. Third, it is within the national context that individuals carry out their daily activities, interact with other individuals daily as concerns their most basic needs, and establish their capabilities. Fourth, it is of practical necessity that individuals reconcile their existence with each other. And fifth, as we have seen by viewing the history of the modern state, individuals have traditionally expected their states to provide for some basic needs.

The state can protect human rights through laws, policies and government action. Some laws, such as international human rights laws, are among the most fundamental rules in society. These rules provide for a humane existence of society. The structure of the state and the constitutional laws that maintain this structure are also laws that are deemed fundamental to our existence. National institutions protecting human rights are thus mechanisms for reconciling individual values and the state.

International human rights law is part of these mechanisms. It is also part of the larger corpus of general public international law. Furthermore, the contribution of each element will depend on the situation. This may be illustrated by reference to the hierarchical relationship between three sources of law with which that most domestic lawyers anywhere in the world are familiar. In this relationship international human rights law is superior to constitutional law, which itself, in turn, is superior to other national laws.

3.1 Legal Obligations

The responsibilities of states for ensuring respect for human rights vary. Under customary international law states are bound by the general principles of public international law concerning state responsibility. These principles, however, as we have seen are mitigated by a government's broad discretion over its own internal affairs. Only when a violation of human rights affects the nationals, or arguably the interests, of third states does international legal responsibility accrue towards these third states. The rules governing this general international responsibility of states are expressed in the International Law Commission's Articles on the Responsibility of States for Internationally Wrongful Acts (ILC Articles) which stress that "[e]very internationally wrongful act of a State entails the international responsibility of that State" and in article 2 establishes a generally accepted definition of international responsibility.

States' obligations differ under different international human rights instruments and other sources of international law. It is useful first to explain the difference between customary and treaty law and then to examine some differences under different treaty regimes. International lawyers tend to divide law into two primary sources: customary international law and treaty law. This is a division perpetuated by the Statute of the International Court of Justice (ICJ) that specifies the sources of law that the ICJ should apply to cases before it. It has little but persuasive authority outside the confines of the ICJ, but is nevertheless an important starting point as it is so often used to illustrate the different sources of law. Article 38, paragraph 1 of the Statute of the International Court of Justice reads:

> 1. The Court, whose function is to decide in accordance with international law such disputes as are submitted to it shall apply:
> a. international conventions, whether general or particular, establishing rules expressly recognised by the contesting states;
> b. international custom, as evidence of a general practice accepted as law;
> c. the general principles of law recognised by civilized nations;
> d. subject to the provisions of Article 59, judicial decisions and the teachings of the most highly qualified publicists of the various nations, a subsidiary means for the determination of law.

This article does not allow much room for accounting for the opinions of individuals, even masses of them. In 1996, for example, while the Court was considering its *Advisory Opinion on the Legality of Nuclear Weapons*, millions of people sent a signed petition to the International Court of Justice expressing their view that nuclear weapons were illegal. Although this may have indirectly had a slight influence on the Court's ultimate decisions to find nuclear weapons illegal in most cases, the members of the Court could not formally take it into account. In a somewhat confused manner, the petition was actually accepted by the Court's registry and carted around to each judge's chambers in several boxes. Do you think the opinions of individuals should be given more weight? If so, how could this be done without disturbing the delicate balance of interests that human rights often affect? Would for example the right of courts that are hearing human rights cases to hear testimony from private individuals be a worthwhile development?

Despite its shortcomings and formal limitations, article 38 of the ICJ Statute has been accepted around the world as reflecting the sources of international law for lawyers and for international political actors. This acceptance has been by international human rights bodies as well. It is thus a good place for one to begin when looking at the sources of states' international legal obligation.

3.2 Treaties

The first source specified by article 38 of the ICJ Statute is general or particular international conventions or treaties. Treaties are written agreements between two or more states or between states and international organizations or between two international organizations. They are expressions of claims and often demands by states on other states. They are also often an expression of how the states party to an agreement expect other states to act. Thus, although there are states that are not members of the United Nations, the Charter of the United Nations may still create rights and duties for these states. International agreements are the "most deliberate form of prescription." By signing and ratifying a treaty a state expressly agrees to an international obligation when the treaty comes into force. Nevertheless, treaties are a source of law that derives from custom and must be "interpreted and applied against the background of customary international law." One general rule that is widely accepted as a principle of customary international law is the principle that is frequently identified by the Latin phrase *pacta sunt servanda*. It means that agreed upon obligations are legally binding. It is the centrepiece of the rules of treaty interpretation found in the Vienna Convention on the Law of Treaties that entered into force in 1980.

Human rights treaties bind states by succession, accession or ratification. Succession describes the assumption of the responsibilities of a previous state by a state that has been created later in time. The responsibilities acquired may include those in human rights treaties that the previous state had held or another state continues to hold. Accession describes when a state that has not automatically succeeded to a previous state's treaty obligations accepts these obligations without ratifying the treaty again. It is a general description of the act of a state expressing the state's consent to be bound by a treaty. And finally, ratification is, according to article 2(1)(b) of the Vienna Convention on the Law of Treaties, "the international act so named whereby a state establishes on the international plane its consent to be bound by a treaty." Ratification differs from the other two means of assuming treaty obligations because it is detached from the existence of a previous state. If the provisions of a treaty allow, any state may ratify a treaty at any time.

The usual procedure is that the state will first consider becoming party to a human rights treaty by discussions within its political organs. The lobbying of individuals and NGOs may influence this discussion. After a decision is made to consent to or become party to a treaty, an individual representing the state will sign the treaty. In some cases this may be all that is necessary for the state to become party, in other cases the state will still have to ratify the convention. Where ratification is necessary the signature of the state still requires that the state do nothing to defeat the object and the purpose of the treaty. How ratification takes place is largely a question on national law. In some countries the legislature must agree to a treaty to express the consent of the state to be bound, i.e. ratification. In other cases this may be done by the mere notification of the signing of the treaty to the state's government. One will have to examine state law, often the constitution, to determine the appropriate means of ratification. When a state has ratified a treaty it will transmit notification of its ratification to the depository of the treaty.

Article 53 of the Vienna Convention on the Law of Treaties is particularly important to international human rights law because many writers have argued that at least some basic human rights are peremptory norms of general international law, *jus cogens*, and thus may never be derogated from by states. The consequence is that states could not enter into agreements that violate these rights. For example, a state may not agree to allow slavery to exists within its borders in a treaty with another country. While the human rights that are *jus cogens* might be few at present and thus not a great limit on states sovereign discretion, there is growing pressure to see all basic human rights (such as those in the ICCPR and ICESCR) as *jus cogens*.

The termination of treaty obligations has been of increasing attention to international human rights lawyers. This is because several states have withdrawn from international human rights treaties and at least one has tried to suspend certain obligations under a human rights treaty. Trinidad and Tobago withdrew from the ICCPR after it was criticized for the manner in which it implemented the death penalty. Their withdrawal was a legal act, which this country was entitled to undertake, but it has led to increasing diplomatic pressure being put on the government.

In 1998 when Peru attempted to withdraw its recognition of the jurisdiction of the Inter-American Court, the Court found Peru could not do so without respecting some basic principles of international law. Peru could have withdrawn from the Convention with proper notice and in accordance with its terms, but elected not to do so because such a move would have brought great political pressure to bear on Peru.

Should a state be allowed to make reservations to human rights treaties? This is a question being dealt with by Allain Pellet as the Rapporteur on the law of reservations for the International Law Commission. It is also a question that the Human Rights Committee has dealt with in its Comment No. 40 on Reservations and Declarations.

3.3 Customary International Law

Another source of international human rights law is customary international law. This law is formed by *opinio juris* and practice—usually, but not always, by states. Just how large a number of states are necessary to create a rule of customary international law is not settled. There are differences of opinion among jurists as to what constitutes *opinio juris* and practice. Generally, practice may be defined as the acts of states on the international plane or concerning matters of international law. It seems clear that a state's action in refraining from or carrying out an armed attack is state practice, but does a state's act of voting for a United Nations General Assembly resolution constitute state practice? And what about the practice of an international organisation in adopting a long line of resolutions taking a specific stance, for example, against nuclear weapons? The same questions are relevant to the concept of *opinio juris*. This concept may be defined as the belief held by a state that certain actions or refraining from certain actions is required by a legal obligation under international law. Again, one may ask if the position of a state in the voting or in an opinion voiced during the negotiating of a United Nations General Assembly resolution constitutes *opinio juris*.

The opinio juris and state practice necessary to form a rule of customary international law must usually be of a general nature—i.e. covering more than a single specific instance. In judicial proceedings it is often for the party claiming that a rule is customary international law to prove that it is. In the *Asylum Case* the ICJ determined that this burden of proof fell upon Columbia when it claimed that Peru was bound by a rule of customary international law concerning asylum.

There are some rules of customary international law that do not allow persistent objectors to avoid their application. The rules of international law that have become *jus cogens* are peremptory norms from which no state may derogate. The prohibitions of slavery, torture, piracy, genocide and the right to self-determination are often accepted as *jus cogens*, although there seems little reason to distinguish these norms from many other basic human rights such as the right to life, the right to health, the right to an adequate standard of living, the right to housing, *et cetera*. When a rule is considered to be *jus cogens* it may not be derogated from by treaty or by any other form of custom. In the words of article 53 of the Vienna Convention on the Law of Treaties a norm that is *jus cogens* is "accepted and recognised by the international community of states as a whole as a norm from which no derogation is permitted and which can be modified only by a subsequent norm of general international law having the same character." In practice the proof of a rule of *jus cogens* is difficult because one must show that states believe a rule allows no exceptions when in reality states are very cautious about restricting their sovereignty in this far-reaching manner. Considerations that may elevate a rule of customary international law to a rule of *jus cogens* include not only a uniform state practice, but also the moral import of a rule. For example, in the *Genocide Case* the International Court of Justice stated that genocide is not only contrary to the practice of states, but that it is also "contrary to moral law and to the spirit and aims of the United Nations."

While *jus cogens* norms do not tolerate objectors, other rules of customary international law may not apply to states that have persistently objected to them and who are thereby known as "persistent objectors". Thus a state that clearly manifests its unwillingness to agree with a rule of customary international law may be able to avoid being bound by that particular rule.

3.4 Other Sources of International Law

The general principles of law recognised by civilized nations are hard to distinguish from rules of customary international law. The most common distinction is to claim that general principles of law are those principles that are shared by the large majority of the world's legal systems. However, if one examines the world's legal systems it will be difficult to find any principles that mean the same thing in all or a large number of legal systems.

The last paragraph of article 38(1) refers to judicial decisions and the teachings of the most highly qualified publicists of the various nations as a subsidiary means for determining the law. The ICJ itself has never referred to publicists in its majority opinions, although they have undoubtedly referred to them and have been influenced by them in deciding the cases. Arbitral tribunals and other international decision making bodies have referred to writers, but their relevance varies widely. References to judicial decisions, on the other hand, have been more numerous and have appeared in the decisions of the ICJ as well as other international bodies. There is no system of binding precedent, even within the ICJ itself as article 59 of its Statute indicates, but a variety of judicial decisions may influence the decisions of the court.

3.5 Affirmative Action

When states act to favour disadvantaged and vulnerable groups they implement programmes of affirmative action, positive discrimination, or reverse discrimination. These are all names for action that discriminates in favour of a group of individuals, but is justified as a legitimate means of ensuring the human rights of the members of the group because there is a history of past discrimination against this group that requires special action to be overcome.

In India the Supreme Court has required the government to take positive actions to redress conditions of discrimination. Several national constitutions have also incorporated provisions allowing for the government to take affirmative action. Perhaps the most prominent expression of support for affirmative action by the international community can be found in article 4 of the Convention on the Elimination of All Forms of Discrimination Against Women (CEDAW).

CHAPTER FOUR
Human Rights and Non-State Actors

4.1 NGOs and Human Rights

Non-governmental organizations (NGOs) have emerged to represent commonly shared interests of individuals in society. In doing so these NGOs reflect a lack of satisfaction among individuals with the way their interests are represented by states. This is as true in developing countries as in the richer developed countries. One reason for this is the recognition that the protection of human rights in the developing world requires a greater sharing of resources by rich countries and non-state actors. The northern and southern NGOs have often joined forces to oppose the policies of governments, especially the United States government, which continue to exploit developing countries by trapping them into a state of almost permanent indebtedness. Together coalitions of NGOs have opposed national policies of exploitation and oppressive domination as well as the abuses of individual rights.

The influence of NGOs has increased substantially in the last thirty years. International NGOs that numbered 109 in 1909 numbered 28,900 by 1993 and have been increasing rapidly in recent years. Many of these are concerned with human rights. The 1993 World Conference on Human Rights was attended by more than three thousand NGOs and there are approximately 1,500 non-governmental organisations that hold consultative status with the United Nations. Arrangements for consultations with non governmental organizations by the Economic and Social Council (ECOSOC) and its subsidiary bodies, including the Human Rights Commission and the Sub-Commission on the Promotion and Protection of Human Rights, are governed by guidelines the Council set in its Resolution 1296 (XLIV) of May 1968. Being accredited with consultative status to ECOSOC allows a non governmental organisation to participate, to varying degrees, in the work of the Council and its subsidiary bodies. Category I organizations may submit written statements, make oral presentations and propose agenda items for the Council's and its subsidiary bodies' consideration. Category II organizations can also submit written statements and make oral presentations. NGOs with Roster status may only submit written statements. Those in Category I and II are required to submit a report on their activities to support the work of the United Nations every four years. To facilitate NGO involvement the United Nations has established an NGO Liaison Office.

As the number of non-governmental organizations continues to grow there is concern about their quality and integrity. To deal with this situation, codes of conduct for NGOs are being promulgated in national, international and local contexts. In the United Nations, the Working Group on NGOs ended several years of debate in March 1996 with weak proposals for regulating the NGOs who have Observer or Roster status with a United Nations body. In the end, ECOSOC adopted Resolution 1996/31 governing the participation of NGOs in the work of the UN.

One of the primary opportunities for NGOs to express themselves is at international conferences. A good example of this is the influence of NGOs in the drafting of the Vienna Declaration and Programme for Action that was adopted by the 1993 World Conference on Human Rights. This Declaration is an explicit expression of support for the role of NGOs in United Nations human rights activities.

Although the Vienna Declaration only explicitly refers to NGOs in a few paragraphs, it is an example of an outcome of a process in which non-state actors made a substantial contribution and influenced the wording of a document adopted by states. The Vienna Declaration may be the best example of NGOs and other non-state actors being able to influence the policies of states in matters of human rights.

The most effective work of human rights NGOs undoubtedly does not take place within the corridors of United Nations buildings or at international conferences, but takes place in the field. NGOs such as Vereniging Humanitaire Projekten, Peace Brigades International, Human Rights Watch and Amnesty International, work to protect individuals' human rights in the field. Sometimes this work is in the form of the political lobbying of governments. Other times it may include actually providing twenty-four hour a day guardianship of individuals who are under threat.

4.2 The Human Rights Defenders Declaration

One of the more relevant instruments concerning the role of non-governmental actors in the protection of human rights is a declaration that was prepared in a Working Group of the Commission on Human Rights of the United Nations. The Declaration on Human Rights Defenders was presented to the Commission, ECOSOC, and then eventually adopted by the General Assembly on 9 December 1998.

In 2000, the Commission also decided to appoint a Special Rapporteur on Human Rights Defenders. The Declaration establishes rights and responsibilities, although there are many more rights than responsibilities. By ignoring to a large degree the responsibilities that non-state actors may have under international law, governments may have denied non-state actors recognition as full participants in the processes of international human rights law. The tradition whereby non-state actors are merely passive subjects of human rights was largely continued. This was even supported by many NGOs because they did not want to be held to additional responsibilities believing that states would use this power to limit their abilities to protect human rights. NGOs and western states believed that the inclusion of responsibilities would devalue the human rights protections and that this is what the southern hemisphere states that sought to have responsibilities included were attempting to do. Is this true? Do the responsibilities of individuals distract from the human rights protections for individuals?

4.3 NGOs and Human Rights Fact-Finding

NGOs fulfil an important function by providing information to international bodies. Larger international NGOs such as Amnesty International as well as governmental bodies such as the Human Rights Committee, the Commission on Human Rights, or the European Union rely on NGOs in the field to provide them with information that they can use to scrutinise states' human rights records. National NGOs on the ground can be of the greatest assistance in this respect because they are there all the time and thus observe with much more consistency. Some NGOs undertake active human rights observance in the country in which they are established and operate, for example, the Egyptian Organization for Human Rights. Other NGOs, for example Amnesty International, have a policy of not involving national offices in national human rights observation.

The techniques used for human rights observation and the use of the acquired information also vary. The International Committee of the Red Cross, for example, is one of the 'best observers of human rights violations' despite its being primarily a humanitarian relief organisation. This is because its mandate takes it into areas of armed conflict and into prisons, both situations where human rights are frequently in danger. Nevertheless, the ICRC does not usually use the information it acquires for public human rights activities. Instead, it usually undertakes cautious diplomacy while trying to negotiate its continued presence and exercise of the powers bestowed on it by the four Geneva Conventions and their Protocols. The ICRC only exposes human rights violations publicly when (1) the information has been observed by an ICRC delegate first hand, (2) the use of the information in public forums will further prejudice the victim(s), (3) the victim consents, and (4) private diplomacy (one on one negotiations with the government) has been tried and failed. Other organizations, for example Human Rights Watch and Amnesty International, publish annual reports and lobby political decision makers. Amnesty International is well-known for its letter writing campaigns whereby masses of individuals are encouraged to write letters to political leaders who have the power to end particular human rights abuses. For fear of jeopardising its own credibility, however, Amnesty International is very particular of which cases it decides to support and only a fraction of those who request support actually become what is known as "Urgent Actions."

Some national NGOs utilize strategies that include class actions, lobbying, demonstrations, education, boycotts, strikes, etc. The activities of NGOs can be divided into two sets. One set includes those that are passive and the other set those that are active. Some NGOs combine both types of activities, while others do not. One can usually, but not always, determine if this is the case by examining the statute of the NGO which should be available to members of the public either through the national body that registers charities or through the NGO itself. NGOs such as the Social and Economic Rights Center in Nigeria and the Center for Economic and Social Rights in New York have begun to look beyond civil and political rights. Amnesty International recently began to do the same.

A unique involvement of NGOs in issues related to economic and social rights can be found in functioning of the International Labour Organization (ILO), which is headquartered in Geneva and is one of the oldest inter-governmental organizations dealing with human rights. Its mandate, however, is limited to human rights that are directly related to labour and other economic means of production. The success of the ILO has nevertheless led to some progress in the participation of NGOs in the proceedings of more general human rights bodies like the UN Human Rights Commission.

4.4 NGOs in the UN System: Is it working?

The proliferation of NGOs has also caused difficulties in being able to exercise control over the integrity of the NGOs activities. Some NGOs are created by governments or intergovernmental organizations to achieve objectives that would be more difficult to achieve otherwise. For example, many National Human Rights Commissions have been set-up by governments to defend them from international criticism. Problems have thus arisen when national human rights commissions established by governments have given their country a relatively clean bill of health, but international NGOs have found clear evidence of human rights violations.

At the 1993 World Conference on Human Rights in Vienna, some apparently independent NGOs took instructions directly from and were entirely financed by governments. The most recent extension of this trend has seen the emergence of NGOs created by inter-governmental organizations. For example, UNHCR and UNICEF now frequently create national NGOs side-by-side with the international affiliate of the organisation that already exists in the country. On the one hand these IGO-NGOs are free to operate without the cumbersome limitations of the bureaucratic decision making organs of the international organisation. On the other hand these IGO-NGOs are removed from the democratic control that is often more frequently apparent in an international organisation and are thus subject to the demands of the highest bidder. Will UNHCR-UK, for example, strive to achieve the goals established by the majority of states acting through the General Assembly of the United Nations or will this IGO-NGO merely strive to achieve the wishes of its most influential donors—that are usually only from rich industrialized countries?

The increasing use of NGOs as the preferred means of accomplishing policy objectives may reflect the belief that NGOs better mirror the values of the individuals who are world society. The fact that billions of individuals, many represented by the thousands of international NGOs around the world almost unanimously subscribe to international human rights law as a shared value, is strong evidence of a convergence of basic universal values outside of the traditional governments structures that had dominated international law. Globalizaton, for example, often heightens the recognition of shared human rights among these non-state actors.

CHAPTER FIVE
Human Rights and the United Nations

5.1 Development of Human Rights in the United Nations

Since the Second World War perhaps nowhere else has the protection of international human rights received so much attention as in the United Nations system. It was under the auspices of the United Nations that the Universal Declaration of Human Rights and the two Covenants were drafted in the early days of the organization. Since then numerous other international human rights instruments have been adopted. Two types of approaches have been taken concerning human rights within the United Nations. One has been based on treaties and the other on the general mandate of the United Nations to promote and protect human rights. This general mandate can be found in articles 1 and 55 of the Charter of the United Nations.

It is wrong to think about human rights within the United Nations System as confined to one part of the United Nations: one office, one official, or one agency. Human rights play a role in the work of almost every United Nations body and they are a responsibility of all the United Nations bodies. Nevertheless, the Office of the High Commissioner for Human Rights (OHCHR), which is part of the Secretariat of the UN, is the UN's focal point for human rights. It coordinates the activities of the United Nations concerning human rights by providing the secretariat for the United Nation's activities such as the Commission on Human Rights. It also provides technical assistance to states. The OHCHR is, however, not the only UN body working on issue of human rights.

5.2 Charter-Based Human Rights Bodies

The Charter-based human rights bodies involved in protecting human rights include the Commission on Human Rights (CHR) soon to be the Human Rights Council; the Sub-Commission for the Promotion and Protection of Human Rights (previously the Sub-Commission for the Prevention of Discrimination and Protection of Minorities), which is a subsidiary body of the CHR, but may disappear when the Council is created; the Special Rapporteurs of the CHR and the Sub-Commission; and, the Office of the High Commissioner for Human Rights. Many other United Nations specialized agencies are also involved in human rights activities. Some, like the United Nations High Commissioner for Refugees (UNHCR), were created by the General Assembly. Others, like the United Nations Educational, Scientific and Cultural Organization (UNESCO), the World Health Organization (WHO) and the International Labour Organization (ILO), were created by their own separate constitutional instruments.

The main political body dealing with human rights issues within the United Nations has always been the CHR. The CHR was a political body consisting of 53 representatives of states who changed regularly after elections held in the ECOSOC. In September 2005, the UN Secretary-General proposed and the heads of states agreed to replace this body with a Human Rights Council that would remain in session throughout the year instead of merely meeting for a few weeks a year. It has been proposed that the Council be made one of the principal bodies of the UN. It is intended that the Council will be put in place after the Commission holds its final session starting in March 2006. While the highly politicised nature of the CHR limited its efficiency, its political nature also provided an unique forum for addressing human rights violations. The meetings of the CHR also provided a forum for the exchange of ideas, information and strategies among state actors and non-state actors. In this regard, it will have to be seen if a standing Human Rights Council will continue to offer these benefits. This smaller and more exclusive Council is envisioned as having the ability to criticize countries with more authority than has been the case with the CHR. An important guarantee for this is intended to be the exclusion of major human rights abusers from membership on the Council. The United States, however, the country that has violated the human right to life of 52 million people in Afghanistan and Iraq by what is widely agreed to be illegal aggression against these countries, does not view itself as being excluded from this body. This in turn has prompted the same criticisms of bias that have plagued the CHR. Can the new Council really be independent? Can a Council that allows one of the militarily and economically most powerful countries to remain a member, but which excludes less powerful, poorer, but more populous countries be an effective protector of human rights?

Non-treaty bodies may also accept individual communications claiming that human rights have been violated. In general, a communication must relate to a widespread violation of human rights and not one isolated instance. Exactly what happens to complaints is often difficult to determine as the processes by which they are handled are usually confidential and the communicator is not kept informed of the progress (or lack thereof). One can try to follow up on a complaint by looking at indications whether it has attained adequate attention by watching for resolutions of the creation of Working Groups or Special Rapporteurs on the issue that was raised. There is also sometimes the opportunity for the Sub-Commission to hold a public debate under the procedure initially approved to deal with the practice of apartheid in ECOSOC Resolution 1235(XLII) and later extended to all issues of widespread human rights violations.

This authority has since been granted to numerous other bodies including the following non-treaty bodies that accept individual communications concerning violations of human rights under the broad formula proposed by Resolution 1235.

The Sub-Commission for the Promotion and Protection of Human Rights consists of 26 experts elected by the representatives of states who make up the Commission on Human Rights. Although these experts sit in their independent capacity, states still maintain a degree of control over them through the election process. The Sub-Commission is authorized to receive individual communications under Resolution 1503(XLVIII) of the Economic and Social Council in 1970. Today this procedure, although still called the '1503 Procedure', is governed by ECOSOC Resolution 2000/3 adopted in 2000. In the futue, this procedure may be combined with treaty-based procedures when the CHR is reformed into the Human Rights Council.

The new procedure calls upon individuals to submit communications to the Working Group on Communications of the Sub-Commission which will determine if the Communications indicates a situation of widespread and serious human rights violations that deserve the attention of the Commission's Working Group on Situations. The CHR/HR Council Working Group on Situations will then recommend action. Ultimately the CHR/HR Council can appoint a Special Rapporteur or the Secretary-General may appoint a Special Representative or a Working Group, Special Process or other means for dealing with the situation may be created. An example is the Working Group on Enforced and Arbitrary Disappearances created to deal with individual communications concerning disappearances. Information directed to the UN by individuals is often forwarded to the Sub-Commission for consideration under one of the procedures described above. The Special Process on Missing Persons in the Territory of the Former Yugoslavia was an example of a process that was created because of the magnitude of the problem in the former Yugoslavia. The mandate of the Special Process was to investigate and address all cases of disappeared and missing persons brought to its attention regardless of whether the victim was a civilian or combatant and regardless of whether or not the perpetrators were state or non-state actors. From the start, the Special Process was handicapped by lack of resources and governmental support; eventually it was absorbed into the United Nations Criminal Tribunals created by the Security Council and that had more adequate funding.

Despite the growth in the number of treaty bodies, non-treaty bodies continue to maintain an important role in ensuring respect for human rights throughout the United Nations system. They are sometimes the only means of redressing human rights violations in states that are not parties to international conventions and may not have accepted the jurisdiction of any relevant human rights treaty bodies. Additionally, they serve as an example for other United Nations bodies to become involved in the common effort to ensure people all over the world enjoy their basic human rights. Today, non-treaty bodies could also be defined to include elements of the peace-keeping and humanitarian missions of the United Nations that have a mandate to promote the reconstruction of society and its civic institutions. Often these missions include, or work hand-in-hand with, human rights monitors, electoral observers, civilian police, trial monitors and legal protection officers. Sometimes United Nations peacekeeping operations are combined with humanitarian assistance operations. The peacekeeping or humanitarian relief operations of the United Nations in Namibia, El Salvador, Cambodia, Mozambique, Guatemala, former Yugoslavia and Rwanda have all included human rights tasks and personnel. The two international criminal tribunals established in the last two examples also contribute to the protection of human rights.

5.3 Treaty-Based Human Rights Bodies

Together with the numerous non-treaty bodies that exist within the United Nations system there is a growing number of treaty related bodies. These bodies are created by international treaties from which they derive their authority. This process also means that states are free to submit themselves to one of the bodies or not to do so merely by not ratifying the treaty concerned. In recent years, however, states have flocked to ratify human rights treaties even if it meant doing so with substantial reservations. The reason for this is mainly political. The failure of a state to ratify a human rights treaty is evidence of that state's unwillingness to respect the human rights therein. This may subject the state to international ridicule, criticism and condemnation. It also often prevents the state from taking advantage of the full range of social and economic development alternatives that may be available to it. Some states 'condition' the provision of development assistance on a state's respect for human rights. While this 'conditionality' principle is seldom applied merely based on a state's adherence to human rights treaties, a state's adherence to human rights treaties is *prima facie* evidence of its good faith.

These treaty bodies deal with inter-state communications, which are possible, but extremely rare, individual communications, and states' initial and periodic reports. The latter are the consequence of obligations in the various human rights treaties that require states to submit reports at specified intervals stating how they have protected the human rights in the treaties. As one might imagine the multiplicity of human rights treaties has put a heavy reporting burden on some states. From the other side, the increasing number of states that have ratified human rights treaties has led to a serious backlog in the consideration of state reports by treaty bodies. To facilitate the better handling of state reports the treaty bodies both individually and jointly have taken several steps. First, they have agreed to allow states to submit one comprehensive initial report that will be circulated by the Office of the High Commissioner for Human Rights to all the relevant treaty bodies. This frees resources so that states' periodic reports can focus on issues of special concern to particular treaty bodies. Second, the treaty bodies have all promulgated detailed guidelines specifying the information they would like to receive from states. And finally, the committees now regularly provide states with lists of issues that they wish to discuss when considering a state's report.

Several treaties concluded under the auspices of the United Nations have created treaty bodies for protecting human rights. The foremost of these is the United Nations Human Rights Committee, created by the International Covenant on Civil and Political Rights (ICCPR) and consisting of eighteen independent experts selected by states. Individuals are entitled to petition this Committee when the state involved in the human rights violation has ratified the Optional Protocol to the ICCPR. The provisions in the ICCPR that establish the Human Rights Committee (HRC) are found in article 28-40. The HRC also has an elaborate Rules of Procedures.

The International Covenant of Economic, Social, and Cultural Rights (ICESCR) also has a Committee on Economic, Social, and Cultural Rights that reviews state reports and may one day accept individual communications as work is currently being done on a protocol to this effect. Although considered a treaty-based body because its mandate is to apply the ICESCR, it was created not by this treaty, but by ECOSOC who was given the responsibility for reviewing reports in the treaty, but decided to delegate this responsibility to a special committee.

Other treaty bodies include the Committee on the Elimination of Racial Discrimination under the Convention on the Elimination of All Forms of Racial Discrimination (CERD) and the Committee Against Torture under the Convention Against Torture and Other Cruel, Inhumane or Degrading Treatment or Punishment (CAT). Both of these committees can accept individual petitions under certain conditions (art. 14(1) CERD and art. 22 CAT). The Committee on the Rights of the Child under the Convention on the Rights of the Child (CRC) and the Committee on the Elimination of

Discrimination against Women under the Convention on the Elimination of All Forms of Discrimination against Women (CEDAW) are treaty bodies that may not review individual complaints, but only periodic state reports. A new Committee that will have the right to both review states' reports as well as to decide individual petitions is the Committee on Migrant Workers' Rights under the Convention for the Protection of the Rights of Migrant Workers and All Members of Their Families (CMWR).

In addition there are more unique types of treaty bodies. The Commission against Apartheid in Sports was set up under the International Convention Against Apartheid in Sports. Some of these treaty bodies are created under the auspices of the specialized agencies of the United Nations. Examples of these types of treaty-based bodies are the ILO Committee on Freedom of Association that can apply numerous ILO treaties and the UNESCO procedures that can examine alleged violations of the right to education. Finally, among the most recent and most significant bodies is the International Criminal Court, which can try individuals for violations of international law.

The procedures in each of these bodies differ, but there are some general comments that are applicable to all the bodies. For example, the rules of procedure that these bodies follow when reviewing the information brought to their attention are less formal, but comparable to judicial proceedings in terms of the evidence that may be produced.

The rules of procedure for communications by individuals or states to the Human Rights Committee were provisionally adopted in 1987, and finally adopted in 1994. The main procedures are periodic reporting procedures (art. 40 of the ICCPR), inter-state communications (art. 41 of the ICCPR) and individual communications (the Optional Protocol). The inter-state communication procedure has never been used by a state.

To familiarize yourself with the procedures of the Committee you should find a copy of the rules of the Human Rights Committee and read through them, answering the following questions as you read:

(1) What entities may submit information (individuals, groups, NGOs)?

(2) May they do so in person during formal or informal hearings?

(3) What type of information may be submitted? That is,

　　a. information involving the violation of an individual's human rights;

　　b. information about gross and systematic human rights abuses; or

　　c. information about policies that appear to violate human rights;

(4) Will entities submitting information necessarily be informed of the results of the consideration of their complaint?

(5) Will the body considering the information make a specific statement about the specific complaints or only consider complaints *en masse*?

Both the reporting and the individual procedure may result in recommendations being made by the Committee. In response to the reports, the Committee will usually issue a short comment on the report. This comment will congratulate states on areas where they are respecting human rights or the improvements they have made to strive towards this goal and the Committee will express its concern at areas where the protection of human rights is still weak. A transcript of a session in which a state report is discussed is sometimes available from the secretariat, but only the brief comments are usually published. State Reports are usually considered over a period of two days that usually takes place between six months and one year after the state has submitted its written report in accordance with the schedule, which is determined by the date of the state's ratification of the ICCPR. On the first day the state will send a government delegation to make representations to the Committee. The Committee members may ask questions during the government's presentation. During the presentation or afterwards the Committee may request either clarifications or additional information. The government representative will answer what questions he or she can, but may wish to delay an answer until the following day after the government has had more time to consider the question or obtain additional information. Finally, the Committee will express its views.

In response to individual communications, the Committee usually meets once with the parties after submission of written proceedings. When this meeting occurs is determined by the length of the Committee's backlog of cases on its docket, the adequacy of the written communication (in many cases additional written information is requested), and the ability of the parties to attend the meeting where they may present information. It is not necessary for the committee to hold oral hearings, although it is common practice that it does. Afterwards the Committee will discuss the case and form its view about whether or not there has been a human rights violation. Usually within several weeks after a hearing the Committee will express its "views". If the Committee determines that there has been a violation it will state so clearly, it will suggest specific action that is required by the government to remedy the violation, and it will request the state to provide information on any relevant measures taken in respect of the Committee's Views within 90 days. The action to remedy the violation may include compensation or the Committee may decide that the mere condemnation by the Committee is sufficient compensation in the particular case.

United Nations committees generally do not hold public hearings on individual communications. They do however, provide NGOs, individuals, and IGOs the opportunity to provide them information and to make short statements to a Committee on one day at the start of each session. Participation in such an information session should be arranged in advance with the Committee. Although a petitioner will not be allowed to argue a case he or she can bring additional information or emphasize information that is relevant to the consideration of individual cases.

CHAPTER SIX
Regional Mechanisms for the
Protection of Human Rights

6.1 The Development of Regional Mechanisms

While human rights have developed within the UN system they have also developed within specific regional contexts that do not include all the United Nations' member states. These regional contexts have sometimes taken steps to secure human rights that go beyond what has been done on the universal level because they can better achieve consensus on particular rights.

As between regional and more universal bodies, it is usually advisable, but not required, that an individual appeal to a regional human rights system first. This is true for several reasons. First, the regional human rights bodies are often better developed, they can offer a victim of a human rights violation better compensation if a breach is found. Second, the regional organisations usually have more influence over the countries that are members because the consensus that was necessary to vest this jurisdiction is usually based on a clearer understanding. This is in turn based on the fact that regional organisations usually emanate from more clearly identified shared values. Third, in light of the first two reasons and because most regional and United Nations bodies exclude each others' competence it is often wise to start at the regional level in case it is one's only shot at redress. Having indicated why it might be more appropriate to bring cases to regional bodies, it should be noted that there are sometimes good reasons to seek redress before an United Nations body. This might be the case when the United Nations body might be free from regional preferences that might influence the determination of a claim adversely or when the jurisprudence of the United Nations body is more favourable.

In each of these forums, there are possibilities for making individual complaints. In some cases, inter-state communications are also allowed, although such communications are rare. The provisions governing the more important and more frequent individual complaints emanate from the primary instruments that created the respective bodies, namely:

1. Article 34 of the European Convention on Human Rights (ECHR) as concerns the European Court of Human Rights (ECHR, art. 34).

2. Both a Declaration of the OAS Foreign Ministers from 1959 and the American Convention on Human Rights (ACHR) as concerns the Inter-American Commission on Human Rights and Article 44 of the ACHR as concerns the Court.

3. Article 55 of the African Charter on Human and Peoples' Rights as concerns the African Commission on Human and Peoples' Rights.

There are also provisions relating to general means of supervision in each regional system. In the Inter-American system this has meant that the Commission has taken the initative to make on-site visits and to issue reports about the situation of human rights in different countries or as concerns different human rights problems of a general interest. The African Commission has copied this practice but with much less success. In the African system, this means of investigation has been rarely used. Instead, the African Commission has relied heavily on its periodic review of state reports.

6.2 AFRICA

6.2.1 African Charter on Human and Peoples' Rights

The African system for the protection of human rights centres on the African Charter on Human and Peoples' Rights (ACHPR). This Charter was concluded under the auspices of the Organization of African Unity (OAU, now the African Union) and opened for signature at a meeting in Nairobi, Kenya on 27 June 1981. The drafting process was one in which senior African statesmen sought to establish their mark on Africa's future. The result was not merely a copy of other regional or universal instruments, but a treaty that is based on African values. This is despite, or perhaps because of, the fact that the drafting took place at a time when many African countries were struggling to emerge from the yoke of colonialism.

The ACHPR entered into force on 21 October 1986. It includes individuals civil, political, economic, social and cultural rights, group rights and responsibilities or duties of individuals. The rights are stated in a short compact form. This is in part due to the diversity of African cultures, societies and states of development. By stating the rights in a general manner, much discretion is left to states in deciding how to implement them. Most rights also do not include limitation clauses, as do almost all the rights in the ECHR and ACHR.

One unusual feature of the ACHPR is that it contains provisions providing for duties of the individual, something it has in common with the Inter-American Convention on Human Rights, but not the European Convention for the Protection of Human Rights and Fundamental Freedoms. Articles 27 through 29 of the ACHPR specify the duties of the individual. These articles compensate in part for the lack of provisions allowing for limitations of each right in the Charter. Instead, the African states decided to express the idea that rights were only limited in as far as the individual's responsibility towards his or her community required.

6.2.2 African Commission on Human and Peoples' Rights

The ACHPR creates the African Commission on Human and Peoples' Rights as the primary organ for ensuring its implementation. It consists of eleven members who are nominated and elected by African states who are party to the Charter and members of the African Union. The members are often senior government officials who continue to hold their positions while they sit on the Commission. A minority of the members have come from NGOs or have been previously recognized for their independent work to protect human rights in their countries.

The tasks of the Commission are drawn very broadly in articles 44-45 of the ACHPR. They include promotion, education, protection, interpretation, and implementation of the ACHPR. The AU Assembly of Heads of State and Government may also assign any other task to the Commission. To fulfil its tasks the Commission has named Rapporteurs; and more recently in 2003, Focal Points on Torture, Human Rights Defenders, Freedom of Expression, and Refugees. There is also a Working Group on Minorities.

The Commission has a broad power to investigate human rights abuses (art. 46) and "may draw, by written communication, the attention of that State to the matter" as well as addressing the communication to the Secretary General of the African Union and the Chairperson of the Commission (art. 47). The accused of a human rights violation then has three months to respond to the enquiring state with a "written explanation or statement elucidating the matter." If the matter is not resolved within the three-month period then either state may submit it to the Commission in accordance with article 48. A state accusing another state of a human rights violation also has the right to bring the accusation directly to the attention of the Commission according to article 49, by addressing "a communication to the Chairman, to the Secretary General of the Organization of African Unity and the State concerned." The Commission's consideration of the complaint can make use of the broad investigatory powers granted under article 46, but is likely to be restricted by resources. States also have the right to make oral representations. Only if the Assembly of Heads of State and Government so decide, will the Commission's views be made public, in contrast to both the former European Commission of Human Rights and the current Inter-American Commission on Human Rights that themselves possessed the authority to make their recommendations or decisions public. However, once its views are made public in accordance with article 59 of the African Charter, it is the Commission's opinion, that they then become binding.

Communications from non-state actors relating to human rights violations may also be submitted to the Commission. These may come from individuals or non-governmental organisations. There is no requirement that the person or body presenting the complaint is the victim of the violation or be located in the country against which the complaint is made.

When an individual complaint is submitted, it must meet the conditions that are stated in article 56. These conditions will often be interpreted in the favour of admissibility, but the petitioner must show that a substantial and good faith effort has been made to satisfy each condition and that it is impossible to do so because the domestic mechanisms are inadequate or will cause undue delay. The Commission has stated the requirement is "the exhaustion of all domestic remedies, if any, if they are of a judicial nature, are effective and are not subordinate to the discretionary power of the public authorities." The Commission has also stated that it "does not hold the requirement of exhaustion of local remedies to apply literally, especially in cases where it is "impractical or undesirable" for the complainants or victims to seize the domestic courts." And where serious and massive violations of human rights have been identified, the Commission has often — but not always — dispensed with the requirement of exhaustion of domestic remedies with the reasoning that the state party has been made aware of the alleged violation and has been given the chance to remedy the situation. Despite this accommodation, the burden of showing that one has met all the conditions of admissibility is often not an easy one and the requirements of article 56 remain extremely important for individuals and NGOs making communications to the Commission.

The Commission will decide whether to consider them by a simple majority. If it decides to consider the complaint, it will decide if there has been a violation. This finding may be made public when the Commission's report is approved for publication by the Assembly of Heads of State and Government of the African Union. To date the Commission has decided about a hundred cases on their merits. The early cases were often confined to statements of whether or not human rights were violated. The cases decided after 1998, however, have contained some of the most creative and advanced legal reasoning to be found in international human rights forums. The case of the *Ogoni People v. Nigeria* (considered in Chapter 13) is one of the most important decisions to come out of an international human rights body to date because it eloquently established the rights of groups and the responsibilities of the state for securing these rights in unambiguous language.

The following is the information that is needed for an individual communication to the African Commission. Note that you will often be requested by the African Commission to provide additional arguments on the admissibility and merits of your communication. Nevertheless, your initial communication with the Commission will be registered and the Commission seized of it, if it includes the following information in sufficient detail to show that one or more human rights protected by the ACHPR have been violated.

6.2.3 Protocol to the African Charter on the Rights of Women in Africa

The newest addition to the growing corpus of African international human rights law is the Protocol on the Rights of Women in Africa. This protocol to the ACHPR was adopted and opened for signature and ratification by states by the Assembly of Heads of State and Government of the African Union meeting in July 2003. Like the UN's CEDAW, the Protocol will primarily protect women against discrimination, but unlike CEDAW, the African Protocol does not have its own implementation mechanism.

The Protocol on the Rights of the Women in Africa provides for a substantial array of rights that are not provided for in other human rights treaties. It therefore differs from the CEDAW, which merely reiterates the duty not to discriminate against women in the enjoyment of already existing human rights. Among the 'new' rights included are: the elimination of harmful practices (art. 5); the right to a separation, divorce or annulment of marriage under certain circumstances (art. 7); the right to peace (art. 10); the expressly mentioned rights of internally displaced persons in wartime (art. 11); reproductive rights (art. 14); the right to food security (art. 15); the right to a positive cultural context (art. 17); widows' rights (art. 20); the right to inherit (art. 21); and special protections for elderly women (art. 22), women with disabilities (art. 23), and women in distress (art. 24). These rights reflect a new generation of human rights. For that reason alone the text of the Protocol is important.

Note that this treaty does not stress the need for affirmative action to address past discrimination being suffered by women, although article 9(1) (b) does call for affirmative action to ensure women equal political rights. Although states have periodic reporting obligations and questions of interpretation may be decided by the African Commission on Human and Peoples' Rights there is no right of individual petition under the Protocol. Article 18 of the ACHPR does, however, allow the African Commission to take into account the Protocol when deciding if women's human rights have been violated.

6.2.3 Other African Mechanisms

As African countries struggle against a wave of globalization that has left them relatively more impoverished then many had been in the years immediately after decolonization, civil society has also pushed the African leaders to consider new standards of rights and mechanisms for securing the basic rights of their citizens. Among the norms are the African Charter on the Rights and Welfare of the Child and Protocol to the African Charter on Human and Peoples' Rights on the Rights of the Women in Africa. The African Commission is one of the mechanisms, but there are also several others that already exist (African Committee of Experts on the Rights and Welfare of the Child) or which are on their way into existence (African Court of Human and Peoples' Rights). Other mechanisms, such as the African Union's NEPAD initiative, also play a role in promoting or hindering human rights in Africa.

6.2.3.1 African Committee of Experts on the Rights and Welfare of the Child

An African mechanism for protecting human rights of children is the African Committee of Experts on the Rights and Welfare of the Child. This body was created by the African Charter of the Rights and Welfare of the Child (ACRWC). In many respects, its jurisdiction duplicates that of the ACHPR because article 18(3) of the Charter refers to other instruments in defining the human rights of the child. Thus while the African Commission may deal with a communication concerning the rights of children, so may the Committee on the Rights of African Children in accordance with article 44 of the ACRWC. To date the contribution of the Committee has been primarily through the examination of state reports. In addition, only fifteen African states had ratified the treaty by 1 January 2003. The contribution of the Committee to the protection of human rights of children in Africa is likely to be determined during the 21st Century. It could, however, be substantial as the plight of African children is perhaps one of the most serious problems facing humanity today.

6.2.3.2 African Court of Human and Peoples' Rights

An African Court on Human and Peoples' Rights was created in 2004 with the entry into force of a Protocol to the African Charter on Human and Peoples' Rights on the Establishment of an African Court on Human and Peoples' Rights. At the meeting of Heads of Government and States in July it was decided to combine this Court with the new African Union Court of Justice. As of mid-2006 this Court is not yet in place.

The new Court will be able to hear cases brought by affected states, the Commission, African intergovernmental organizations, and, with the leave of the Court, individuals and non-governmental organizations, if the state against which the complaint is brought has entered a declaration under article 34(6). The Court will make legally binding decisions that must be implemented by the state parties. The Court will also be vested with the authority to grant advisory opinions and to encourage friendly settlements. In making its decisions the Court may apply "any ... relevant human rights instruments ratified by the States concerned." While the binding nature of its opinions is its primary contribution to the protection of human rights in Africa, a weak point will be its lack of authority to take effective action if its judgments are not implemented. However, given the respect generally shown by African countries for other legal mechanisms to date this problem may be overcome.

The protocol provides the Court with the authority to decide cases with legally binding effect and to provide advisory opinions at the request of states or the Commission. These will be the most significant contributions made by the Court to the protection of human rights in Africa. However, as the practice of the African Commission and the Inter-American Court has shown the authority of the Court will *de facto* depend on the member states and their willingness to respect it. Finally, in 2004 AU states agreed to combine this Court with the AU Court of Justice.

6.2.3.3 African Union

At their meeting in Lome, Togo, the 39th Assembly of Heads of State and Government decided to dissolve the OAU and to form the African Union as a successor organization. The new AU was based on a Constitutive Act of the African Union (CAAU) adopted on 11 July 2000; however, this act was not implemented until August 2002.

The African Union was created to provide a push towards African integration in the economic and social spheres. By the end of the 20th century, the OAU had become dulled and relatively ineffective due in large part to the apathy of its members. To remedy this situation Libya's Colonel Qadafy proposed the creation of a renewed and more energetic African

Union. If for no other reason then because of its origin, the proposal was first viewed with much suspicion. Colonel Qadafy's commitment to the idea, however, eventual overcame the obstacles. However, to counter Qadafy's apparent success, several others states initiated alternatives that eventually became known as NEPAD, which is discussed below. Because of Qadafy's enthusiasm and investment of resources, the AU was formed as an international organization while NEPAD became a somewhat ambiguous 'project' of the AU. Thus, the two competing ideas were reconciled, although many problems persist.

Much of what can be said about the African Union's contribution to human rights is mere speculation at this point or based on what we know about the human rights activities of the OAU. The latter are relevant because the African Commission of Human and Peoples' Rights, which was created by a separate treaty, will continue to exist as the most prominent human rights body in the AU. Indeed, because the AU is the legal successor to the OAU and many of its organs continue to exist and to carry out the responsibilities given to the equivalent former OAU organs. It is thus expected that the main organs of the AU will continue to contribute to the work of the ACHPR very much in the same way that those of the OAU did previously. For example, the treaty responsibilities of OAU organs under the African Charter of Human and Peoples' Rights will be automatically taken over by organs of the AU.

Perhaps the greatest challenge facing human rights in Africa is the New Partnership for African Development. The NEPAD framework for development is championed by a collective of African states led by Algeria, Senegal, Nigeria, South Africa, and Egypt. It materialized through the consolidation of several other regional initiatives, namely South Africa's Millennium Action Plan and Senegal's New African Initiative in October 2001 and has since been adopted as a project of the AU. It was originally conceived at the same time that the AU was conceived by Libya, undoubtedly as part of a response to Colonel Qadafy's idea. It was a response particularly encouraged by the United States' pressure for Africa to choose a more American-friendly leader to which it might attribute its future. Evidence of American involvement is replete through the framework document as well as by its close resemblance to the American initiated former Conference for Security and Cooperation in Europe or the United Nation's Commission on Human Rights. Both of these bodies began as mechanisms in which politics play a greater role than normative mandates. So it appears to be the case with NEPAD. While some observers have suggested that NEPAD could play an important direct role in promoting human rights in Africa, it lacks the clear mandate to do so and has also not yet illustrated such a will.

6.3 AMERICAS

The Inter-American system came into being gradually as the Organization of American States (OAS) developed. The OAS was created in 1948 by an intergovernmental conference in Bogotá, Colombia. The Charter of the OAS, sometimes known as the Charter of Bogotá, entered into force in 1951. The headquarters of the OAS are in Washington, D.C. in the United States of America. At the same conference, the states adopted the American Declaration of the Rights and Duties of Man. This Declaration is non-binding, but expresses the aspiration of the American States.

In 1959, the Inter-American Commission was created as an autonomous body outside the scope of the OAS. It was intended that the Commission would apply the American Declaration. In 1965, the Commission's Statute and Rules were amended to allow individual petitions. In 1967, the Commission was incorporated into the OAS system becoming its principle human rights organ. In this capacity, the Commission applies both the American Declaration (to states that have not ratified the ACHR) and the ACHR (to states that have ratified it).

Although a human rights declaration was adopted in 1948, the history of the development of the human rights mechanisms stretched over a longer period of time and can be understood as a result of a combination of commitment to ensuring human rights in democratic societies and attempts to avoid outside interference. The theme that runs behind this combination is the influence of the government of the United States. Since its creation the OAS has been heavily influenced by the policy concerns of the United States government. This has had the effect of encouraging some states to make commitments to respect human rights in the hope that they could avoid American intervention in their internal affairs. On the other hand, the United States has not been the best example of human rights protection itself, as it has not ratified the ACHR.

6.3.1 The Inter-American Commission

The Fifth Meeting of Consultation of Ministers of Foreign Affairs in Santiago, Chile in 1959 created the Commission on Human Rights and vested it with a responsibility for human rights. When the ACHR entered into force the Commission received the additional responsibilities for dealing with human rights cases. The provisions of the ACHR providing for these additional responsibilities of the Commission and creating the Court are found in articles 33 through 69.

The work of the Commission is summarised annually in its report to the General Assembly of the OAS. These reports have stressed the connection between human rights and democracy, as well as the political nature of this connection. In its Annual Report for 1985-1986 the Commission stressed that "experience" has confirmed, "authentic social peace and respect for human rights can only be found in a democratic system." The Commission puts much emphasis on the form of government that is necessary in order to achieve respect for human rights. The preferred form is a democracy.

The Commission has broad investigatory powers in both general situations and in specific cases that have been brought to its attention. It has also not been shy in applying its authority to request and make on-site visits and to enquire about human rights situations where information has come to its attention. These visits are often planned well in advance and the result of substantial attention from OAS states to a particular situation of human rights abuses. Nevertheless, the Commission has come out with sometimes harsh reports and has even made press releases while a mission is on-going calling on a government to respect human rights and cooperate with the Commission.

The Commission has a broad mandate to promote and protect human rights in the Americas. At the same time, it operates on a budget that is greater than that of the African Commission, but less than that of the European system. In 2000, the Commission's budget was around three million dollars and there were fifteen professional staff working at the Commission. Although it initially began with visits and political interaction with governments to address human rights abuses, by the end of the 20th century the Commission now concentrates on individual cases.

As noted above, individual applications are possible under the Commission's wider jurisdiction to invoke the American Declaration of the Rights and Duties of Man. There is also a treaty-based authority to receive individual applications in accordance with article 46 of the American Convention on Human Rights.

The Commission may also make onsite visits. This power arises under a broad reading of article 41 and its subsidiary function as the main organ for promoting and protecting human rights under the American Declaration of Human Rights and within the Organization of American States. Initially the Commission used onsite visits as its primary means of promoting and protecting human rights, towards the end of the twentieth century it began to spend more energy on deciding individual cases.

The Commission also has an important role of reporting to the General Assembly of the Organization of American States. These reports are made to the annual meeting of the General Assembly and are public documents. Initially the Commission decided to include states based on it own, often politicized, criteria. In Chapter VI of its report to the General Assembly in 2000, the Commission established five criteria for deciding what topics or countries upon which it will report. These five criteria are: 1. states that do not have elected governments, 2. states that have suspended some rights of the ACHR and the ADRDM, 3. a state for which there is clear and convincing evidence of massive and grave violations of human rights, 4. states that are in transition from any of the three previous situations, and 5. states in which temporary and structural situations seriously impair the enjoyment of human rights.

The Commission has occasionally used its powers to make often broad and bold statements such as criticizing the United States for its embargo of Cuba and making less controversial recommendations that include requesting states to ratify the Statute of the International Criminal Court.

The Commission may also name Rapporteurs on different subjects — women's rights, indigenous persons, displaced persons, migrant workers, *et cetera* — who do reports that the Commission then publishes. The Rapporteurs are usually members of the Commission. These Rapporteurs have been somewhat responsive to the concerns of NGOs and have tried to involve them in their investigations.

The Commission's decisions are not binding, according to the Inter-American Court of Human Rights in the *Genie Case*, (Preliminary Objections), Ser. C, No. 21 (27 January 1995), but some states have implemented laws that require the state to comply with the recommendations therein. When adopting its new rules in May 2001 the Commission codified its somewhat inconsistent practice of following-up some cases by codifying this practice in the hope that it would be used more often. Furthermore, in contrast to the African Commission that must request the Assembly of the African Union to publish its recommendations or decisions, the Inter-American Commission possesses this ability itself according to article 51(3) of the ACHR.

The Commission's activities — like that of the African Commission described above — have been somewhat handicapped by the failure of states to provide the Commission with adequate resources.

6.3.2 Inter-American Court of Human Rights

The Inter-American Court of Human Rights is a body with legally binding authority that may only be invoked when the Commission has referred a case to the Court in a contentious case. The Court and the Commission has not always been on good terms, although they form two parts of the same system for the protection of human rights. They have often, despite differences complemented each other's work. In this cooperation, the Commission has often been able to defuse highly political situations, while the Court has shielded human rights from dilution through political compromise.

According to article 64 of the ACHR, the Court can also entertain requests for advisory opinions. There are two types of advisory opinion jurisdiction enjoyed by the Court, which in keeping with the intention of the drafters, have been interpreted liberally. The first, found in Paragraph 1 of article 64, provides for the right of states or organs of the OAS acting within their competencies to ask advisory opinions. This provision allows the Commission to request advisory opinions. According to paragraph 2 of article 64, member states only may also request the Court to express its opinion on the compatibility of their laws with their international obligations under Inter-American human rights treaties. In the Advisory Opinion on the *Enforceability of the Right to Reply or Correction*, Advisory Opinion OC-7/86, 29 August 1986, IACtHR, Ser. A, No. 7 (1986), held that this unusual right was indeed legally enforceable before it. Note that because this right is not protected in any other international human rights instrument, an advisory opinion by the Inter-American Court is perhaps the only means by which this issue could have been clarified.

The Inter-American court has reiterated that it has the exclusive right to decide its competence to review cases. The Court re-iterated that this competence was part of the longstanding practice of international tribunals. The issue arose because the Peruvian government feared that the Court would uphold the decision of the Commission by a binding judgment in several cases. One of those cases involved Peruvian President Alberto Fujimori's dismissal of all the Constitutional Court Judges and his replacing them in a manner that allegedly contravened the Constitution of Peru. The dismissed judges brought this matter to the attention of the Inter-American Commission that held that Peru had violated its obligations under the ACHR. The Commission then referred the case to the Inter-American Court. To avoid an adverse finding by the Inter-American Court, the government of Peru sought to withdraw from the jurisdiction of the Court, which it had previously accepted. Although the Court could not prevent Peru from withdrawing, it did hold Peru to its obligations in cases that were already before the Court and that a withdrawal had to satisfy certain conditions. *Constitutional Court Case*, IACtHR, Ser. C, No. 55 (1999).

6.3.3 Human Rights Treaties in the Americas

The central legal obligations concerning the protection of human rights in the Inter-American system flow from the American Convention on Human Rights (ACHR) from 1969. The ACHR lists numerous human rights and, like the African Charter, it contains references to the duties of individuals. The ACHR is the broadest of the human rights instruments in the Inter-

American system, but it is not the only human rights treaty. Other human rights treaties include the Protocol of San Salvador, Concerning Economic and Social Rights from 1988, but not yet entered into force; the Protocol to the American Convention of Human Rights to Abolish the Death Penalty from 1990; the Inter-American Convention to Prevent and Punish Torture from 1985; the Inter-American Convention on Forced Disappearance of Persons from 1994; the Inter-American Convention on the Prevention, Punishment, and Eradication of Violence against Women from 1994 and the ground breaking Inter-American Convention on the Elimination of All Forms of Discrimination Against Persons with Disabilities from 1999. There is also the American Declaration of the Rights and Duties of Man that is not a legally binding treaty, but which includes broad declaratory statements about human rights. This Declaration is important because the Commission, but not the Court, has jurisdiction to decide if states have acted contrary to its provisions even if the state is not party to the ACHR. Thus, the Commission has applied the Declaration as reflecting customary international law among OAS states and has thereby made it *de facto* legally binding on OAS member states that have not yet ratified the ACHR.

The ACHR was adopted in 1969 and entered into force in 1978. It contains a broad selection of civil and political rights. Articles 3 through 26 contain rights while articles 1 and 2 establish the general legal effect of these rights. Article 1 specifies that states must respect these rights for every person within their jurisdiction and article 2 requires legislation to be put in place ensuring such respect. There are also some rights that do not frequently appear in other treaties such as the right to reply (art. 14), the right to a name (art. 18), the right to compensation (art. 10), and the right to judicial protection (art. 25). There is also an emphasis on democratic participation in government, especially article 23, which is emphasized in much of the work of the OAS. And like the ACHPR (art. 14), the right to property is protected in the ACHR (art. 21).

Article 26 must be read in conjunction not only with the Charter of the OAS, which itself refers to economic and social rights, but also with the Declaration of the Rights and Duties of Man and the Protocol of San Salvador both containing several economic, social and cultural rights. The economic and social rights in the Declaration will be applied by the Commission to states that have not ratified the ACHR and thereby remain bound by the general authority vested in the Commission to apply the Declaration. The Protocol of San Salvador entered into force in 2001 and allows individual petitions regarding the rights of trade unions (art. 8: the right to establish a trade union, the rights of individuals to join and the right of trade unions to function freely) and education (art. 13).

Unlike the African Charter, but similar to the European Convention, the ACHR contains a general article concerning the suspension of guarantees (art. 27). Paragraph 2 of this article lists the rights that may not be suspended. The list is broader than the ECHR and the ICCPR and thus prevents states from derogating from a large number of human rights.

Like the African Charter, the ACHR considers the responsibilities of the individual towards other individuals in article 32. While the African Charter considers individual responsibilities towards the State as well as "other legally recognised communities," the ACHR is more vague in specifying that the responsibilities are to one's family, community and mankind.

The ACHR is implemented by several organs within the OAS. First, there are the general organs of the OAS that include the General Assembly, the Meeting of Ministers of Foreign Affairs, the Permanent Council, the Inter-American Economic and Social Council and the Inter-American Judicial Committee. In addition, there is the Human Rights Commission and the Court that are the primary bodies for dealing with human rights in the Inter-American system. There are also six specialized organizations in the OAS; the most prominent of these dealing with issues of human rights are the Inter-American Children's Institute, the Inter-American Commission of Women, and the Inter-American Indian Institute.

The primary institutions concerned with the protection of human rights in the Inter-American system are the Judicial Committee, the Commission and the Court. The Judicial Committee advises the OAS on points of law and on the development of international law, including human rights law. The primary focus of the Judicial Committee in recent years has not been the development of international human rights law.

The Inter-American Commission on Human Rights has been the primary body dealing with human rights in the Inter-American system for the protection of human rights. Its prominence is due in part to it having a very extensive mandate. It is also the only body to which individuals under the jurisdiction of the United States can appeal.

The other body responsible for contributing to the promotion of human rights in the America's is the Inter-American Court of Human Rights. This body has gained significant respect through its more neutral handling of the legal issues in human rights cases. Its interpretation of the Convention and its willingness to address difficult issues has given it an important place in the development of international human rights law. Still, the Court has often been handicapped both by a lack of resources as well as by the lack of support from member states who have not often backed up their already thin rhetoric with action. The Inter-American Court of Human Rights has both an advisory as well as contentious case jurisdiction. Its advisory opinions have been very important in developing the law.

Additional Inter-American bodies concerned with the protection of human rights include national officials, the Unit for the Promotion of Democracy, the Inter-American Institute of Human Rights, the Pan-American Health Organization (an independent international health organization that is part of both the United Nations via the World Health Organization or WHO and the OAS families), and other NGOs. In addition, the Inter-American Defense Board and the Inter-American Defense College have done comparative research on institutional human rights teaching and the successful training of law enforcement officers. Finally, the OAS's Secretariat has provided countries with expert technical assistance to evaluate and initiate programs involving human rights.

The Inter-American system for the protection of human rights is one of the most developed in the world and only second to the European system in terms of the respect it enjoys by its state parties. The main shortcoming, however, is the failure of the United States and Canada to fully join the system. This failure has prevented the Inter-American system from developing to the extent that the European system has developed. At the same time, it shows a significant disrespect for the development of human rights by some of the richest and most influential countries in the world. It is also embarrassing for these countries internationally as while even the newest states in the Council of Europe have readily accepted the jurisdiction of the European Court of Human Rights, states that publicly pride themselves as being the beacons of democracy are openly flaunting the most basic principles of a striving democracy, respect for human rights.

6.4 EUROPE

There are several international organizations concerned with the protection of human rights in Europe: the Council of Europe (CE), the European Union (EU) and the Organization for Security and Cooperation in Europe (OSCE). Each of these is discussed separately below.

6.4.1 The Council of Europe

The primary forum for the protection of human rights in Europe is the Council of Europe. This international (intergovernmental) organization, headquartered in Strasbourg, France was established after the Second World War by five states, but it quickly grew to 45 states. It consists of a Council of Ministers, a Parliamentary Assembly and a Secretary-General. The mandate of the Council of Europe is very broad. It includes a broad range of social policy that is coordinated with Europe's other major regional organization, the European Union. Initially, neither the Council of Europe nor the European Union dealt with issues of (military) defense. Defense policy was a task that was left to NATO and the fledgling Western European Defense Union.

Article 3 of the Treaty Establishing the Council of Europe (not to be confused with the European Convention on Human Rights) does, however, provide a clear responsibility for protecting human rights. Initially, the Council of Europe's primary means of protecting human rights was to expel a country. This has never happened, although it almost did in the *Greek Colonels Case*, but Greece withdrew from the Council of Europe before it could act.

During its early years, the Council of Europe was not very prominent even in Europe as well as in wider international affairs. In 1951, the Council of Europe took steps to strengthen the means by which it could protect human rights. The major step it took was to draft a European Convention on the Protection of Fundamental Freedoms and Human Rights. Even this did not have an immediate impact. The first president of the European Court of Human Rights never heard a case and the then-existing European Commission of Human Rights heard only a few dozen cases a year in its early days. Nevertheless, European states still prize membership in the Council of Europe. Although not as economically attractive as membership in the European Union, membership in the Council of Europe still provides many benefits. Among these benefits are involvement in political decision making concerning issues such as immigration, police, security, crime prevention and, of course, human rights. To become a member of the Council of Europe a state must agree to operate as a democracy that respects the rule of law and human rights. Additionally states must agree to cooperate with the Council and its bodies on these matters. In practice, these requirements have been interpreted as requiring states to ratify the ECHR and its protocols and to agree to submit to the procedures for individual and inter-state complaints.

Originally, the Committee of Ministers had the last word on human rights matters. Even cases decided by the Court could be sent to the Committee of Ministers. In several cases referred to it, however, the Committee could not take action because of the requirement that two-thirds of the Committee, which is made up of state representatives, was not in support of action. Finally, action was taken to try to strengthen the system at the same time that the Council was expanding. In addiiton to the members of the Council of Europe a number of states had been invited to be 'guests' — a special status that is meant for states preparing for membership. At the same time, Protocol No. 11 from 1998 largely removes responsibility for human rights from the domain of the Committee of Ministers and gives the Court more power. The Committee of Ministers retains a residual role in ensuring that the judgments of the Court are respected.

Other entities exercising human rights competencies under the auspices of the Council of Europe include the Secretary-General and (European) High Commissioner on Human Rights. The former has the right in accordance with article 62 of the ECHR to request reports on human rights matters from states. In 2000, for example, the Secretary-General asked the Russian Federation to report on how it had implemented certain articles under the ECHR. The European High Commissioner for Human Rights has a more ambiguous role. He may act to protect human rights in states of the Council. The first High Commissioner, a Spaniard, was criticized for failing to criticize governments when he reported on the situation of the ETA in Spain and was, according to critics, very uncritical of the government of Spain.

The main human rights body in Europe, the European Court of Human Rights, accepts both individual and inter-state complaints. There is also a European Committee on Torture under the European Convention for the Prevention of Torture and Inhuman or Degrading Treatment or Punishment and a Committee of Experts under the European Social Charter. The European Committee on Torture does not deal with individual complaints, but it has the right to visit countries without notice, which have become parties to the European Convention on Torture. It may visit prisons or other enumerated places and then writes a report on its visit. The weight of these reports has varied.

The Committee of Experts under the European Social Charter is also unable to receive complaints from individuals. This Committee may only accept complaints from expressly enumerated non-governmental organizations — usually trade unions. The Committee of Experts makes a decision that is then communicated to a state. The state should implement; if it does not sanctions may follow.

6.4.1.1 Human Rights Protected Under the ECHR

The human rights protected in the European system are primarily civil and political rights, economic, social and cultural rights are protected to a lesser degree. The difference is mainly in the types of procedures that litigants may invoke to protect their rights. An exception is the right to education that is found in article 2 of Protocol No. 1 to the ECHR. The jurisprudence or case law of the European institutions interpreting and applying the human rights in the ECHR is some of the most developed of any international human rights mechanisms. This is largely because of the large numbers of cases that have been brought by private individuals through individual application procedures in the ECHR.

The European Court has been perhaps the most developed in interpreting and applying international human rights law. This does not mean, however, that it has been the most progressive. Indeed, the European Court of Human Rights is perhaps the most conservative of all the international human rights bodies in the interpretations it gives to rights. This in turn, might be due to the fact that the European Court has greater authority in the national legal systems and therefore does not want to threaten that authority by attempting to push states too far. Is this a legitimate view for a human rights body to hold? Is it a realistic one? What might be the long-term consequences? In the Court's defense it should be pointed out that it has never explicitly stated that it is or should be giving restrictive interpretations of human rights in the ECHR. Nevertheless, the often-criticized doctrine of "margin of appreciation" does just this.

The doctrine of margin of appreciation allows the Court to defer to the judgment of states when weighing individual rights against the interests of the state. It does not preclude the Court from reviewing a state's decision to ensure that it is in accordance with the ECHR, but it can be used by the Court to limit its review when it believes that a decision is better made by a government and has been reasonably made. The Court will review the government's exercise of discretion, even in one of the most sensitive areas of state competence, national security. *Tinnelly & Sons v. United Kingdom*, ECtHR, Appl. No. 62/1997/846/1052–1053. This indicates an important intersection of human rights and politics as well as the restrictions international human rights bodies recognize when going into such areas.

6.4.1.2 The European Court of Human Rights

There are both political and judicial procedures for the protection of human rights under the auspices of the Council of Europe. The principle political body is the Committee of Ministers that is the meeting of Prime Ministers (or the highest political officials) or the Foreign Ministers. Although the ministers themselves only come together at intervals, a permanent working group meets with more regularity. The principle judicial organ of the Council of Europe is the European Court of Human Rights. Previously there was a Commission that screened cases going to the Court, but this was abolished in 1998 by Protocol No. 11. At that time individuals were given the right to petition the Court directly.

The European Court of Human Rights was created by the original ECHR. Its procedures were revised in November 1998 when Protocol No. 11 entered into force and will be revised again after Protocol No. 14, which was open for ratification in 2004. The Court is composed of one judge from every country for a total of 45 judges. Under the new procedures, individual judges may decide on admissibility. Otherwise the Court sits in Chambers or ultimately a Grand Chamber to consider cases. Any individual, including a company or corporation, may bring a complaint to the Court (art. 34 ECHR) as may a state (art. 33). This difers from the Inter-American human rights mechanisms that only allow individuals to bring cases.

The general rules of admissibility apply before the ECHR. An applicant, for example, must exhaust domestic remedies and submit his or her application within six months of having done so (art. 35 ECHR); must be personally affected – although this has been interpreted broadly; and must meet the formal requirements of an application — such as signed, not anonymous, not in disparaging language, not before another international human rights body, and pertaining to a human right in the ECHR (art. 35). Protocol No. 14 will also give the Court the power to dismiss cases where it deems that the damage being done to a Petitioner is not significant enough.

The Court Registry will register an application that meets the formal requirements for admissibility. The application is then referred to a Committee of a Chamber of the Court for consideration of other aspects of admissibility. The Chamber will assign a judge to be Rapporteur for the case. The Rapporteur will make a report determining whether the case should be declared admissible. Although the Rapporteur's determination is not binding, the three members of the Chamber of the Court usually follow it. The Rapporteur is usually the national judge from the country against whom the petition has been brought. If the case is declared admissible then the parties will be asked to submit further written pleadings to a Chamber of seven judges. Eventually a hearing will usually be held and the Chamber of the Court may make a judgment that is binding on the state and from which there is no appeal. When a case involves an important point of European human rights law or when a party can make an overwhelmingly convincing argument, the Chamber of the Court may refer a case to the Grand Chamber (art. 30 and 43 ECHR). It is important to remember that decisions of the Grand Chamber are final and there is no appeal from them.

Third parties may not intervene in a case, but may be invited to provide an *amicus curiae* brief to the Court after a case has been declared admissible. In addition, a litigant whose case has been declared admissible (and not before) may claim legal aid from the Council of Europe if they are able to show that they cannot pay the costs of litigation themselves. The costs of all proceedings up to and including the decision on admissibility, however, must be borne by the applicant. An applicant who believes that his or her human rights have been violated can often find a NGO to champion his cause.

Cases that come before the Court must have exhausted domestic remedies and must be filed within six months of the exhaustion of domestic remedies. It can take an additional several months for the Court to deal with a case and only the minority of cases are granted an oral hearing. If irreparable harm might be caused before a case can be heard and decided the Court can decide to grant interim measures (or what is called precautionary measures or preliminary measures, which are similar to injunctive relief under domestic law). To provide these measures, however, the Court must be provided with reliable information indicating that a violation of human rights is about to take place. It will then direct the state concerned to take steps to prevent the violation from occurring. The interim measures, by their very nature are temporary. They lapse once the Court has taken a final decision, although a finding of a violation may require that the state make the temporary measures permanent. The Court has used interim measures to prevent deportations and extraditions. Thus where a person is threatened with imminent deportation to a country where he or she might suffer torture, cruel, inhumane or degrading treatment or punishment, the Court may order the state not to deport the person until it has had the opportunity to review his or her claim in more detail. Although such orders are not mentioned in the ECHR — but instead are found in the Rules of the Court — they are binding and failure to observe them constitutes a breach of an international obligation. Originally, the Court had held in the *Cruz Varas v. Sweden, Cruz Varas and Others v. Sweden*, ECt. HR, Application Number 15576/89, Judgment of 20 March 1991 at para. 102, that the interim measures of the Commission were not binding. In *Öcalan v. Turkey*, European Court of Human Rights, Application Number 46221/99 Judgment of 14 December 2000, the Court granted interim measures requiring the Turkish government to give guarantees that the Petitioner would have a fair trial. The Turkish government responded by first disputing the Court's ability to grant such measures, but eventually complied by delaying the execution of the prisoner. The binding nature of interim measures is discussed by the Court in the case of *Mamatkulov and Abdurasulovic v. Turkey*, ECtHR, App. Nos. 46827/99 and 46951/99, Judgment of 6 February 2003. In this case the Court held that its interim measures were binding.

Another important aspect of the Court's powers is its jurisdiction. The European Court, like the Inter-American Court of Human Rights, has the right to decide upon its own jurisdiction (*"competence d'competence"*). In exercise of this competence, the Court has found that the United Kingdom could limit the jurisdiction of the Court by entering a derogation to the ECHR. Somewhat problematically, the Court held that this prohibits it from continuing to deal with cases that have been filed. The Inter-American Court has taken almost the opposite view holding that states that accept its jurisdiction can no longer withdraw except by renouncing the ACHR *in toto* and even then already pending cases remain under the jurisdiction of the Court. *Constitutional Court Case*, IACtHR, Ser. C, No. 55 (1999).

The Court also deals with inter-state complaints. *Ireland v. United Kingdom*, ECtHR, Ser. A, No 25 (18 January 1978) is one of the rare examples of an interstate complaint before the European Court of Human Rights. This example also contains a good discussion of jurisdiction in which the Court holds that it may decide a case even if the state party has agreed to cease the violation.

In practice, there have been few cases by states against other states. Most of the Court's case law has been based on petitions brought by private individuals. To bring a case, an individual must have exhausted his or her domestic remedies. Often the government will challenge on admissibility of a petition claiming that a claimant has not exhausted domestic remedies. *Deweer v. Belgium*, ECtHR, Judgment of 27 February 1980 a Belgium Butcher who failed to abide by pricing guidelines that were applicable to his wares. The Butcher claimed he had made a mistake and had rectified it when it was brought to his attention, nevertheless, he was fined and received a letter in which the government threatened to close his shop if he did not pay the fine. To avoid closure he paid the fine under protest. Instead of appealing the fine to higher administrative authorities, he complained to the then-existing European Commission and eventually the case went to the Court. His claim was based on the inappropriate nature of the domestic remedies for his claim under article 6 of the ECHR. The Court, however, gave a broad margin of appreciation to the government and found Deweer inadmissible.

6.4.2 Other Instruments Relevant to the Protection of Human Rights in Europe

As mentioned above, the Council of Europe strives to ensure human rights through both political and judicial mechanisms. An example of a political decision is the Parliamentary Assembly's Recommendation 1201 from 1993 concerning minorities that recommends an additional protocol to the ECHR to protect minorities or same the Parliamentary Assembly's recommendation for an additional protocol on cultural rights.

The Commissioner for Human Rights of the Council of Europe is concerned with the protection of human rights of both the minority and majority populations in member states. His role is to provide technical support, education, and advice to governments on issues related to human rights. The Commissioner visits countries, dialogues with states, and receives solicited and unsolicited information on human rights in member states from a variety of sources. His reports have won praise from both member states and NGOs alike and play an important role in the protection of human rights in Europe. He has been especially active in countries that are in situations of conflict or state of emergency and might therefore have derogated from their obligations under some provisions of human rights treaties.

The Council has also adopted fourteen protocols additional to the ECHR. Some of these contain substantive rights and some deal with procedural matters. The right to enjoyment of one's property, to freedom of movement, and not to have the death penalty imposed in peacetime, have been added to the ECHR in protocols. For example, Protocol No. 12 from 2000 extended the prohibition on discrimination found in article 14 beyond the remit of rights in the Convention, to any rights "set forth by law". This makes the ECHR's prohibition of discrimination as broad as the prohibition in article 26 of the ICCPR.

The Council of Europe has also adopted several specialized human rights Conventions. The European Convention for the Prevention of Torture and Inhuman and Degrading Treatment or Punishment from 1989 strengthens the mechanisms for ensuring compliance with the already established prohibition of torture. Its outstanding feature is that states agree to submit to on-site visits by the European Committee for the Prevention of Torture. The Convention, however, does not contain a definition of torture.

There are almost 200 treaties that have been concluded under the auspices of the Council of Europe and many of them deal with issues of human rights. Other specialised conventions include the European Convention on the Exercise of Children's Rights, the Framework Convention for the Protection of National Minorities, and the European Charter for Regional or Minority Languages. All of these conventions are drafted in very broad terms. The first adding little to the mechanisms for ensuring already existing rights of the child in the widely ratified United Nations Convention and the second leaving the definition of who is a minority up to each government. The Framework Convention also includes the provision for a Committee of Experts, which may review state reports. Nevertheless, this Convention has not functioned well in practice because some states, such as France, have claimed that there are no minorities on their territory.

Finally, there is the European Social Charter that has been in force since 26 February 1965 in one form or another. It provides for social and economic rights and is ratified by about two dozen states of the Council of Europe. The Charter includes some general principles applicable to all who ratify it and then some specific rights of which states must choose at least five of seven that they will undertake to respect. These rights include: (1) the right to work, (2) the right to organize trade unions, (3) the right to bargain collectively, (4) the right to social security, (5) the right to social and medical assistance, (6) the right of a worker's family to social, legal and economic protection, and (7) certain rights for migrant workers. An Additional Protocol in 1992 added several rights having to do primarily with equal employment opportunities. A European Committee of Social Rights examines state reports and oversees the implementation of the Charter. The Additional Protocol enhances the powers of this Committee to enable it to meet with states and to request information from them. Above this Committee, there is the Governmental Committee that reviews and approves its reports and ultimately the Council of Ministers who may adopt recommendations based on the approved reports. Protocols from 1991 and 1995 revised the monitoring mechanisms, including creating a limited collective compliant procedure. In 1996 a Revised European Social Charter was promulgated taking into account many of the above-mentioned developments.

The Europe Social Charter is likely to become increasingly important as resources become more scarce around the world and both Council of Europe and European Union expand their membership. Despite this increasing importance the means for bringing petitions for specific cases of violations of social rights in Europe are limited and the test remains complex. The means for bringing a petition are limited by the fact that some rights cannot be the subject of complaints and even for the protection of those rights that may be the subject of petitions the entity that bring a petition is very limited. The complexity of the text is the result of political negotiations, a fragmented text, and the failure of more than a third of the Council's member states to ratify any of the instruments that make up the ESC.

6.4.3 European Union

The European Union (EU) was established as an economic community. Thus, the human rights protected by its institutions must be related to economic undertakings. In the 1990's, the European Union's jurisdiction expanded with a series of treaties including the Maastricht Treaty, the Single European Treaty and the Amsterdam Treaty. In 2004 the Union grew from 15 to 25 member states. The preamble to the latest treaty calls for the European Court of Justice to take into account human rights. This is also a principal of the new draft European Constitution that has not yet entered into force. Nevertheless, the main basis for jurisdiction is still the Treaty of Rome Establishing the European Economic Community that deals with economic matters. The new treaties very much expand the areas in which the EU may become involved. In 1999, the European Union adopted a Charter of Fundamental Human Rights that expressly allows the European Court of Justice in Luxembourg (not to be confused with the European Court of Human Rights in Strasbourg) to apply the human rights in the ECHR, although the claims must still meet the requirements for admissibility that are found in the EU Treaty. The result is that both the European Court of Justice and European Court of Human Rights may deal with the same claims and petitioners may do forum shopping.

Decisions by the European Court of Justice usually focus on economic concerns, but this does not mean that they cannot also concern issues involving human rights. To date, however, the Court of Justice has only looked to international human rights law where there is a question involving a right granted under the European Union treaty. This has changed now that the European Union has adopted a resolution stating that the Court of Justice should apply the international human rights in the ECHR and adopting the Charter of Fundamental Rights of the European Union. This

Charter was adopted after the Court of Justice ruled that the European Union could not become a party to the ECHR.

The European Court of Justice has held that fundamental human rights are part of community law when they are related to an issue to which community law was applicable. *Nold, Kohlen- und Baustoffgrosshandlung v. Commission of the European Communities*, Case 4/73, Eur.Ct. of Justice, [1974] *ECR* 491, [1974] 2 *CMLR* 338 (14 May 1974), involved a challenge to the European Commission's ability to authorize an interference with the purchasing rights of the Nold company. The Commission had taken a decision that re-classified the Nold business as a purchaser of coal so as to put it in a worse position than it had previously been because under the new classification it had to buy coal from a middle party and could no longer buy coal directly from a major supplier. Among the grounds that Petitioner argued when challenging the Commission's decision was that it interfered with its property rights. This ground was dismissed, but the importance of the case lies in it being the leading precedent in which the European Court of Justice applied human rights.

The Charter of Fundamental Rights of the European Union contains a broad array of civil, political, social, and economic rights. It also contains a human right to asylum (art. 18), environmental rights (art. 37), consumer rights (art. 38), a right to good administration (art. 41), and a right to diplomatic and consular protection (art. 46). These rights are much broader then the protections provided for in the ECHR, although, according to article 51, the rights are only directed towards "Member States ... when they are implementing Union law" and the "Charter does not establish any new power or task for the Community or the Union, or modify powers and tasks defined by the Treaties."

6.4.4 Organization on Security and Cooperation in Europe

The Organization on Security and Cooperation in Europe (OSCE) can be traced back to the Helsinki Final Act from 1975. This act includes general declaratory statements about human rights, democracy and security. These statements reiterate many existing human rights, but are not themselves intended to create binding legal obligations.

Until 1990, the OSCE functioned as the ill-defined Conference on Security and Cooperation in Europe (CSCE). At a meeting in Paris in 1990 the CSCE became the OSCE and three institutions were formed: (1) the CSCE Secretariat in Prague, (2) the Conflict Prevention Centre in Vienna and (3) the Office for Democratic Institutions and Human Rights (initially named the Office for Free Elections) in Warsaw. The Office for Democratic Institutions and Human Rights (ODIHR) has been active in election observation in emerging democracies. Such services may be requested by a government, or initiated by a request from the ODIHR. Fifty-three states participate in the work of the OSCE, including states from outside Europe. To date however its influence has been marginal.

One of the major accomplishments of the OSCE is the Office of the High Commissioner for National Minorities. The mandate of High Commissioner extends to (1) the collection and dissemination of early warning information, (2) the collection of information about minority issues, and (3) visits to countries. The High Commissioner is answerable to the Committee of Senior [Government] Officials and may make recommendations and reports on particular situations. The High Commissioner may also accept and consider information from any source, including NGOs and individuals, in carrying out his tasks.

The focus of the OSCE has been on dialogue and security measures. Since the collapse of the Soviet Union, it has been dominated by the United States, whose human rights interests concentrated on civil and political rights. Nevertheless, the 1989 Vienna Declaration of the then Conference on Security and Co-operation in Europe (now the OSCE) declared that "...the promotion of economic, social, cultural rights...is of paramount importance for human dignity and for the attainment of the legitimate aspirations of every individual" and states guarantee the "effective exercise" of these rights. Thus, at least in theory, economic, social and cultural rights should be a concern of the OSCE. In the recent attempts by the OSCE to ensure human rights, however, this has not been the case. The OSCE's work in the former Yugoslavia is a prime example.

The OSCE has major human rights responsibilities under the Dayton Agreement, which suspended the war in Bosnia and Hercegovina by introducing a NATO occupation force into the country during 1996. The work initially focused on the elections that were held in late 1996, but there is also a longer-term human rights component. Unfortunately, this operation was organized from Washington, D.C., in the United States, rather than from the ODIHR in Warsaw, that has experience with election and human rights observation in emerging democracies in Eastern Europe. The decision to bypass the ODIHR with less experienced individuals led to many difficulties in the Bosnian operation. Under the Dayton Agreement the OSCE is mandated to ensure that conditions for elections are present and, with other organizations, to monitor human rights. Additionally, the Ombudsperson is appointed by the Chairman-in-Office of the OSCE. Initially, it had been planned to provide up to 500 human rights monitors, but this number was reduced to around fifty. In addition, there are about 250 staff members employed on the project to prepare for the elections. The OSCE human rights observers who are in the country are based in Sarajevo and in regional centres in Banja Luka, Bihać, Mostar, Sokolac and Tuzla. The priorities of both the election and human rights observers are human rights concerned with the elections, that is, freedom of movement, expression, association and assembly and the prohibition of discrimination.

The OSCE's field missions have no ability to investigate specific cases, unless they are specifically designated observer missions. They may and should, however, always bring situations involving violations of human rights to the attention of UN bodies. The OSCE also plays a role in developing the institutions of democracy in member countries, including training activities and support for education. The OSCE's work has usually been hindered by the lack of knowledge of international human rights law among OSCE observers and trainers and the failure of the OSCE to cooperate fully with the UN OHCHR. Funding on the other hand, has been less of a problem as several countries in the OSCE are among the wealthiest in the world.

6.4.5 The Commonwealth of Independent States

In 1992, after the break up of the former Soviet Union several of the newly independent states created the Commonwealth of Independent States (CIS), a regional intergovernmental organization headquartered in Minsk, Belarus. The CIS was created by the Charter of the CIS and a Protocol on the Establishment of the CIS on 21 December 1991. Eleven of the former USSR states agreed to this apparently feeling more secure cooperating among themselves than with outsiders who had challenged their way of life for decades. The CIS, however, did not prevent cooperation with other international bodies and all members are also members of the United Nations. Since its inception, the primary goal of the CIS has been to provide a forum for discussing issues related to the social and economic development of the newly independent states. Among its goals is also the promotion and protection of human rights in CIS member states. Initially efforts to achieve this goal consisted merely of statements of good will.

The Charter of the CIS created, in article 33, a Human Rights Commission sitting in Minsk, Belarus. This was confirmed by decision of the Council of Heads of States of the CIS in 1993. Just two years later in 1995, the CIS adopted a human rights treaty that includes civil and political as well as social and economic human rights. The CIS treaty is modelled on the ECHR, but lacking the implementation mechanisms of the latter. In the CIS treaty, the Human Rights Commission has very vaguely defined authority, but according to the statute creating the CIS Human Rights Commission it may receive inter-state as well as individual communications.

To date this Commission has not functioned very effectively. Instead it has been met with hostility not only by the CIS states that created it, but also by European states who have criticized it as distracting from the work of European institutions such as the European Court of Human Rights.

This criticism, however, failed to note that there are many CIS states that cannot become party to the European mechanisms. For example, the five central Asian states—Uzbekistan, Kazakhstan, Turkmenistan, Tajikistan, and Kyrgyzstan—do not have other regional human rights mechanism to which they may currently become a party. Although most of these states have ratified the most important United Nations human rights treaties, to deprive them of the CIS is to deprive them of membership in a regional human rights body that may be more effective and which will undoubtedly better understand the problems of these states. This criticism also fails to recognize that many rights protected in the CHR of the CIS are not protected in the European human rights treaties.

The states party to the CIS human rights regime have also been unenthusiastic about promoting the functioning of this treaty regime. Even trying to obtain information about the CIS human rights system is an elaborate task. Trying to communicate with the CIS Commission on Human Rights is almost impossible. In part these difficulties are a reflection of the failure of the states who created the mechanisms and who ratified the treaty to take their obligations seriously. The CIS in general remains under-funded and its member states have failed to disseminate adequate information about it. As a result not a single complaint has been dealt with by the Commission on Human Rights.

6.5 THE MIDDLE EAST AND ASIA

Some of the most prominent human rights documents have emanated from the Islamic world. The degree of compatibility of these instruments with the more universally accepted instruments has varied. For example, the Arab Charter of Human Rights from 1993 is a document of the League of Arab States. This document includes rights similar to those in the Universal Declaration of Human Rights. The Arab Charter for Human Rights is striking because of its contribution to the recognition of human rights in Islamic countries. The 1990 Cairo Declaration adopted by the Organization of Islamic Conferences in 1994 also contains human rights, but subordinates them to Islam by using vague language while the Universal Declaration of Human Rights under Islam adopted by the Islamic Council in 1981 is more explicit. The French version of the latter document that was handed over to the UNESCO at an official ceremony appears to accord with established international human rights law, however, the Arabic text, which, according to the document itself is authoritative, makes it clear that Islamic law is superior to international human rights law. Since then there have been several human rights documents dealing with this issue and an important United Nations Conference held in Geneva, Switzerland in November 1999 on Human Rights and Islam that was organized by the Organization of Islamic Conferences and the

United Nations' Office of the High Commissioner for Human Rights. At the moment none of these instruments has become legally binding on states because either they are not intended to be legally binding, or, as is the case concerning the Arab Charter of Human Rights, they have not received sufficient ratifications. Nevertheless, the Arab Charter serves to illustrate the broad consensus that is being reached on international human rights law, both regionally and universally.

It is not the Middle East, but Asia that is perhaps the area of the world with the fewest adherents to international human rights instruments. In part, this may be explained by the attitudes of some Asian political leaders who have objected to human rights as being anti-communal (*see* Chapter One). This argument, based on cultural relativism, has been used to deny the relevance of human rights in Asian society. It has also been used to deny the validity and usefulness of international human rights instruments. These arguments have only received the support of a few Asian elites and then usually for overtly selfish reasons.

In 1982 when the United Nations organized a seminar in Colombo, Sri Lanka, to consider establishing an Asian Human Rights Convention, the political leaders of Asian countries rejected the idea despite the fact that many Asian NGOs supported it. This contributed to stifling the development of an Asian human rights regime. Thus, the area of the world where the largest proportion of people live does not have a regional regime that reflects that area's cultural preferences. The universal human rights instruments have, however, been ratified by several countries—all Asian countries have, for example, ratified the Convention on the Rights of the Child—and thus many of these countries are bound to the human rights shared by all or most other countries in the world.

By the end of the 1980's there were sub-regional approaches in Asia. For example, in 1989, the Law Association of Asia and the Pacific proffered a Pacific Island Human Rights Charter and the Regional Council on Human Rights in Asia was formed by ASEAN. During the 1990's, however, there was little progress. The little progress that could be seen was not the result of governments as much as of non-governmental organizations. Asian civil society began to re-evaluate its understanding of community and to consider requiring that its governments guarantee some basic rights for all the individuals in the country.

The ASEAN declaration reflects the increasing pressures from civil society in Southeast Asian countries to have human rights given more attention. In addition, interaction with the western world is increasingly requiring Asian countries to adopt basic human standards whether or not they have ratified international human rights treaties. The Law Association for Asia and the Pacific, for example, is an NGO that frequently cooperates with western NGOs and professional associations of lawyers to try to encourage the role of law in the protection of human rights. On 22 July 2000, the Working Group for an ASEAN Human Rights Mechanism forwarded a Draft Agreement on the Establishment of an ASEAN Human Rights Commission to the Senior Officials and Ministers of the Association of Southeast Asian Nations. This text had not been adopted by the end of 2003. The text foresees a seven person Human Rights Commission with the ability to review both individual and inter-state complaints and the mandate to "promote and protect human rights" in the ASEAN region. Although the Commissioners are to be elected by the Ministers of Foreign Affairs of the states parties, they are guaranteed tenure for a single five-year term, and would serve as independent experts. The Commission, however, lacks binding authority to enforce its decisions and only makes recommendations to the states. Nevertheless, its broad powers to study and report on situations of alleged human rights abuses and to make recommendations could prove to be at least as potent as the similar powers of the African Commission on Human and Peoples' Rights.

Often one of the greatest disadvantages suffered by individuals in regions that have not created their own human rights bodies is their inability to contribute fully to the development of international human rights law. This in turn causes some individuals in these regions of the world to feel as if some human rights have been imposed on them. In other words, regional organizations help individuals from a particular region participate and make known their views on human rights. With greater participation in the development of international human rights law through regional organizations, it is likely that both the individuals in the particular region as well as at international forums will be benefited. It is also likely that human rights might be better shaped to take into account the need and concerns that might be more important to a particular region of the world.

6.6 Other Regional or Other Initiatives for Protecting Human Rights

There are some initiatives aimed at protecting human rights that cut across regions. The OSCE is one of these and has already been discussed above in the section on European mechanisms because it is primarily related to this region of the world. The OSCE, however, includes countries from the Americas and from Asia. It does not include, however, legally binding mechanisms for interpreting, promoting, or enforcing the rights in the aspirational instruments that OSCE countries have agreed upon. Moreover, it is substantially controlled by the American government and its allies and often does their policy bidding around the world, even when this policy may be inconsistent with human rights.

Another cross region organization that concerns itself with human rights is the Commonwealth of countries who were former colonies of Great Britain. The meetings of the fifty-four Heads of States of the Commonwealth have sometimes dealt with human rights issues. The Commonwealth Secretariat, based in London, has also compiled valuable materials on human rights in its member countries and published reports relevant to human rights protection.

In the Islamic world, the Organization of Islamic Conferences (OIC) that consists of more than fifty states has been involved in raising the profile of the human rights of the Palestine people in international forums. For example, in 2004 the OIC was invited to make representations to the International Court of Justice as it considered its advisory opinion on the legality of Israel's wall through the occupied territories. Its presentation to the Court highlighted the grave human rights abuses by Israel against the Palestinians that were ongoing and would be intensified by the wall and those which would directly result from the building of the wall.

The Commission on Peace and Justice of the Roman Catholic Church has also sometimes promoted the protection of human rights in international forums, usually in support of the policies of the Vatican, in which it is based, but also reflecting a the views of Catholics around the world.

While none of these regional or faith-based initiatives are solely concerned with human rights, they often make substantial contribution to the attention given to issues of human rights in forums devoted to the development of international human rights law such as the UN Commission on Human Rights.

CHAPTER SEVEN
The Limits of Human Rights

7.1 The Limits of Obligations

States may limit their responsibility for ensuring human rights. First, a state may fail to ratify a treaty or withdraw from one. Second, a state may enter a reservation or declaration when it ratifies a treaty. Third, a state may rely on one of the general derogation provisions in a specific human rights treaty. And fourth, a state may rely on the permissible limitation of a right that is built into the definition of that right. Each of these is discussed further in this Chapter. It should be understood, however, that these means of limiting a state's obligations are applicable only to treaty law, which is the main source of international human rights law.

Since a state does not explicitly consent to customary international law, it cannot usually avoid the application of this law. The only exception to this general principle is in the case of a 'persistent objector' — a state that objects to a principle of customary international law from the time of its creation. To be a persistent objector it is essential that the state makes its objection known as soon as other states begin to accept the principle as customary international law. The International Court of Justice recognized the existence of the legal principle of persistence in the *Asylum Case (Columbia v. Peru)*, ICJ Reports 276 (1950). In this case, Columbia had argued that Peru was bound to recognize Columbia's right to grant diplomatic asylum to a Peruvian national who had sought asylum in the Colombian embassy in Peru. Columbia argued that the large number of states that had ratified a

Latin American treaty on diplomatic asylum had created a rule of customary international law. Peru argued that it was not a party to the treaty and had objected to the rule permitting diplomatic asylum from the time of its creation. The ICJ agreed with Peru. Regional customary international law may also be limited in its geographical application. That is, it may not bind states that are situated outside of the particular region in which the rule of regional customary international law is formed. Finally, as noted in Chapter Three, a rule of customary international law that has become *jus cogens* never admits derogation.

7.2 Failure to Ratify a Convention or Withdrawal

A State may avoid its treaty obligations by failing to ratify a convention. As treaties only bind states that have ratified them, a state's failure to ratify a treaty means that no legal obligations are incurred under the treaty. There are several exceptions to this rule, however. The first exception is when a state that is party to the Vienna Convention on the Law of Treaties has signed, but not yet ratified or positively withdrawn its intention to ratify the treaty. In this case, article 18 of the Vienna Convention incurs an obligation on the state not to act to frustrate the object and purpose of the treaty. The second exception is when an obligation has become *jus cogens* and thus is binding on all states in the international community whether or not they have agreed to it in a treaty. There may also be a third obligation for states under customary international law. Some authorities hold that a state may object to a customary rule by failing to sign a convention. Other writers hold that any rule of law concerning human rights that has become customary international law binds all states because of the importance of human rights to all of humanity. It would appear that this second opinion is more consistent with the general objects and purposes of international human rights law. Nevertheless, as has been shown in the earlier chapter discussing states' responsibilities for human rights most states still seem to act as if human rights obligations flow primarily from treaties.

As the *Asylum Case* indicates, the failure of a state to ratify a convention may also be evidence that the particular state is objecting to a particular principle of international law. The fact that Peru had not ratified the Montevideo Convention, for example, was held to be rebuttal evidence that Peru objected to a rule that Columbia was claiming to be customary international law. States may also limit their obligations by withdrawing from a treaty after they have ratified the treaty.

7.3 Reservations, Declarations, and Understandings

When ratifying a treaty, states may enter reservations, understandings or declarations to the treaty. A reservation is a statement by a government it will not apply one or more provisions of the treaty. An understanding expresses a state's belief that a provision of a treaty has a certain generally accepted meaning. And a declaration states that a provision of a treaty has a particular meaning in relation to that state. All three of these instruments limit a state's responsibility under a treaty. All three must be made when ratifying a treaty and only at that time. Generally, the discussion of reservations, which are considered below, applies equally to understandings and declarations as well.

Reservations, understandings and declarations are important to international human rights law because much of this law is found in treaties. Many of the rules of international law concerning reservations and declarations have been codified in the widely accepted Vienna Convention on the Law of Treaties (UN Doc. A/CONF.39/27, entered into force 27 January 1980), which in large part reflects customary international law. This instrument contains specific provisions on reservations. The rules in the Vienna Convention are general guidelines. One must also examine the human rights treaties themselves to determine if they contain *lex specialis* rules concerning reservations.

The *Advisory Opinion on Reservations to the Convention on the Prevention and Punishment of the Crime of Genocide*, I.C.J. Reports 15 (1951), preceded and influenced the expression of rules in the Vienna Convention. In this case the General Assembly asked the International Court of Justice whether or not states making reservations were to be considered parties to the Convention. The Court held that "a State cannot be bound without its consent, and that consequently no reservation can be effective against any State without its agreement thereto," but also that human rights treaties were made with the special intention of encouraging as many states to become parties as possible. Thus a government which has made and maintained a reservation which has been objected to by one or more of the parties to the Convention but not by others, can be regarded as being party to the Convention if the reservation is compatible with the object and purpose of the Convention. In other cases, according to the Court, "a State cannot be regarded as a party to the Convention...if a party to the Convention objects to a reservation which it considers to be incompatible with the object and purpose of the Convention, it can in fact consider the reserving State is not a party to the Convention...if, on the other hand, a party accepts the reservation as being compatible with the object and purpose of the Convention, it can in fact consider that the reserving State is a party to the Convention."

It only partly applies these principles in Article 19, stating in the negative that a valid reservation is one (1) not prohibited by the treaty; (2) not prohibited because the provisions of the treaty allow only certain reservations, and (3) not contrary to the object and purpose of the treaty.

It would appear, however, that these general rules of international law only apply in part to international human rights treaties. An expression of the special nature of human rights treaties is the Human Rights Committee's General Comment 24(52) adopted on 2 November 1994 which states that reservations to human rights treaties should receive special treatment under international law. Thus the general international rule that a state not accepting a reservation was entitled to set aside the operation of the treaty between itself and the reserving state is not applicable to human rights treaties. The Human Rights Committee expressed its view that "[t]he normal consequence of an unacceptable reservation is not that the Covenant will not be in effect at all for a reserving party. Rather, such a reservation will generally be severable, in the sense that the Covenant will be operative for the reserving party without benefit of the reservation." Both the United States and the United Kingdom have responded to this General Comment, claiming that it goes beyond the authority of the Human Rights Committee to express such an opinion and stating that the HRC narrowly interprets the opinion.

Nevertheless, the general consensus that has emerged from the different opinions concerning reservations is that reservations to international human rights treaties must receive special consideration. Because human rights are not merely rights between states, but are the basic rights of the individuals in states they must be interpreted so as not to allow states to easily avoid their obligations. The test applied by the International Court of Justice in its *Advisory Opinion on Reservations to the Convention on the Prevention and Punishment of the Crime of Genocide* was adopted by the European Court of Human Rights in *Belilos v. Switzerland*, ECtHR, Ser. A, No. 132 (29 April 1988), when it held invalid Switzerland's attempt to exclude a whole category of offenses from the protections of due process in article 6 of the ECHR.

In a later case, *Weber v. Switzerland*, Ser. A, No. 177 (22 May 1990), an attempted reservation to Article 6 by Switzerland was again held invalid. This time the problem was that Switzerland had failed to append a brief statement of the law with which the reservation was concerned. The Court stated this about the reservation and the conditions in article 64 of the ECHR that a reservation must fulfil:

> 38. Clearly it does not fulfill one of them, as the Swiss Government did not append 'a brief statement of the law [or laws] concerned' to it. The requirement of paragraph (2) of Article 64 [ECHR], however, 'both constitutes an evidential factor and contributes to legal certainty'; its purpose is to 'provide a guarantee' — in particular for the other Contracting Parties and the Convention institutions — that a reservation does not go beyond the provisions expressly excluded by the State concerned...Disregarding it is a breach not of 'a purely formal requirement' but of 'a condition of substance'...The material reservation by Switzerland must accordingly be regarded as invalid.

Other international human rights bodies have also had to deal with the question of reservations to human rights treaties. The Inter-American

Court of Human Rights has commented on reservations in two advisory opinions: The *Advisory Opinion on the Effect of Reservations on the Entry into Force of the American Convention,* (IACtHR, Advisory Opinion No. OC-3/83 (8 September 1983)) and the *Advisory Opinion on Restrictions to the Death Penalty* (IAmCtHR, Advisory Opinion No. OC-3/83 of 8 September 1983). In both of its opinions, the Court applied the Vienna Convention on the Law of Treaties, although in a manner particular to human rights treaties. These particularities have to do with the object and purpose of human rights treaties. The Inter-American Court has held that although reservations were authorized under the ACHR this

> makes sense only if it is understood ... to enable States to make whatever reservations they deem appropriate, provided the reservations are not incompatible with the object and purpose of the treaty ...
> 37. Having concluded that reservations expressly authorized by Article 75 [of the ACHR] ... all reservations compatible with the object and purpose of the Convention, do not require acceptance by the States parties, the Court is of the opinion that the instruments of ratification or adherence containing them enter into force, pursuant to Article 74 [of the ACHR], as of the moment of their deposit.
> 38. The States parties have a legitimate interest, of course, in barring reservations incompatible with the object and purpose of the Convention ...
> 40....The Court is of the opinion, by unanimous vote, that the Convention enters into force for a State which ratifies or adheres to it with or without a reservation on the date of the deposit if its instrument of ratification or adherence.

In its *Advisory Opinion on Restrictions to the Death Penalty* the Inter-American Court was again asked to interpret a reservation. Once again, the primary test applied by the Court was whether the reservation was compatible with the object and purpose of the treaty.

Reservations, Declarations and Understandings remain important instruments by which states can choose the human rights they wish to be bound by in a human rights treaty. Is this ability of states justified by the fact that more states might ratify a treaty to which it can make reservations?

7.4 Derogations

States may derogate from international human rights for certain reasons that are identified in the human rights treaties and that can be broadly described as being in the interest of preserving the authority of the state. Derogation by a state means that it is trying to avoid an obligation by claiming that a situation exists requiring the state to exercise special powers in the public interest. In contrast to a restrictive interpretation of a human right, a derogation can apply to more than one human right.

The general conditions with which a derogation must comply are the following: (1) the state must show proof of an emergency situation, (2) the derogation must be limited by the necessity of the situation, (3) the state paries to the treaty must have been informed, and (4) the derogation must be limited in time to the duration of the emergency. In addition, some human rights such as the prohibition of torture, the right to life, the freedom of conscience, thought and religion, are non-derogable. In some human rights treaties, the right to fair trial is also non-derogable.

Derogation clauses can be found in article 15 of the ECHR, article 4 of the ICCPR and article 27 of the ACHR. Nevertheless, the rights that may not be derogated from are not always the same from one treaty to another. For example, the rights for which derogation is allowed in the ICCPR are different from those in the ECHR.

The derogation provisions in the ICCPR have been interpreted in the Siracusa Principles that were produced by individual academics and practitioners and later adopted by the United Nations. The second part of these Principles addresses derogation, This instrument reiterates that derogations are only allowed when required by the necessity of national security or public order

One of the leading cases to come before the European human rights mechanisms is the *Greek Colonels' Case*, 12 *Yearbook of the European Convention* 4 (1969). This case concerned a challenge by Denmark, Netherlands, Norway and Sweden against the regime of the Greek Colonels for their actions, which included torture and suspending judicial due process guarantees, after taking control of the country in the 1960's in a *coup d'etat*. Two petitions were submitted, one in 1967 and one in 1970. The petitions are some of the few examples of inter-state complaints under human rights instruments. The case was heard by the Commission using its investigatory powers to hear witnesses and to do an on-site investigation. The outcome of the case — the decision of which is reproduced below — found the Greek government's human rights observance to be lacking. The crux of the Greek government's case was that they were entitled to derogate from the obligations under the ECHR to protect public order and the security of the state. In this case, the now-defunct European Commission began to define the general derogation clause in article 15.

In interpreting article 15 of the ECHR, the European Court of Human Rights has generally allowed a broad margin of appreciation in reviewing a state's exercise of discretion. The *Lawless Case*, Ser. A, No. 3, ECtHR (1961), involved the detention of an Irish citizen suspected of being a terrorist with the Irish Republican Army (IRA). Under Irish law, it was possible to detain a person for an extended period without a trial. The applicant was detained for five months. The applicant claimed that several of his human rights under the ECHR were violated including his right to liberty (art. 5), the prohibition on retroactive criminal punishment (art. 6) and the right to fair trial (art. 7). The Irish government denied that the applicant's rights were violated, but also that its actions were justified because a public emergency existed. In addition, to allow the applicant to rely on his rights would amount to sanctioning the violations of others' rights because the applicant was known as a terrorist. The European Court of Human Rights held that in this case the restrictions were justified because an emergency existed. A "war or other public emergency" in article 15 of the ECHR was defined as "an exceptional situation of crisis or emergency which affects the whole population and constitutes a threat to the organised life of the community of which the state is composed." The existence of an emergency could be reasonably deduced from the level of violence that had taken place in the recent past and the difficulty the government was having in controlling it.

The Inter-American Court has considered derogations most extensively in the *Habeas Corpus in Emergency Situations*, Advisory Opinion, OC-8/87 of 30 January 1987, Ser. A, No. 8 (1988), where it advised that because the "writs of *habeas corpus* and of "*amparo*" are among those judicial remedies that are essential for the protection of various rights whose derogation is prohibited by Article 27(2)"they may not be suspended. The Court also emphasized that a state has a heavy burden of justifying the suspension of any human rights because the human rights in the ACHR "are to be guaranteed and enforced unless very special circumstances justify their suspension." Nevertheless, the court admitted that it "cannot be denied that under certain circumstances the suspension of guarantees may be the only way to deal with emergency situations and thereby, to preserve the highest values of a democratic society." While the opinion did not contradict the clear words of the ACHR, it interpreted them very restrictively to allow the Court to limit the discretion of states seeking to derogate from the provisions of the ACHR.

In striking contrast to the derogation provisions of the ACHR and the ECHR is the African Charter on Human and Peoples' Rights. This treaty does not contain derogation provisions and as a consequence the African Commission—the body with the authority to interpret the treaty—has found that the African Charter is non-derogable *in toto*. *Commission Nationale des Droits de l'Homme et de Libertés v. Chad*, Comm. No. 74/92 (10 July 1996). After stating that the Charter was non-derogable, the Commission went on to find Chad in violation of the right to life, human dignity, physical integrity, fair trial and freedom of expression even though it was embroiled in a civil war.

Finally , the Human Rights Committee's General Comment makes clear that states' ability to derogate from internationally protected human rights is limited. Note also that the Committee finds that it has not only a right to review states' derogations to determine if they are in accordance with the Covenant, but a duty to do so even if a state has not notified them that it is derogating.

7.5 Restrictive Interpretations

The phrase "restrictive interpretations" refers to the practice of states interpreting specific human rights provisions narrowly to justify a limitation. Such an interpretation may stem from a general provision of a treaty or from limitation provisions concerning particular human rights that appear in the definition of the right itself. Article 5 of the ICCPR is an example of the first type of limitation clause. It is general and applies to numerous human rights scattered in numerous articles in the ICCPR.

Similar provisions appear in all other human rights treaties. Briefly review the treaties at the end of the Coursebook and try to identify similar provisions. The other form of limitation that appears in all human rights treaties is restrictions on particular articles. An example is paragraph 3 of article 19 of the ICCPR that protects the freedom of expression. After two paragraphs defining, the right paragraph three provides some discretion to the state for limiting the right. Note, however, the restrictions put on the state's right to limit this human right. They are often present in the expression rights and frequently invoked by states seeking to limit the exercise of these rights.

The Siracusa Principles drafted by a group of lawyers and politicians provide some assistance for understanding restrictive interpretations based on the limitations provisions in particular treaty articles. Although these Principles are not binding they reflect understandings that can be argued before international human rights tribunals and which have to date been often adopted as accepted understandings of the limitation provisions in human rights treaties.

7.6 Human Rights and Terrorism and Jurisdiction

The American NGO, the Lawyers Committee for Human Rights, writes in October 2003 in its Report on Human Rights in the United States that "[c]ounterterrorism has become the new rubric under which opportunistic governments seek to justify their action, however, offensive to human rights." Although states have the right and responsibility to protect their citizens from acts of terrorism, in cases where action is being taken against terrorism, states must ensure that international human rights norms are respected. The foremost role of international human rights in cases involving terrorists is thus the protection of the accused terrorist's human rights. As the Inter-American Commission has pointed out in its lengthy *Report on Terrorism and Human Rights* in 2003, in undertaking initiatives against terrorism "states are equally obliged to remain in strict compliance with their other international obligations, including those under international human rights law and international humanitarian law."

In most cases—where no armed conflict exists or where an armed conflict exists but the relevant state cannot or has not made a derogation for a right as prescribed by the relevant human rights treaty—international human rights law will continue to apply. Where no armed conflict exists, or arguably, when the state alleged to have violated the law has illegally started an armed conflict, international human rights law will have full effect without mitigation. When a legal armed conflict exists, it may be necessary to interpret human rights law by reference to international humanitarian law, thus although this law can not be applied by the international human rights tribunal it may influence its interpretation of the applicable law.

In some instances states have gone further than merely arguing that their action against terrorism or a recalcitrant state. They have tried to avoid their international human rights obligations altogether by arguing that they are not responsible for action taking place outside of their territory. To justify their failure to abide by the restriction of the ECHR, European states have claimed that their human rights obligations do not apply outside of their territories. The leading case in which they made this claim came before the European Court occurred in the context of the bombing of the former Yugoslavia by coalition under a North Atlantic Treaty Organization (NATO) umbrella. In this case, all the respondents were NATO member states, but some NATO member states were not included because they were not party to the ECHR. The Applicants were individuals injured by the NATO strikes and the relatives of person killed by the strikes. The Court held applicants' petition to be inadmissible based on an unfortunately restrictive interpretation of the ECHR that confined its reach to territory of the member states, except in exceptional circumstances that the Court found not to be present.

In the pertinent part of its judgment, the Court in *Bankovic and Others v. Belgium and 16 Other Contracting States*, Decision of the Grand Chamber, No. 52207/99, ECHR 2001-XII., stated that as concerns

> ...the 'ordinary meaning' of the relevant term in Article 1 of the Convention, the Court is satisfied that, from the standpoint of public international law, the jurisdictional competence of a State is primarily territorial. While international law does not exclude a State's exercise of jurisdiction extra-territorially, the suggested bases of such jurisdiction (including nationality, flag, diplomatic and consular relations, effect, protection, passive personality and universality) are, as a general rule, defined and limited by the sovereign territorial rights of the other relevant States....
>
> Accordingly, for example, a State's competence to exercise jurisdiction over its own nationals abroad is subordinate to that State's and other States' territorial competence... In addition, a State may not actually exercise jurisdiction on the territory of another without the latter's consent, invitation or acquiescence...

In keeping with the essentially territorial notion of jurisdiction, the Court has accepted only in exceptional cases that acts of the Contracting States performed, or producing effects, outside their territories can constitute an exercise of jurisdiction by them within the meaning of Article 1 of the Convention.

The decision appears to be at odds with the generally accepted understanding of international human rights bodies that they will interpret the provisions of human rights treaties to provide as much protection to individuals as possible. The Court rested its decision on the interpretation of Article of the ECHR that it believed states had intended in 1951 when they ratified the treaty, despite the fact that such a restrictive interpretation is refuted by many other cases including the Court's own jurisprudence. In any event, it is unlikely that the Court's jurisprudence will be followed by other international human rights bodies that have found the provisions of human rights treaties to apply beyond the borders of the member states when the actors are clearly under the authority of a state party to the relevant human rights treaty.

The European Court itself appeared to have doubts about its earlier decisions in the case of *Öcalan v. Turkey*, Application number 00046221/99 of 12 March 2003., when it unequivocally refuted the suggestion that *Bankovic* prohibited the application of the ECHR outside of Europe stating that

> 88. The Court accepts that an arrest made by the authorities of one State on the territory of another State, without the consent of the latter, affects the person's individual rights to security under Article 5 §1 (*see*, to the same effect, *Stocké v. Germany*, 12 October 1989, Series A, No. 199, opinion of the Commission, p. 24, § 167).

The Öcalan Court further stated that

> 92. Independently of the question whether the arrest amounts to a violation of the law of the State in which the fugitive has taken refuge – a question which only falls to be examined by the Court if the host State is a party to the Convention – it must be established to the Court "beyond all reasonable doubt" that the authorities of the State to which the applicant has been transferred have acted extra-territorially in a manner that is inconsistent with the sovereignty of the host State and therefore contrary to international law...

The Court found that the Turkish authorities had violated some of Mr. Öcalan's human rights by the arrest. It is also relevant to note that in this case the arrest of Öcalan not only took place outside of Turkey, but outside of the territory of any Council of Europe state in Kenya.

The UN Human Rights Committee has also long held that "it would be unconscionable to so interpret the responsibility under article 2 of the Covenant as to permit a State party to perpetrate violations of the Covenant on the territory of another State, which violations it could not perpetrate on its own territory." This was clearly stated in the case of *Casariego v. Uruguay* involving a person abducted abroad and brought to Uruguay. On 1 September 2006 the United Nations' Working Group on Arbitrary Detention issued an opinion finding both the governments of the United States and Iraq to be violating international law by conducting an unfair trial before the Iraqi Special Tribunal, which had been trying members of the former Iraqi government under former Iraqi President Saddam Hussein. *Saddam Hussein v. United States/Iraq*, WGAD Opinion 31/2006.

Perhaps the best argument for ensuring that human rights treaties are applied as broadly as possible — and to all acts of states parties that are carried out by persons under the control of that state — is not legal, but is logical. If the law is not respected, individuals will begin to take justice into their own hands. Indeed, it is hard to argue that individuals are not justified in fighting back when states are massively violating their human rights with impunity. Such a situation may breed terrorism or freedom fighters, depending on whether you take the perspective of the recalcitrant state or the victims of human rights abuses.

CHAPTER EIGHT
Economic, Social, and Cultural Rights

8.1 Rights in the International Covenant of Economic, Social and Cultural Rights

One of the first clear expressions of economic, social and cultural rights pre-dated the United Nations, in fact appearing in the Treaty of Versailles, which ended the First World War in 1919. This treaty established the International Labour Organization (ILO) whose goal it was to strive to abolish "hardship, injustice and privation" and to guarantee workers "fair and humane conditions of labour." The 1944 Declaration concerning the Aims and Purposes of the International Labour Organization reaffirmed, *inter alia,* that "poverty anywhere constitutes a danger to prosperity everywhere" and that "all human beings, irrespective of race, creed or sex, have the right to pursue both their material well-being and their spiritual development in conditions of freedom and dignity, of economic security and equal opportunity."

When, in the aftermath of the Second World War, countries set about constructing the United Nations, the Universal Declaration of Human Rights and the two Covenants economic, social and cultural rights were very much at the front of their minds. The pre-war period had been marred by years of depression and economic hardship. The conditions of minorities and of the people to exercise their cultural rights had been highlighted by the treatment of minorities after the First World War, which was the cause for an array of minority treaties whose provisions have been too seldom used. And the expectation of a social net had been reinforced by a series of post war ILO treaties providing for workers rights. Thus in the Charter of the United Nations not only are economic, social and cultural rights referred to in Chapter IX on

International Economic and Social Co-operation but they are also stated in the more general and programmatic provisions of the Preamble and the first article. In the Preamble the "Peoples of The United Nations" express their determination "to promote social progress and better standards of life in larger freedoms" and "to employ international machinery for the promotion of the economic and social advancement of all people." And as a purpose of the United Nations Article 1 states "international co-operation in solving international problems of an economic, social and cultural, or humanitarian character, and in promoting and encouraging respect for human right and fundamental freedoms for all without distinction as to race, sex, language, or religion." Finally, the obligations of states in articles 55 and 56 are enhanced by the functions of the Economic and Social Council of the United Nations in Chapter X, which include the examination of human rights in general and social and economic development in particular.

In the drafting of the Universal Declaration on Human Rights the UN Commission on Human Rights was strongly influenced by American President Franklin Delano Roosevelt's "Four Freedoms Speech" and 1944 "State of the Union" address. The 1944 address to the United States Congress sets out rights ranging from the right to "a useful and remunerative job" and the "right to earn enough to provide adequate food and clothing and recreation" to "the right of every family to a decent home," "the right to adequate medical care," and "the right to a good education." His wife, who chaired the Commission on Human Rights during the drafting process, strongly supported the inclusion of economic, social and cultural rights. At the same time, however, she distinguished between the civil and political rights that states had the power to guarantee and "the case of other rights, such as the right to work, the right to health and the right to social security [over which] there are widely different theories and practices in different parts of the world as to the manner in which the Government can best facilitate the desired end." This argument was to set the tone for the debates leading to two separate covenants with as their main difference the matter of implementation or realization of the rights contained therein in practice. The question as to why economic, social and cultural rights are important is crucial to deciding how to implement, and indeed, how to view these rights in the large agenda of priorities confronting the international community.

One argument for a relatively high place for these rights among the priorities of authoritative decision makers in the world society is based on statistics concerning the conditions of human beings. An increasingly recognised and referred to source of these statistics is UNDP's annual *Human Development Report 1995* that states:

> *1.3 billion people in developing countries and 100 million in developed countries live below the poverty line;
>
> *the poorest 40% of the households in developed countries get only 18% of the total income;

> *more than a third of the children in the developing world are malnourished and under weight; and
> *nearly 800 million people in developing countries do not get enough food and about 500 million are chronically malnourished.

Despite the gains that have been made in the last fifty years, these figures still paint a grim picture of the economic and social position of a large portion of the world's population. The 1995 Report concludes that while "between two-thirds and three quarters of the world's people live under relatively pluralistic and democratic regimes," nevertheless "poorer nations as well as rich are afflicted by growing human distress—in the forms of a weakening social fabric, threats to personal security and a spreading sense of individual isolation."

8.2 The Right to an Adequate Standard of Living Including Food, Clothing and Housing

One of the broadest rights is the right to an adequate standard of living in Article 11 of the International Covenant of Economic, Social and Cultural Rights. This right expressly consists of the rights to adequate food, clothing and housing. The right to food has been the subject of much discussion. In large part, this discussion emanates from the existence of more than enough food to feed everyone in the world, but a failure in the processes of distribution to accomplish this goal. The right to clothing has not received substantial attention, but the right to housing has been the subject of a great amount of international activity, especially in light of the Habitat Conference in Istanbul in 1996. At this conference, states discussed urban and rural planning policies for housing. A major issue was the reiteration of the right to housing as a human right. The United States opposed the reference to the right to housing in the Conference Declaration and Plan of Action, but finally bowed to international pressure and agreed to recognise that it was a consensually accepted human right.

Concerning the right to housing, the Special Rapporteur of the Sub-Commission stated at the beginning of his June 1993 Report that "[i]n spite of the considerable legal foundation of housing rights that exist...housing and living conditions continue to worsen the world over. Of special concern in a world where free market economics are fashionable is the Repertoires finding that "[t]he continued indulgence by the world's Governments of citizens who are already better off and the failure to reorder fiscal policies, including taxation, budgetary allocations and policies for subsidization of the disadvantaged sector, towards meeting the needs of those denied housing rights remains an area requiring change."

The right to housing is found in the ICESCR, art. 11(1), the CERD, art. 5(e), the CEDAW, art. 14, the CRC, art. 27, the MWC, art. 43, the ILO Convention No. 115 (concerning workers' housing from 1961; in addition there are thirty-seven ILO conventions or recommendations that refer to the right to housing), the ILO Convention No. 117 (Concerning Basic Aims and Standards of Social Policy from 1962). Other treaties provide this right for specific groups such as refugees, RC, art. 21 (which provides that refugees must be treated as "favourable as possible" and at least as aliens generally in same circumstances), and SC, art. 21 (that provides the same for stateless individuals as the RC does for refugees). This right is also discussed in international declarations and General Comments.

Furthermore, this right is linked to the right to an adequate standard of living, the right to health and even the right to life. The particular aspects of the right to housing have been defined in terms of the following concepts:

1. Legal security of tenure;
2. Availability of services, materials and infrastructure;
3. Affordable housing: attainment of other basic needs not threatened;
4. Habitable housing: physically safe and minimally comfortable;
5. Accessible housing: vulnerable individuals can apply and get housing;
6. Location: allows access to employment and other services;
7. Culturally adequate housing.

The monitoring and development mechanisms which exists as concerns the right to housing include Habitat, which has produced a Global Strategy for Shelter to the Year 2000 and which requires governments to report specific indicators every two years to the Commission on Human Settlements. The Committee on Economic, Social and Cultural Rights requires state reports every five years.

8.3 The Right to Health

The right to health is one of the most widely recognized of human rights. Article 25 of the Universal Declaration of Human Rights states that the right includes food, clothing, housing, medical care and necessary social services. The later Declaration on Social Progress and Development in 1969, in articles 10 (d) and 19 (a), emphasised access to basic health services to be provided free of charge, if possible. However, a different view was taken by the American Declaration of the Rights and Duties of Man in 1948 and the Cairo Declaration on Human Rights in Islam in 1990. Article XI of the American Declaration declares the right is required "to the extent permitted by public and community resources." Likewise, article 17(b) of the Cairo Declaration requires the right to health be recognition in so far as the limits of a state's available resources permit.

The binding legal instruments that followed these declarations adopted the latter approach of balancing the right with the resources of the state. Thus, Article 12 of the International Covenant of Economic, Social and Cultural

Rights lists examples of steps that states are required to take, but must be read in the shadow of article 2(1) and 2(3) of the Covenant that provide a link to a states available resources. Paragraph 1 of article 2 does this by providing that states should strive to achieve respect for the social, economic and cultural rights therein progressively and to the maximum of their available resources. This stands in contrast to the obligations of states in the International Covenant of Civil and Political Rights that are immediate and cannot be avoided because of lack of resources. In both treaties, however, discrimination is not allowed, in the ICESCR this prohibition is found in article 2, paragraph 2 and the duty in paragraph 1 must be read in light of it. In paragraph 3 of article 2, developing countries are given an additional dispensation allowing them to delay or avoid securing the rights for non-nationals when this would have an adverse impact on their national economies.

Other international provisions such as article 16 of the ACHPR, article 10 of the Protocol of San Salvador to the ACHR , and article 11 of the European Social Charter, although sometimes providing a short list of steps states should take, nevertheless leave the legal obligations vague and subject to wide ranging interpretations. For example, article 16 of the ACHPR states that everyone has a right to health and those states should take all necessary measures to protect the health of their people and to ensure access to health care. It does not elaborate on what these measures may be.

Several regional instruments do not include the right to health. The Arab Charter of Human Rights, the ECHR, and the ACHR all do not include this right, although the latter two are supplemented by regional instruments that do include the right.

Several human rights treaties applying to specific categories of individuals also include the right to health. The CRC is the foremost among these. Article 24 of this Convention contains an extensive description of the right. Furthermore, this article was emphasised and elaborated upon in the Declaration and Plan of Action of the World Summit for Children a year later in 1990. The World Summit documents, although not legally binding, are valuable interpretations and/or specifications of the rights in the CRC. For example, article 24(2) (a) of the CRC requires states to "diminish infant and child mortality." The Declaration then restates this priority by defining it in terms of a task and commitments, although both equally as vague as the CRC provisions. Finally, point number 5 of the Plan of Action provides both specific goals, for example, states are urged to reduce "under-5 child mortality rates by one third or to a level of 70 per 1,000 births" by the year 2000 and to strengthen health care interventions. A similar goal of halving child mortality rates in the forty-two most seriously effected countries was established by states at the turn of the century as one of the Millennium Development Goals. In each cases these goals were to include follow-up and monitoring mechanisms, but it is herein that the failure of many social and economic rights may be recorded. The ILO and the WHO have also promulgated treaties protecting certain aspects of the right to health.

There is no body with the binding legal authority to make decisions as concerns the right to health. The African Commission which comes the closest to such a body has not to date expressed a coherent jurisprudence about the right to health. The Commission has found that this right has been violated upon occasion, but with such brief reasoning that their rationale remains mysterious.

The most extensive interpretation of the right to health and legal obligations it creates for states has been the General Comment of the UN Committee on Economic, Social and Cultural Rights. This body has explained that article 2 of the ICESR provides real and immediate duties for states despite the fact it allows for some discretion as to what specific steps states need take. The Committee points out, for example, that a state that has not achieved adequate respect for an economic and social right must do more immediately. In other words, if a state has not been able to achieve consistent reductions in child mortality it must invest more resources in accomplishing this task. Thus a state may be required to re-direct resources away from defence, space exploration, economic investment, and other similar budget items to health care because health is a human right.

The understandings reflected in this General Comment become even more important for states that have ratified the CRC. Unlike the Covenants, and like the ACHPR, the CRC requires all ratifying states (almost all the states in the international community) to implement its provisions without derogation and as quickly as possible. Thus, although states may have some discretion as to how much they must do in respect of the general right to health, they have much less discretion as concerns children's right to health.

It is also noteworthy that the Human Rights Committee, created under the ICCPR, has interpreted the right to life in article 6 of that Covenant as including aspects of the right to health. In its General Comment No. 6, the Committee has expressed its view that the right to life has often been interpreted too narrowly and it cannot properly be understood in a restrictive manner. According to the Committee the right to life requires states to take positive steps including measures to reduce child mortality, increase life expectancy, and eliminate malnutrition and epidemics.

Similarly, the CEDAW Committee has also issued a General Recommendation stating that it affirms that access to health care, including reproductive health is a basic right under article 12 of the CEDAW. The Committee then consequently adopted a general recommendation on article 12 of the Convention specifying in more detail what the right to health means for women and what the obligations of governments are towards women in respect for this right.

8.4 Right to Education

Although the right to education is important for the development of every country in the world, it is particularly important for individuals in developing countries where access to education is one of the few means by which individuals can extricate themselves from the scourge of poverty. The right to education often consists of the right to receive a free primary education, the right to equal access to a higher education (and in some cases a free higher education, if for example, financial constraints are the main obstacle) and the right to provide education.

The right to education is found in numerous articles in several human rights treaties. For example, article 26 of the UDHR, article 2 of Protocol 2 to the ECHR, article 27 of the CHR of CIS, article 13 of the San Salvador Protocol, and article 17 of the ACHPR. Sometimes it is defined generally and sometimes it is defined specifically in the same instrument. The ICESCR, for example, contains both a general right to education (art. 13) and a specific right to primary education (art. 14). The ACHPR also includes a duty on the state to provide human rights education (art. 25) as does article 26(2) of the UDHR, article 13(1) of the ICESCR, article 7 of CERD, article 29(1) of the CRC, article 13(2) of the ESC and article 13(2) of the San Salvador Protocol. In general, however, the state does have the duty to impose a certain type of education, but must ensure that any restrictions it places on the provision of education do not deny the right to education.

In its General Comment on the Right to Education the UN CESCR has indicated the breath and relevance of this right found in Article 13 of the ICESCR. States undoubtedly have the primary responsibility for ensuring respect for the right to education. Most leaders have openly expressed the opinion that education is among the most important requirements for development. When a state has a knowledgeable and competent workforce it can compete with other states. Thus a state committed to the development of its population will often prioritise education, and conversely, a state that does not prioritise education may be indicating to its population and the world that it is not committed to its country's development. Nevertheless, several states have decided to follow the lead of the United States and have left education to market economics.

The ACHPR contains not only a general right to education (art. 17), but also imposes upon countries the obligation to ensure human rights education (art. 25). The African Commission has also reviewed the right to education in Article 17 of the ACHPR finding that the closing of universities and secondary schools for two years and failing to pay teachers constitute a violation of article 17. *World Organisation Against Torture, Lawyers' Committee for Human Rights, Union Interafricaine des Droits de l'Homme, Les Témoins de Jéhovah v. Zaire*, ACHPR, Comms. 25/89, 47/90, 56/91, 100/93.

Other regional human rights treaties containing the right to education include the ACHR's Protocol of San Salvador (art. 13) and the ECHR's Protocol 1 (art. 2). Individuals in states that have ratified the ACHR and the San Salvador Protocol (in the Americas) or the ECHR (in Europe) can bring individual petitions to these two regional bodies concerning the right to education.

The leading international organzation dealing with the right to education is UNESCO — an IGO based in Paris, France with a cooperative agreement with the United Nations. Several treaties have been adopted under UNESCO's auspices concerning this right, most notably is the UNESCO Convention against Discrimination in Education. This convention protects the right to education.

The right to education is also promoted by the activities of international organizations like the World Bank and the International Monetary Fund. These organizations might have a positive effect on a country's ability to provide adequate education by providing loans or grants for that purpose and by encouraging countries to invest in education by making loans conditional upon such investment. International financial institutions might also contribute to the violation of human rights when they force countries to repay loans at rates that prevent a country from investing in basic education for its population. Although the obligation remains one of the state in question, an international organization can be complacent in a violation of human rights by urging policies that it knows, or has good reason to believe, will cause a government to inadequately invest in education.

8.5 The Right to Social Security

The human right to social security refers to the right of individuals to receive services and money from the state when they cannot provide for themselves. It is found in article 22 of the UDHR, article 9 of the ICESCR, article 6 of the CRC, article 5(e) (iv) of the CERD and articles 11(1) (e) and 13(a) of CEDAW, article XVI of the ADRDM, article 9 of the San Salvador Protocol to ACHR, article 16 of the CHR of CIS, articles 13(3) and 18(4) of the ACHPR, articles I(12) and II (30) of the ESC, and article 34 of the Charter of Fundamental Rights of the EU. The Arab Charter will also include this right in article 30 that provides the entitlement to "comprehensive social security." Instruments, such as the MWC provide for this right for specific groups of persons and can be seen as supplementary to the just named provisions. Many of these articles are linked to other articles indicating once again the interdependence of human rights. For example, in the ADRDM articles XXXV and XXXVI and in the ACHPR article 29(6) provide for individuals' duties to cooperate with the state for ensuring these rights can be paid for out of public funds.

In most cases, this right applies to individuals who are retired, disabled or otherwise prevented from working. It also often applies to individuals who are unemployed. While the level of social security that a state is expected to provide may vary. The level must be enough to provide individuals with an adequate standard of living, although it may be either through payments of money or in kind services. There is also no common adequate standard of living that applies to everyone everywhere, but this standard must be determined in consideration of the specific vulnerabilities related to the persons concerned. The right to social security is equally, in practice, dependent on the particular circumstances prevailing in a state. The right to social security is also protected by numerous ILO treaties including the ILO Social Security (Minimum Standards) Convention (No. 102) of 1952 that requires that governments provide information about their social security system.

The right to social security benefits is also one of the few social or economic human rights that has been the subject of international authoritative decision making in individual cases. In first instance this happened indirectly in the HRC's decision in *S.W. Broeks v. Netherlands*, UN HRC, Comm. No. 172/1984 (12 May 1999), which found distinctions between social security benefits between men and women to be discrimination prohibited by Article 26 of the ICCPR. In addition, the UN 's CESCR, has expressed its highly regarded view on the right in its General Comment 6 concerning older persons. According to the UN CESCR, the information should include a description of the forms of benefits: medical care, cash sickness, maternity, old-age, invalidity, survivors', employment injury, unemployment and family.

The Committee of Experts under the European Social Charter that is empowered to receive communications from select enitites has found France to have violated this right. It has done so finding that alleged reforms of the *Aide médicale de l'Etat* (State medical assistance law) and the *Couverture maladie universelle* (Universal sickness coverage law) deprive a large number of adults and children of sufficient resources for medical care.

As the case against France indicates, the right to social security has become more controversial as governments are being pressured to cut social spending by rich governments such as the United States and by international financial organizations. Since 2000, several Latin American countries have been faced with strong internal political opposition to economic cutbacks on social programs that have been required by international bodies such as the IMF and World Bank. Countries like Argentina have stood up to these organizations and refused further cuts even if it meant reneging on debt payments. This has in turn pressured rich lenders to either stop their profitable loans or accept more moderate or even delayed repayment schedules. The link between social security and the international economic mechanisms is unmistakable, yet it is rarely expressed as an issue of human rights by western observers or observers sharing the perspectives of rich governments.

The governments of developing countries trying to protect the right of their citizens to social security have frequently argued to richer countries that their citizens have a human right to social security. Despite these advances, the right, however, remains controversial because of the opposition of rich countries, especially the United States.

8.6 The Right to Work and to Appropriate Work Conditions

The right to work is divided into a right to employment and a right to appropriate conditions once one is employed. Although the right does not require that a government provide a job to every person in the country, being a social and economic right, it does require that a government take immediate and progressive steps towards achieving the right. The right to work and to appropriate conditions of work appears in articles 23 and 24 of the Universal Declaration of Human Rights, articles 6 and 7 of the ICESCR, articles XIV and XV of the ADRDM, article I of the ESC, articles 6 and 7 of the San Salvador Protocol to the ACHR, article 14 of the ACHPR, article 14 of the CHR of CIS, and several ILO conventions.

In societies that ascribe to socialist or communal principles the right to work has been viewed as very important because it symbolizes the individual's contribution to society as well as one of his or her most basic benefits: remuneration. The right requires the government to have policies that aim at allowing everyone under their jurisdiction to find work. It has not been interpreted to require the government to give everyone any job they want, but it does require the government to produce and begin to implement a policy that would enable everyone to work in a job for which they are qualified.

Perhaps the most widely accepted facet of the right to work is the right not to be discriminated against when being considered for employment. Of course, this means that only certain forms of discrimination are prohibited and the degree of permitted discrimination may depend on the status of the employer or the employment. In the first case, the prohibition of discrimination combines with the right to work to prohibit discrimination on grounds such as race, religion, ethnic background, national origin, etc. This may not, however, prevent a state from limiting the employment opportunities, and even rights, of migrants. In the second case, the fact that an employer is a government may mean that the employer has less discretion in deciding upon the criteria for recruitment then does a private entity.

The right to work and appropriate conditions of work is also relevant to special groups of persons. In the European context, European Union nationals have a right to work that is equal to that of nationals of the member state in which they find themselves. The European Committee of Experts under the Social Charter has dealt with several cases involving child labour in a number state parties. In *International Commission of Jurists v. Portugal*, Report to the Committee of Ministers, Complaint No. 1/1998, Strasbourg (9 September 1999), the Committee found a violation of the right to appropriate work conditions and the protection of children from exploitation. Although the decisions of the European Committee of Social Rights are non-binding, they are passed on to the Committee of Ministers who may adopt a binding resolution.

As the numerous treaties promulgated under its auspices indicate, the International Labour Organization has an important role to play in the attainment and protection of the right to work. At a normative level, it promulgates treaties that states can ratify and has thereby contributed substantially to creating international law protecting workers. Many of the ILO treaties create rights for workers. At the level of implementation, there are several committees within the ILO that provide for workers' rights. These matters are decided by bodies made up of representatives of employers, employees and state officials. Thus, not only the government's point of view is represented in decision-making processes.

Significant protection of workers rights has also been granted within economic blocs, most notably the European Union. Not only are states of the European Union required to admit each others' nationals they are also required to ensure that these nationals have relatively equal conditions of work. For example, both female and male parents must be able to take maternity leave after the birth of a child.

8.7 Right to Form Trade Unions and the Right to Strike

Human rights related to labour have long been championed by socialist's perspectives of international human rights law. This includes not only communist perspectives, but also the social democratic perspectives that prevail through most of the world. In recent years, however, some countries have challenged the legitimacy of trade unions in favour of deferring more to employers' discretion. Nevertheless, the rights to form trade unions and to go on strike remain important to securing other basic human rights for workers.

While the right to form trade unions is sometimes combined with the right to freedom of association (see Chapter 11) in article 22 of the ICCPR, article XXII of the ADRDM, article 11 of the ECHR, article 16 of the ACHR, article 10 of the ACHPR, articles I(5) and (6) and II(5) and (6) of the ESC, and article 22 of the CHR of the CIS; it is also a separate right found in article 24 of the UDHR and article 8 of the ICESCR. Similarly the right to strike is included implicitly in the freedom of expression or as part of the right to form trade unions as in article 8(1) (d) of the ICESCR. Perhaps the primary protection of this right has come from the ILO Committee on Freedom of Association which has held that a general prohibition on strikes is not consistent with ILO Convention No. 87 (concerning freedom of Association and the Right to Organize from 1949), which is widely ratifed. Other ILO conventions also protect these rights.

In the ICESCR, the right to form and join trade unions extends not only to domestic labour unions, but also to the right of domestic unions to "join international trade union organizations." The right to strike is only allowed in conformity with law. Another exception to these rights is specifically reserved for members of the armed forces, police or the "administration of the State." In their reports, states are requested to provide detailed information about the conditions that must be satisfied to join trade unions. In the periodic reports that follow the first report, states are asked to "give a short review of changes, if any, in national legislation, court decisions, as well as administrative rules, procedures and practices during the reporting period affecting the rights enshrined in Article 8 of the ICESCR.

Interpretation of the right to form trade unions has not been uniform. Article 11 containing the freedom of association in the ECHR has been interpreted narrowly by the European Court of Human Rights allowing the state a margin of appreciation in deciding whether police are entitled to go on strike. *National Union of Belgian Police v. Belgium*, ECtHR, Ser. A, October 1975. At the same time article 10 the freedom of association in the ACHPR has been interpreted broadly to prevent a state from restricting lawyers from forming a bar association independent of government control. *Civil Liberties Organisation in respect of the Nigerian Bar Association v. Nigeria*, African Commission on Human and Peoples' Rights, Comm. No. 101/93 (1995).

8.8 The Right to Cultural Life

The right to participate in one's culture is a right that allows individuals to develop their ethnic, religious, linguistic, national or other identity. It protects individuals in the exercise of cultural traditions and obliges the state to foster such exercise. It is found in article 15 of the ICESCR, article 14 of the ACHR, article 17(2) of the ACHPR, and article 21 of the CHR of the CIS. Ethnic, religious, and linguistic minorities enjoy this right under article 27 of the ICCPR. Declaratory statements on cultural rights include article 27(1) of the UDHR and article XIII of the ADRDM. Cultural property is protected by several instruments relevant to international humanitarian law, most notably, the Convention for the Protection of Cultural Property in the Event of Armed Conflict from 1954 and the Pan American Union (now OAS) treaty on the Protection of Artistic and Scientific Institutions and Historic Monuments from 1935. The right of members of minorities to enjoy, individually and in community with others, their own culture is guaranteed in article 27 of the ICCPR and the right of children to enjoy their culture is provided for in article 30 of the CRC.

In a world in which individuals increasingly move across borders and often settle in countries with cultures that are much different from those in which they were raised, this right provides individuals the ability to retain a link to their heritage. In many cases, the right is uncontroversial and actively promoted by governments; the problems usually arise when an expression of culture might arouse political sensitivities that are unwelcome by a government or particular elites. When this happens, governments sometimes have to be reminded that their citizens have a human right to enjoy their own culture even if it is not the culture of the ruling elite or the majority. Several additional declarations have been adopted by governmental and or non-governmental bodies reminding states of these responsibilities.

The right to participate in one's culture is often most important to individuals in societies with rich cultural traditions that go back thousands of years. It is often a point of shared pride among different members of a minority. It is also especially important to people subjected to alien occupation or other forms of foreign domination. For these people their cultural heritage and respect for this heritage is sometimes the only source of pride they have left and the source of inspiration for their struggle against the oppression they are suffering.

CHAPTER NINE
Discrimination, Security of Person, and Fair Trial

The previous Chapter concentrated on rights that might be referred to as economic, social and cultural rights or needs based rights. In this Chapter, the rights that can be referred to as civil and political or dignity enhancing rights are considered. However, be cautious with the application of these academic distinctions, because as one can clearly see there are many overlaps and much intertwining between the two areas of rights. Because these rights are protected in regional and international contexts in which there are adjudicatory bodies there are also more authoritative decisions from particular cases illustrating how these rights apply. When reading the materials that follow try to train your attention on the similarities rather than the distinctions, although it will be necessary to understand the distinction as well to decide cases in which these rights are threatened or violated.

9.1 Prohibition of Discrimination

The principles of non-discrimination and equality are some of the most basic principles of international law. They are found in almost every international human rights instrument in one form or another. It is found, among other places, in article 1, paragraphs 2 and 3 of the UNC; article, 2(1) of the

ICCPR; article 2(2) of the ICESCR; article 14 of the ECHR and Protocol 13 of the ECHR; article 1 of the ACHR; article 2 of the ACHPR; article 20(2) of the CHR of the CIS; article 3 of the RC in relation to refugees; article 2 of the CRC in relation to children; article 1 of the MWC for migrant workers and their families; the whole of the CERD in relation to racial discrimination; and the whole of the CEDAW in relation to women. Article 2 of the UDHR and article II of the ADRDM also prohibit discrimination.

The principle of non-discrimination expressed in article 26 of the ICCPR, according to the UN HRC, "constitutes a basic and general principle relating to the protection of human rights." The Committee has stated that "[a]rticle 26 not only entitles all persons to equality before the law as well as equal protection of the law but also prohibits any discrimination on any ground such as race, colour, sex, language, religion, political or other opinion, national or social origin, property, birth or other status."

The Committee has interpreted the breadth of the application of article 26 broadly finding it to imply a prohibition of "any distinction, exclusion, restriction or preference which is based on any grounds such as race, colour, sex, language, religion, political or other opinion, national or social origin, property, birth or other status, and which has the purpose or effect of nullifying or impairing the recognition, enjoyment or exercise by all persons, on an equal footing, of all rights and freedoms."

It must also be noted that while other prohibitions of discrimination apply to specific rights or sometimes only to those rights protected in a particular treaty, Article 26 does not specify such limitations. Article 26 thus prohibits discrimination in law or in fact in any field regulated and protected by public authorities.

The importance of the prohibition of discrimination was emphasized by the Permanent Court of International Justice in *Minority Schools in Albania*, P.C.I.J., Advisory Opinion, Ser. A/B, No. 64 (1935). This case involved the closing of (Christian) minority schools in Albania by the Muslim dominated government by amendment of the Constitution to provide for complete public education and outlawing private schools. The Court was asked to decide whether the closings violated the obligation to provide minorities the same treatment as the majority in terms of the right to education. The Court found discrimination to exist.

The *Minority Schools in Albania case* sets out an important understanding concerning discrimination: that it is prohibited in fact and in theory. Thus a state may be in violation of the prohibition against discrimination even if its laws prohibit discrimination. To avoid such condemnation and to abide by its international obligation to prohibit discrimination — an obligation that is likely part of customary international law — a state must ensure that discrimination is in fact prohibited.

More recently other international human rights tribunals have applied the prohibition of discrimination in broader terms. Most notable among the case law has been a series of cases brought against the Netherlands under article 26 of the ICCPR applying the prohibition of discrimination to the enjoyment of economic and social rights that are not even covered in that instrument. The UN HRC found that the Netherlands was acting discriminatorily because the right had been created under domestic legislation and the general prohibition of discrimination required that any right created by the government be recognized for all persons equally. *F.H. Zwaan-de Vries v. Netherlands*, UN HRC, Comm. No. 182/1984 (28 September 1984).

Several international conventions provide protection against discrimination. A convention that provides specific protections against a specific form of discrimination is the International Convention on the Elimination of All Forms of Racial Discrimination (CERD). While the ICCPR provides a general protection against discrimination, the CERD provides protection against discrimination only when it is based on race. The Committee created by the CERD issues General Recommendations interpreting the prohibition of discrimination.

The prohibition of discrimination is found in both treaty and customary law. Both Article 14 of the ECHR in conjunction with the 12th Protocol to the ECHR and article 26 of the ICCPR prohibits discrimination in general terms. The prohibition of some forms of discrimination, most notably racial discrimination, is undoubtedly customary international law. These grounds likely include race, colour, sex, language, religion, political or other opinion, national or social origin, property, and birth. Non-discrimination is a principle, which in the view of the UN HRC, entitles aliens "to equal protection of law" and provides that "[d]iscrimination may not be made between different categories of aliens" in regards to procedures involving removal from the country.

In all cases, it is important to understand that both discrimination 'in fact' and 'in law' are prohibited. Nevertheless, for a government to be found to be discriminating, it must be shown that either there is a prohibited distinction being made between various groups of people in the law or in the application of the law. In other words, an act of discrimination based on a private person's action may not constitute a violation of human rights as long as the government does not condone or allow it.

The prohibition of discrimination is often prominent. The European Court of Human Rights stated the following in regards to the principle of non-discrimination in *Belgian Linguistics Case*, ECtHR, Ser. A, No. 6, para. 9 (23 July 1968):

> Article 6 of the Convention does not compel States to institute a system of appeal courts. A State which does set up such courts

consequently goes beyond its obligations under Article 6. However it would violate that Article, read in conjunction with Article 14, were it to debar certain persons from these remedies without a legitimate reason while making them available to others in respect of the same types of actions.

In such cases, there would be a violation of a guaranteed right or freedom as it is proclaimed by the relevant article read in conjunction with article 14. In *Abdulaziz, Cabales and Balkandali v. United Kingdom*, ECtHR, Ser. A, No. 94, para. 82 (28 May 1985), the European Court of Human Rights dismissed the United Kingdom's arguments that discrimination based on sex was a legitimate form of action for limiting "primary immigration" which in turn would, according to the government, harm Britain's labor market. In the same case, however, the difficulty with arguments of discrimination is illustrated by the Court's willingness to accept a distinction based on birth. The Court accepted that there "are in general persuasive social reasons for giving special treatment to those whose link with a country stems from birth." Thus, the distinction was "an objective and reasonable justification" in particular because it was proportional to the "unquestionably legitimate" goal of avoiding hardship for women with close ties to the United Kingdom. In this case, the applicants also argued that the government had lied about its motives, but this argument was summarily dismissed.

Many types of discrimination are prohibited. One of the most recent areas of concern is discrimination against persons with disabilities. At the end of 2001, the UN General Assembly established an Ad Hoc Committee to consider proposals for treaty protecting the human rights of persons with disabilities. Consequently, several reports have been promulgated on the situation of disabled persons and their existing and future protection. There already exists a thirteen-paragraph Declaration on the Rights of Disabled Persons from 1975 that sets out what these rights should be and a declaration on the rights of persons with mental disabilities. The focus of the Declaration on the Rights of Disabled Persons is non-discrimination. In other words, it merely reiterates the existing rights that all individuals have and reminds us that disabled persons have these rights as well.

Groups that have been a specific concern of non-discrimination norms under international human rights law include physically and mentally disabled persons, women, refugees, and persons living with HIV/AIDS.

9.2 Right to Security of Person

This human right that is found in article 9 of the ICCPR, article 6 of the ACHPR, article 7 of the ACHR, article 5 of the ECHR, article 5 of the CHR of the CIS, and article 16 and 37 of the CRC. It is also expressed as a human right in articles 3 and 9 of the UDHR and articles I and XXV of the

ADRDM.

The right to security of person is a right that adheres to individuals, to persons in detention or deprived of their liberty. The right to security and liberty of person is applicable to "all deprivations of liberty," according to General Comment 8(16) at para. 1 of the HRC. Paragraph 4 of this General Comment states that any individual deprived of his or her liberty "by arrest or detention shall be entitled to take proceedings before a court, in order that the court may decide without delay on the lawfulness of his [or her] detention and order his [or her] release if the detention is not lawful."

The clearest villatins of this right may occur in cases involving massive arrests without charge or explanation or detention without trial or charge, *Amnesty International on behalf of Orton and Vera Chirwa v. Malawi*, ACommHPR, Comm. No. 78/92 (1995); or in cases in which a state is attempting to act to protect national security. *Commission Nationale des Droits de l'Homme et des Libertés v. Chad*, ACommHPR, Comm. No. 74/92 (1995).

The most elaborate interpretations of this right have been put forward by the European Court of Human Rights. In *Winterwerp v. Netherlands*, ECtHR, Ser. A, No. 33 (24 October 1979), the Court held that this right is violated by the failure to provide a person incarcerated for their own good on the basis of a mental disease, the right to regular review of their incarceration by a competent court.

As Chapter Seven has indicated, governments sometimes have the right to derogate from their human rights obligations for specified reasons. Article 15 uof the ECHR, for example, provides governments this right when the existence of the state is concerned.

Although the human right to security of person is, together with the right to life and the prohibition against torture, one of the most basic rights of the individual it may be temporarily derogated from under the special procedures of most major human rights treaties. However, when a government has not derogated from this right it must take all necessary measures to protect it. Furthermore, when found to have violated the right a government must quickly conform its actions to the requirements of the law or face the loss of trust of its citizens and others under its jurisdiction.

9.3 Right to Fair Trial

The right to fair trial is one of the most expansive and most complicated of all the human rights protected under international law. Because it is such an important human right, it is often protected in more than one article in human rights treaties and in a variety of manners. Provisions protecting rights of fair trial can be found in article 14 and 16 of the ICCPR, articles 3, 7 and

26 of the ACHPR, articles 5, 6 and 7 of the ECHR and articles 2 to 4 of the 7th Protocol to the ECHR, article 3, 8, 9 and 10 of the ACHR, articles 6 and 7 of the CHR of the CIS, and article 40 of the CRC. The right to fair trial is also promoted in numerous declarations, resolutions and minimum standards that are themselves not binding, but which reflect customary international law because of their widespread acceptance. Articles 6, 7, 10 and 11 of the UDHR, articles II, XVII, and XXVI of the ADRDM are examples.

Among the general fair trial protections are (1) the right to be heard by a competent, independent and impartial tribunal, (2) the right to public hearing, (3) the right to be heard within a reasonable time, (4) the right to counsel, and (5) the right to interpretation. The rights of fair trial may be derogated from in circumstances enumerated in the respective treaties. The prohibition of *ex post facto* laws, which according to the ECHR and the ACHR is non-derogable, is found in separate articles in most treaties. The aim of these guarantees is to ensure the proper administration of justice. Both the European and Inter-American courts have made it clear that these guarantees apply to all types of judicial proceedings. In other words, the guarantees of fair trial apply to administrative as well as judicial proceedings. Whenever an individual's legal right is at stake, then there must be a fair procedure to determine disputes about this right.

Of particular importance among the guarantees is the adequate time and facilities for preparation of one's defense. This includes the right to be able to communicate with counsel of one's own choosing. The communications between the accused and his or her lawyer must be given full respect for its confidentiality and lawyers "should be able to counsel and represent their clients in accordance with their established professional standards and judgment without any restrictions, influences, pressures or undue interference from any quarter." *See* General Comment 13(21) of the UN HRC at para. 9. Furthermore, the law must allow the accused or his or her lawyer "to challenge the conduct of the case if they believe it to be unfair." *Id.* at para. 11. As judicial remedies play a central role in the protection of human rights these protections are some of the most important in the ICCPR The failure of a government to provide for them, therefore, creates a serious situation and indicates an environment where other human rights may be in jeopardy.

The first step in deciding which protections of fair trial are applicable is the determination of the type of proceedings and which provisions are applicable. In the European system for the protection of human rights this has meant that the European Court of Human Rights must determine whether a civil or criminal proceeding exists and if a civil right or obligation is involved. The application of fair trial in article 6 of the ECHR has been gradually extended by the European Court of Human Rights to apply to all civil rights and obligations, including those created by domestic law. *Apeh Uldozotteinek Szovetsege and Others v. Hungary,* ECtHR, Appl. No. 32367/96, 5 October 2000.

Special proceedings might also be subject to scrutiny under article 6. For example, in *Mills v. the United Kingdom*, App. No. 35685/97 (5 June 2001), a court-martial was considered to be subject to article 6 scrutiny because of the serious criminal nature of the crime with which the defendant had been accused (in this case assault with a weapon and wounding).

The African Commission on Human and Peoples' Rights has often dealt with cases involving grossly unfair trials of civilians by military tribunals for serious crimes. In *Constitutional Rights Project v. Nigeria, Constitutional Rights Project v. Nigeria*, Communication No. 60/91, *Eighth Annual Activity Report of the African Commission on Human and Peoples' Rights 1994-1995* (Doc. No. ACHPR/RPT/8th/Rev.I, Annex VI at 4, the Commission held that military courts *prima facie* do not provide due process for civilians. The African Commission has also held that the right to counsel of one's own choosing is also an essential part of the right to fair trial and particularly relevant to a citizen's access to his or her country's courts. It is a right enshrined in most human rights treaties, including article 7(1)(c) of the ACHPR. The African Commission recognized the importance of this right holding that "[c]itizens who cannot have recourse to the courts of their country are highly vulnerable to violation of their rights" The Commission has also stated that "[t]he right to freely choose one's counsel is essential to the assurance of a fair trial. To give the tribunal the power to veto the choice of counsel of defendants is an unacceptable infringement of this right." Finally, the African Commission has held that sometimes a state's judiciary is in such a state as to be considered inadequate for providing a fair trial.

9.3.1 Criminal Proceedings

The protections of the right to fair trial are greater in criminal proceedings where the consequences for the individuals involved are greater than in civil processes. In criminal proceedings the following guarantees apply in addition to the general guarantees already mentioned: (1) the right to be notified of charges against one in a timely manner, (2) the right to adequate time and means for the preparation of one's defense, (3) the right of an accused to defend him or herself personally or to be assisted by legal counsel of his or her own choosing, and to communicate freely and privately with his or her counsel, (4) the right to call witnesses in one's defense and question witnesses against oneself, (5) the right not to incriminate oneself, and (6) the right to appeal a judgment of a court of first instance to a higher court. The right to security of person will provide some additional protections for criminal defendants. As will special rights that are sometimes found in other articles such as the prohibition of trying a person for the same crime twice.

The most litigated of the array of rights provided for under the general heading of fair trial has been the right to a trial within a reasonable time and the right to a determination by an independent and impartial tribunal. The length of time has often been one of determining whether the government has been responsible for delays in ensuring justice. Italy is the country that has most often been criticized for delays in its judicial procedures. The period of time that will be reasonable will depend on the complexity of the case. Generally it is necessary that a criminal defendant be arraigned quite quickly — within a matter of days. The requirement of an independent and impartial tribunal is also important to criminal trials and requires that judges be both *de facto* impartial and independent as well as appear to be impartial and independent. The fact that a judge may also initially investigate a case has caused some concern in civil law countries.

The right to a fair trial might also encompass the right of an individual to be recognised before the law as is established in article 16 of the ICCPR. The right to recognition of legal personality is established in article 16 of the Covenant. According to this article, everyone is entitled to be recognised as a subject, and not object, of the law. This protection allows no derogation and admits of no exceptions.

Although some of the most difficult cases arise concerning persons in special situations, the protections of article 6, of course, apply to all individuals under jurisdiction of the state. *Saunders v. the United Kingdom*, ECtHR, Ser. A., No. 6 (November 1996). The right to fair trial is one of the most litigated of all human rights. It is also perhaps one of the most important because without it a violation of a human right is unlikely to be remedied in domestic procedures. As shown above it is especially important in relation to the criminal charges.

* * *

Although these rights constrain states from violating the human rights of persons under their jurisdiction it is unclear whether the human rights bodies that enforce these provisions themselves are constrained by the rights. It would certainly make sense that the defenders of human rights themselves respect human rights, but this is not always the case and even some members of international human rights tribunals have suggested that they are not bound. If such a state of affairs becomes the norm it will substantially undermine the credibility of international human rights law. Furthermore, sometimes human rights bodies have, in practice failed to abide by the standards they are enforcing upon states. Again, such action seriously undermines the functioning of these international human rights bodies.

CHAPTER TEN
Torture, Life, Slavery

10.1 Prohibition of Torture and Other Inhuman or Degrading Treatment

All individuals under the jurisdiction of a state are protected against torture, cruel, inhuman and degrading treatment and punishment under international human rights law. This protection can be found in Article 7 of the ICCPR, article 1 of the CAT, article 3 of the ECHR, article 5 of the ACHPR and article 5 of the ACHR, article 3 of the CHR of the CIS and articles 19, 32-37 of the CRC. Both article 5 of the UDHR and article XXV of the ADRDM also prohibit torture, cruel, inhuman and degrading treatment. It appears in almost every human rights treaty. In addition, most national constitutions containing provisions on human rights prohibit torture and inhumane and degrading treatment or punishment. This prohibition is also customary international law.

Whether an act constitutes inhuman degrading treatment or punishment depends on the circumstances of the case, the African Commission, for example, has stated that the prohibition of torture, cruel, inhuman, or degrading treatment or punishment is to be interpreted as widely as possible to encompass the widest possible array of physical and mental abuses. The prohibition in article 5 of the ACHPR has been held, therefore, to include actions that "humiliate the individual" as well as detention in a "sordid and dirty cell," "being detained arbitrarily, not knowing the reason or duration of detention," and "added to this deprivation of contact with the outside world and health threatening conditions." The African Commission has even included laws that insulate government actions from legal challenge by declaring that nothing authorized by law can be inhuman and degrading treatment as possible violations of this prohibition.

In practice the assessment of whether an act violates the prohibition of torture, cruel, inhuman, or degrading treatment or punishment focuses on whether the act achieves a significant degree of severity. In the view of the European Court even a lawful punishment may be degrading and thus prohibited as a violation of human rights, but "the humiliation or debasement involved must attain a particular level and must in any event be other than the usual element of humiliation..." The European Court has also explained that "[t]he assessment of this minimum is, in the nature of things, relative; it depends on all the circumstances of the case, such as the duration of the treatment, its physical or mental effects and, in some cases, the sex, age and state of health of the victim, etc." For a punishment carried out by the state, the threshold "depends on all the circumstances of the case and, in particular, on the nature and context of the punishment itself and the manner and method of its execution." The threshold for cruel, inhuman, and degrading punishment is thus crossed when an act creates "feelings of fear, anguish and inferiority capable of humiliating and debasing" the victim."

Acts such as lashings for petty crimes have been determined to achieve such a level of severity that they violate article 5 of the African Charter according to the African Commission. While the European Court of Human Rights in *Tyler v. United Kingdom*, 26 ECtHR (Ser. A) (1978), 2 E.H.R.R. 1 (1979-80), applying article 3 of the ECHR has similarly held even for lashings that were carried out in private, with appropriate medical supervision, under strictly hygienic conditions.

An act that constitutes torture, cruel, inhumane, or degrading treatment or punishment cannot be justified for any reason, even public opinion, public health, public morals or the protection of rights of others. This has been most clearly stated by the European Court of Human Rights stating in *Chahal v. UK*, ECt.HR, Judgment of 15 November 1996 and *Ahmed v. Austria*, ECtHR (17 December 1996), when it decided that even if the United Kingdom was correct in its suggestion that a single person could threaten the national security of the United Kingdom it could not treat the individual in a manner that would violate this human right. In this case, the treatment in question was deportation to India, where the applicant had argued he might be arrested and tortured because he is a Sikh. The European Court repeated this concern in a case involving corporal punishment stating that although "it might well be that one of the reasons why ... [a] penalty [is viewed] as an effective deterrent is precisely the element of degradation which it involves ... a punishment does not lose its degrading character just because it is believed to be, or actually is, an effective deterrent or aid to crime control." Thus, while the sentiments of the people of a particular country and even region within a country may be relevant for a state when deciding which of two or more rights to give priority, this is not the case as concerns cruel, inhumane and degrading acts. Once an act is found to cross the threshold and found to be cruel, inhumane, or degrading, there cannot be any justification for that action, it is a violation of the prohibition.

Furthermore, a particular measure is not excluded from being cruel, inhumane, or degrading because the measure has been in use for a long time or even meets with general approval. Similarly in *Tyler* the European Court found that "even assuming that local public opinion can have an influence on the interpretation of the concept of 'degrading punishment' ... the Court does not regard it as established that judicial corporal punishment is not considered degrading" because it is supported by public opinion.

A widely recognised treaty definition of torture is found in the UN Convention Against Torture and Other Cruel, Inhuman or Degrading Treatment or Punishment. Article 1 of this treaty defines torture in one of the most cited definitions stating that

> ... the term "torture" means any act by which severe pain or suffering, whether physical or mental, is intentionally inflicted on a person for such purposes as obtaining from him or a third person information or a confession, punishing him for an act he or a third person committed or is suspected of having committed, or intimidating or coercing him or a third person, or for any reason based on discrimination of any kind, when such pain or suffering is inflicted by or at the instigation of or with the consent or acquiescence of a public official or other person acting in an official capacity. It does not include pain or suffering arising only from, inherent in or incidental to lawful sanctions.

The article provides a broad definition of "torture" but immunizes lawful sanctions from being violations of the CAT. The CAT also creates a Committee against Torture made up of eighteen independent experts with the power to accept individual (art. 22) and inter-state (art. 21) complaints against states that have made the requisite declarations and the power to initiate investigations that may include on site visits to a state (art. 20). States must also submit periodic reports to the Committee (art. 19). The CAT also allows states to create national bodies that may deal with complaints before they are submitted to the Committee. A recent protocol to CAT enhances the investigative authority of these bodies.

The most widely accepted prohibition of torture, cruel, inhuman and degrading treatment and punishment is found in article 7 of the ICCPR. The purpose of this article is to protect the integrity and the dignity of the individual. To this end, it is "not sufficient for the implementation of this article to prohibit such treatment or punishment or to make it a crime" ... [and] ... States must ensure "effective protection through some machinery of control," according to the UN Human Rights Committee.

Among the safeguards which may make control effective are provisions against detention incommunicado, granting, without prejudice to the investigation, persons such as doctors, lawyers and family members access to the detainees; provisions requiring detainees should be held in places that are publicly recognised and that their names and places of detention should be entered in a central register available to persons concerned, such as relatives ...." Thus the "scope of protection required goes far beyond torture as normally understood. It included the prohibition of treatment such as the deprivation of human rights for extended periods of time. In *M.V. Massera v. Uruguay*, see decision reproduced in McGoldrick, D., *The Human Rights Committee* 365, para. 9.6 (1994), the Committee held that inadequate provision of food and unhealthy working conditions for a detainee had weakened her state of health to such an extent as to constitute a violation of Article 7. In *Selçuk and Asker v. Turkey*, (24 April 1998), the European Court of Human Rights held that the destruction of a person's home by the army constituted cruel, inhuman or degrading treatment. In another case involving Uruguay, the Committee expressed the view that harsh conditions of detention were torture. *Conteris v. Uruguay*, UN HRC, Comm. No. 139/1983 (17 July 1985), UN Doc. Supp. No. 40 (A/40/40) at 196 (1985). The Committee found that the state has a positive obligation to "ensure protection by the law against such treatment even when committed by persons acting outside or without any official authority" and that each of the three prohibited activities in article 7 defines different actions that depend on "the kind, purpose and severity of the particular treatment."

The protections in paragraph 1 of article 10 are similar to those in article 7, but are especially directed to people who have been deprived of their liberty. Article 10 applies to individuals "not only in prisons but also, for example, in hospitals, detention camps or correctional institutions." General Comment 9(16) at para. 1. This article also applies during war time to detained civilians and prisoners of war, including for example the individuals being held in Guantanámo Bay by the United States government.

The cases before the Committee illustrate that a broad exercise of discretion is appropriate in determining what constitutes torture, inhumane or degrading treatment. The Committee will look to the applicant to determine the facts giving rise to the alleged violation. If the facts are agreed upon then the Committee evaluates the treatment against a standard that takes into account the effect of the treatment on the individual and the Committee's prevailing view of humane treatment. If the treatment, which has been factually established, is considered torture, inhumane or degrading, it need only be determined that the acts are attributable to the state. In this regards, it may be the acts themselves or the states' failure to prevent, investigate or punish them, which constitutes a violation of the prohibtion.

The prohibtion of torture prohibits a state from deporting, expelling or extraditing them to a state where they will be tortured or treated inhumanly. This prohibition will apply even if the treatment will not come from the first state to which the person is removed, but there is reason to believe that this state will send the person on to a state that will accord inappropriate treatment.

The prohibition of inhuman and degrading treatment prevents a state from denying an individual the means of basic subsistence. For example, when the state prohibits an individual from receiving benefits and from working, thereby forcing the individual to live in abject poverty, this right may be violated, according to the English High Court. See *R. v. Secretary of State for Social Security ex parte B and Joint Council for the Welfare of Immigrants*, [1996] 4 All ER 385. The violation of article 3 of the ECHR could result from the combination of the denial of benefits and the refusal of the right to work.

The leading case in which this right or prohibition is discussed is the inter-state complaint brought by the government of Ireland against the United Kingdom before the European Court of Human Rights. *Ireland v. United Kingdom*, ECtHR, Ser. A, No 25 (18 January 1978). This case involved an inter-state complaint. The government of the Republic of Ireland complained that the United Kingdom's laws and procedures for dealing with terrorism violated several provisions of the ECHR. In August and October 1971, 14 persons had been arrested by British soldiers and attempts were made to extract information from them. They were interrogated by the United Kingdom authorities. The interrogation involved the use of five techniques, namely: 1. keeping detainees hooded except during interrogation; 2. making detainees stand 'spreadeagled' against a wall for long periods of time; 3. accommodating the detainees under conditions where they were subject to continuous and monotonous noise; 4. depriving the detainees of sleep; and 5. restricting their diet to one loaf of bread and one pint of water provided every six hours. These 'five techniques' were sometimes applied together and there was evidence that they were part of a government policy. The techniques were applied for several days. As a result the detainees suffered physical and mental suffering and injuries. The Court found that the five techniques were a violation of Article 3 of the ECHR prohibiting torture.

Torture or inhumane treatment often occur in the context of imprisonment or police activities. One reason for this is that human rights are traditionally understood as the rights individuals have against or vis-à-vis a state and it is through police actions that states exercise their coercive powers. The United States government's actions in Abu Gharib and Guantanámo Bay are additional examples of situations where the unbriddled authority of a detaining power has escalated into torture.

Because torture most often occurs in places of detention, an Optional Protocol to the 1984 Convention against Torture and Other Cruel, Inhuman or Degrading Treatment or Punishment has been drafted that attempts to provide more effective monitoring of these places. It does this by adopting a system similar to that in the European Convention Against Torture. The Optional Protocol calls upon states that are parties to the ECHR to allow visits to prisons and other places of detention by a newly formed Subcommittee on Prevention of Torture and Other Cruel, Inhuman or Degrading Treatment or Punishment which is under the supervision of the already existing Committee Against Torture, and the designation of a national preventive committee that will act as a liaison to facilitate the work of the Subcommittee.

Note that in *Ireland v. UK* the Court defined torture as "deliberate inhumane and degrading treatment causing very serious and cruel suffering." There are three elements to this definition. First, the acts must be deliberate, inflicted intentionally. Second, the acts must already have crossed the threshold of what is prohibited by Article 3 of the ECHR and be inhumane or degrading treatment. And third, they must cause very serious and cruel suffering. This suffering can be physical or mental. The three elements are those identified by the European Court on Human Rights.

Similar elements have been established as concerns Article 7 of the ICCPR that prohibits torture, inhumane and degrading treatment. The purpose of this article is to protect the integrity and the dignity of the individual. To this end, it is "not sufficient for the implementation of this article to prohibit such treatment or punishment or to make it a crime." States must ensure "effective protection through some machinery of control." The UN Human Rights Committee has specified that several conditions that must be satisfied in particular cases stating:

> Among the safeguards which may make control effective are provisions against detention incommunicado, granting, without prejudice to the investigation, person such as doctors, lawyers and family members access to the detainees; provisions requiring detainees should be held in places that are publicly recognised and that their names and places of detention should be entered in a central register available to persons concerned, such as relatives ...

Thus, the "scope of protection required goes far beyond torture as normally understood. It included the prohibition of treatment such as the deprivation of human rights for extended periods of time. The prohibited activities in article 7 depend on "the kind, purpose and severity of the particular treatment."

Sometimes the acts which constitute inhuman or degrading treatment are not acts of physical torture, but cause other forms of hardship to the individuals involved. This type of torture is often more difficut to provide as the leading cases of *East African Asians v. United Kingdom*, Report of the European Commission of Human Rights from 14 December 1973, Applications Nos. 4403-19/70, 4422/70, 4434/70, 4443/70, 4476-78/70, 4486/70, 4501/70 and 4526-30/70, indicated. In this case the European Commission of Human Rights decided that the applicants who were discriminatorily refused admission to the United Kingdom on the basis of their colour or race did not amount to "degrading treatment" in the sense of Article 3, although it was prohibitied discrimination.

It is important to remember that most human rights treaties — the CAT is an exception with its definition of torture in Article 1 — prohibit cruel, inhuman or degrading treatment and punishment. In addition, it is also clear that such treatment is prohibited even if it will not be carried out by the state, but even by another state or by private individuals over whom the state has control. This problem has usually arisen in the context of cases involving an individual in one country who might be treated inhumanly in another. In these cases, the first country is the country against whom the case is brought and the object of the case is to prevent this country from sending an individual to the other country. See *Jabari v. Turkey*, EurCtHR, (Fourth Section), App. No. 400035/98 (March 2000) and *Soering v. United Kingdom*, ECtHR, Ser. A, No. 161 (7 July 1989). But see *Kindler v. Canada*, UN HRC, UN Doc. No. CCPR/C/48/D/470/1991 (1991).

In *Soering v. United Kingdom* the European Court of Human Rights held that the United Kingdom violates article 3 by agreeing to allow the United States to exercise jurisdiction over and individual who could receive the death penalty. After the Court's judgment the United States gave the assurance that the applicant would not be executed and the applicant was turned over.

The UN HRC has had to decide several cases whereby the death penalty and its manner of execution have been challenged as violating the human right to be free from cruel, inhumane or degrading treatment or punishment as is provided under Article 7 of the ICCPR. In expressing its views on several communications concerning Jamaica, the UN HRC has found that the death penalty violated the right to life because there are not sufficient procedural guarantees for a fair trial, but did not find it violates article 7 of the ICCPR. *Reid v. Jamaica*, UN HRC, Communication No. 250/1987 and *Berry v. Jamaica*, UN HRC, Communication No. 330/1988. In the case of *Pratt and Morgan v. Jamaica*, UN HRC views expressed on 6 April 1989, the Committee, however, found that there could be a violation of article 7 stating that it considers that "a delay of close to 10 hours from the time the stay of execution was granted to the time the authors were removed from their death cell constitutes cruel and inhumane treatment within the meaning of article 7."

Although all the regional treaties that protect human rights generally contain specific provisions prohibiting torture, there are also specific treaties prohibiting only torture in the regional context. One of these regional treaties is the European Convention for the Prevention of Torture and Inhuman or Degrading Treatment or Punishment. The outstanding feature of the European Torture Convention is its implementation mechanism. This Convention creates a European Committee on Torture that has the power to visit state parties without an invitation, something that has only recently been followed by the more universal CAT. In the Americas there is the Inter-American Convention to Prevent and Punish Torture.

Perhaps the most striking element of the prohibition of torture, cruel, inhuman and degrading treatment is the fact that once an act or a threatened act is found to pass the definitional threshold for this violation of human rights, then there can be no justification for the act. The prohibition of torture is therefore sometimes said to be the most important and sacrosanct of all human rights because of its absolute nature: once an action of a state, or an action allowed by a state is found to constitute torture, cruel, inhumane or degrading treatment it cannot be justified even by the security interest of the state.

10.2 The Right to Life

The right to life appears in article 6 of the ICCPR and in its Second Optional Protocol, article 4 of the ACHR, article 4 of the ACHPR, article 2 of the ECHR and Sixth and Twelfth Protocols, article 2 of the CHR of the CIS, and article 6 of the CRC. It also appears in article 3 of the UDHR and article I of the ADRDM. In all cases, the right to life protects against arbitrary deprivation. In the case of the protocols to the ICCPR and the ECHR, it is the death penalty that is prohibited. The right to life is one of the most fundamental rights because without it other rights are meaningless. Furthermore, there can be little doubt, that if the prohibition of torture is a principle of customary international law, so too is the right to life.

The clearest forms of violation of this right involve direct government participation in killing. For example, in *Association Internationale des Juristes Democrates v. Rwanda*, ACHPR, Comm. No. 27/89, 46/91, 49/91, 99/93 (1996) the Rwandan government was held to have participated in arbitrary arrests and summary executions that were carried out by the government.

In some cases the government may be acting for a legitimate end, but may have over reacted. For example while a government may use limited force to control prisoners, it may not use excessive force. In such cases, United Nations instruments on the use of force by police and other government forces are relevant to determining the legitimacy of the use of force. In *Niera Alegría, et al, v. Peru*, IAmCtHR (19 January 1995), the Inter-American applied United Nations guidelines in conjunction with the right to life to find the latter right was violated by the Peruvian government's excessive use of force against riotiing prisoners. The case concerned the use of excessive force by the Peruvian government in putting down a riot at San Juan Bautista Prison. Detainees at this prison were alleged terrorists. The government had delegated control of the prison to the Armed Forces when the riot broke out. As a result, the areas were sealed off and the riot suppressed with the use of force. The case was brought by the relatives of three people at the facility on whom no information was forthcoming from the authorities.

While it is clear that the right to life is violated when the state engages in the arbitrary deprivation of life, the right also extends to cases where the state fails to protect an individual from a situation where his or her life might reasonably be considered threatened. In *D. v. United Kingdom*, ECtHR (9 May 1997), the United Kingdom sought to deport a citizen of St. Kitts to his homeland for having committed a crime for which deportation is allowed under English law. The complicating factor was that the man was dying of AIDS and in St. Kitts for a mixture of socio-economic and political reasons he would not receive medical care for his illness. In fact, counsel for the petitioner described the conditions in St. Kitts as denying the very existence of AIDS. It was argued before the Court that the removal of the man to St. Kitts would violate his right to life because he would be denied the basic medical treatment he was able to receive in the United Kingdom and thus almost certainly he would die sooner than if he had remained in the country. The Commission agreed that there would be a violation of the right to life, however, the Court found only that there would be a violation of article 3 (inhuman and degrading treatment) and consequently that no question arose under article 2. The finding under article 3 is similar to the *Soering Case*, discussed above. However, it is interesting to speculate whether the European Court would have found a violation of the right to life in Soering as it is protected in the Sixth Protocol to the ECHR prohibiting the death penalty, if the United Kingdom had been party to this Protocol at the time.

The right to life is concerned with actions or threatened action by a state that would lead to the death of the individual whose rights are in question. Challenges to government action that is claimed to have indirectly violated the right to life have not been successful before the European bodies. For example, the claim that Italy was violating the right to life of a mine-clearer who was an Iraqi national and who had been severely injured by a landmine manufactured and sold by Italy to Iraq was declared inadmissible. *Tugar v. Italy*, ECtHR, First Chamber, Application No. 22869/93 (18 October 1995). Similarly another complaint claimed that a voluntary public vaccination scheme which had led to the deaths of some children had violated their right to life, but was considered inadmissible. Professor David Harris, Micheal O'Boyle and Colin Warbrick have argued, however, that "where a state takes on a responsibility such that involves the operation of a public vaccination scheme, it will be liable under Article 2 for any negligence that results in death." Indeed the Court has held that states sometimes have an obligation to take action (not merely refrain from action) to protect the right to life. See, for example, *L.C.B. v. United Kingdom*, ECHR, Reports of Judgments and Decisions 1998-III, p. 1403, § 36 (9 June 1998). There is not, however, a duty upon states to allow people to take their own life or to be assisted in doing so by others, according to the European Court of Human Rights in *Pretty v. UK*, ECHR, Appl. No. 2346/02 (29 April 2002).

In other forums an extended interpretation of the right to life has also been accepted. For example, the UN HRC has stated that:

> the right to life has been too often narrowly interpreted. The expression "inherent right to life" cannot properly be understood in a restrictive manner, and the protection of this right requires that States adopt positive measures. In General Comment 6(16), the UN Human Rights Committee has stated that it considers that it is desirable for States parties to take all possible measures to reduce infant mortality and to increase life expectancy, especially in adopting measures to eliminate malnutrition and epidemics.

Appropriate reasons for interpreting the right to life in Article 2 of the ECHR in the broad manner suggested by the Human Rights Committee can be found in the values that are at the foundation of international human rights law. According to this broad interpretation it would appear that a country violates an individual's right to life when it deprives that person of the basic rights of subsistence. In addition, as this right does not allow derogation or provide for progressive implementation, states are bound to ensure it immediately and cannot defer their responsibilities.

The right to life is protected in all major human rights instruments. Like the prohibition against torture it is non-derogable. Nevertheless, it is a right which has been interpreted to allow the exception of killing in wartime and the death penalty. In both cases there are conditions attached. Killing in wartime must be done in accordance with the laws of war or international humanitarian law. Thus indiscriminate killings, the killing of civilians, the killing of other protected persons such as wounded or surrendering soldiers, *et cetera*, are prohibited. As concerns the death penalty, this must also be carried out with respect for procedural guarantees and in a humane manner. What is a humane manner of intentionally killing another human being?

Article 6 of the Covenant states that "[e]very human being has the right to life." In its comment on the right to life the Committee has stated that this right is "the supreme right from which no derogation is permitted even in time of public emergency which threatens the life of the nation" and it "is a right that should not be interpreted narrowly." In this last respect, the applicants rely on a broad interpretation of the right to life, whereby action or inaction perpetuating inhumane conditions under which individuals are forced to live constitutes a violaton of their right to life. Such an interpretation is in accordance with the Committee's determination that "protection of this right requires that States adopt positive measures" and the example given by the Committee of taking "all possible measures to reduce infant morality and to increase life expectancy, especially in adopting measures to eliminate malnutrition and epidemics."

Article 2 of the ECHR appears to provide the same right. However, it is questioned whether it will be interpreted as broadly as the Human Rights Committee's comment indicates it may be. The failure of the claim against the Italian government for selling landmines, discussed above, indicates a narrower interpretation. The European Court of Human Rights, however, has found that killing terrorists without proper safeguards violates the right to life. *McCann and Others v. United Kingdom*, ECtHR, Ser. A, No. 324 (March 1996) was the first case in which a violation of the right to life was found by the Court. Despite finding a violaton of the right to life, note that the Court dismissed the applicants' claims for compensation finding it inappropriate to make such an award because, in the opinion of the Court, the three applicants were planning to bomb Gibraltar. The *McCann Case* was based on a finding not that the soldiers acted negligently, but that the United Kingdom had acted negligently in the manner it had trained and instructed the soldiers. This broad indictment of the United Kingdom's terrorist combat policy has caused much irritation among British policy makers and has reiterated to them that even matters of national security must be dealt with without the trampling of human rights of individuals who are suspected of causing the threat.

Although states may use force as legitimate combatants involved in an armed conflict, the right to life may be violated when armed force is used in a manner that contravenes the laws of war, for example, against civilians — who are defined as non-combatants — or, when the war itself is illegal — a violation of *jus ad bellum*.

The right to life is one of the most important human rights because the enjoyment all other rights depend upon it. It is the driving force behind the movement to abolish the death penalty and nuclear disarmament.

10.2.1 Death Penalty

The death penalty has been a long-standing problem for both developed and developing countries. Second Optional Protocol to the ICCPR prohibits the death penalty. In Europe the death penalty is now prohibited by virtue of the 6th and 13th Protocols to the ECHR. The latter abolished the death penalty without exception. In Africa there is no prohibition on capital punishment in the regional human rights treaty. In the Americas, the prohibition of the death penalty is somewhat vague as article 4 of the ACHR only requires states parties not to re-establish the death penalty and to limit its application to the most serious crimes. In 1989, the OAS member states adopted a Protocol to the ACHR that abolished the death penalty generally, although it allows exceptions in time of war.

The jurisprudence in Europe has only addressed the death penalty indirectly. In the *Soering Case* the European Court of Human Rights determined that the length and indeterminate nature involved in executing the death penalty in the United States (in Virginia) constituted inhumane and degrading treatment. At the time the Sixth Protocol to the ECHR had not entered into force for the United Kingdom.

In the Americas, the Inter-American Court has reviewed the death penalty in advisory opinions. In 1978, the Court issued an *Advisory Opinion relating to the Death Penalty in Guatemala,* Advisory Opinion No. OC/3 (1978), whereby it limited the means by which the death penalty could be applied. In 2000, the Court found the application of the death penalty to aliens in violation of Article 37 of the Vienna Convention on Consular Privileges and Immunities — which required notification of an alien's consular officials — *ipso facto* violates the right to due process of a person receiving the death penalty. IACtHR, Advisory Opinion No. OC/16 (2000).

The Inter-American Commission (IACommHR) has dealt with the greatest number of death penalty cases and the greatest number of issues involving the death penalty. These cases have concerned the US and several Caribbean countries. In December 1996, the IACommHR adopted a report finding the US to have violated the right to life because a conviction for which the petitioner had been sentenced to the death penalty appeared to have been unfair based on a note that a jury member had left behind in the deliberation room indicating prejudice. *William Andrews v. United States,* Case No. 11.139, Report No. 57/96, OAS Doc. No. OAE/Ser.L/V/II.95, Doc. 7 rev. at 570 (1997). The US had nevertheless executed the Applicant while the process was pending before the IACommHR and refused to compensate the next of kin even after the decision of the Commission suggested it do so. In 2000, the Commission found that a juvenile could not be executed by the United States, but again while the process was pending before the IACommHR the US executed the victim. *Gary Graham v. United States,* Case No. 11.193, Report No. 51/00 (15 June 2000).

A series of cases before the IACommHR have forced Caribbean govern-ments to commute the death sentences of persons who were on death row for more than five years. This prompted Trinidad and Tobago to with-draw from the ACHR in 1998, although there are still several cases pend-ing before the Court and the government stated that it would re-ratify the ACHR with a reservation. The issue of mandatory death penalties is per-haps the area of law where there is the most agreement. The UN Human Rights Committee has also held mandatory death sentences and sentences passed after unfair trials to be violations of the right to life as is guaran-teed in Article 6 of the ICCPR.

In *Ng v. Canada*, Views adopted by the UN HRC (5 November 1993), the author of the communication was a British subject who was resident of the United States of America. He had been arrested and charged with theft and murder of a security guard in Canada. After becoming aware of his arrest the United States requested his extradition for alleged crimes of kidnapping and murder in California. These crimes carried the death penalty in the United States. Having exhausted his appeals in Canada the applicant applied to the Human Rights Committee claiming that his right to life and to freedom from torture and other inhumane and degrading treatment would be violated if he was extradited. The Committee disgreed stating that "while States must be mindful of their obligations to protect the right to life when exercising their discretion in the application of extradition treaties, the Committee does not find that the terms of Article 6 of the Covenant necessarily require Canada to refuse to extradite or to seek assurances." From the Committee's decision concerning in Article 6 in *Ng* it appears all that is required for a decision to extradite to a state where the individual may get the death penalty is that the decision not be "taken summarily or arbitrarily."

The IACommHR has considered numerous cases in which death penalty, even when not absolutely prohibited, was applied contrary to international law. Some of these cases involved the execution of children. Several cases involving the execution of persons who were children at the time they committed the crime have been brought against the US. The most well known of these is *James Terry Roach and Jay Pinkerton v. United States*, IACommHR, Case No. 9647, Res. 3/87 (22 September 1987), in which the United States was found to have violated the right to life by executing a person who was a minor at the time of the commission of his crime. In deciding this case, however, the Commission was asked to find the prohibition of execution of persons under 18-years of age to be contrary to *jus cogens*, but the Commission declined to so find. In *Dominques v. the United States*, IAmCommHR, Report N° 62/02, Case 12.285 (22 October 2002), the Commission was asked to reconsider this case and especially its finding as concerns *jus cogens*. This time the Commission found that the prohibition of executing minors had solidfied into a rule of *jus cogens*.

10.2.2 Nuclear Weapons

One of the areas that unavoidably implicates the right to life is that of nuclear weapons. The law on this has been somewhat unclear. Although the UN Human Rights Committee has stated that nuclear weapons "should" be illegal, the International Court of Justice has held that despite the overwhelming *opinio juris* to the contrary, nuclear weapons are not illegal. Nevertheless, the ICJ did not decide the matter conclusively. Instead, it held that nuclear weapons would probably always be illegal, but there may be an exception when the life of a nation is threatened. In the Court of fifteen judges, five appended separate declarations to the judgment of the Court, three wrote separate opinions, and six dissented. Furthermore, the Court began by finding that the World Health Organization, which together with the General Assembly had requested the Advisory Opinion, did not have the standing to do so because nuclear weapons did not concern legal issues related to health. In final analysis both those who support and object to the possession and use of nuclear weapons, claimed that the opinion supported their position. Judge Christopher Weeramantry attached a dissenting opinion to the ICJ case in which he argued forcefully over eighty pages for the illegality of nuclear weapons. Unfortunately, the scourge of nuclear weapons does not appear to be likely to disappear in the near future and it may well even be that a human rights body will one day be asked to judge the legality of the use of nuclear weapons.

10.2.3 Genocide

The right to life is necessarily implicated in the prohibition of genocide because genocide consists of serious and widespread threats to life or the widespread taking of life. Genocide as an international crime was first defined in the Convention on the Prevention and Punishment of the Crime of Genocide from 1951. This definition has since been adopted by the ICTFY ICTR and ICC.

The term genocide entered the vocabulary of international law when it was coined by Raphael Lemkin in the wake of Europe's Second World War. He described the hideous act as

> ... a coordinated plan aimed at destruction of the essential foundations of the life of national groups so that these groups wither and die like plants that have suffered a blight. The end may be accomplished by the forced disintegration of political and social institutions, of the culture of the people, of their language, their national feelings and their religion. It may be accomplished by wiping out all bases of personal security,

liberty, health and dignity. When these means fail the machine gun can always be utilized as a last resort. Genocide is directed against a national group as an entity and the attack on individuals is only secondary to the annihilation of the national group to which they belong.

The Genocide Convention preserves this definition in large part in article II. The crucial addition is the requirement of intention to destroy a group. Rarely will a government state that it intends to destroy a national, ethnical, racial or religious group. Although at the start of American invasion of Afghanistan American President George W. Bush did publicly state that the United States goal was to destroy the Taliban, an ethnic and religious group, by killing or capturing every member of the Taliban. Was this an admission of the intention to commit genocide?

Eight persons have been convicted of genocide by the International Criminal Tribunal for Rwanda (ICTR) as of the end of 2003. Convictions have been more elusive before the International Criminal Tribunal for the Former Yugoslavia (ICTFY), although there has been one.

The first ever conviction of a person for the crime of genocide came in 1998 when former Rwanda Prime Minister Jean Kambanda became the first former government leader to be convicted of the crime of genocide. His conviction by the ICTR was based on his own agreement as to his actions. He was subsequently jailed for life.

10.3 The Prohibition of Slavery and Forced Labour

The abolition of slavery was one of the first undertakings of the international community as regards human rights. The 1926 Slavery Convention and its Protocol was an attempt to "prevent and suppress the slave trade" with the goal of bringing about "progressively and as soon as possible, the complete abolition of slavery in all its forms." It included obligations to prevent the transfer of slaves through ratifying states' territory. It did not anticipate the immediate abolition of slavery. Slavery was defined in Article 1 as "the status of condition of a person over whom any or all of the powers attaching to the right of ownership are exercised." In 1930, the International Labour Organization adopted Convention No. 29 that prohibits forced labour for political coercion or education, discipline, punishment for a strike or as a means of racial, social national or religious discrimination. The Universal Declaration of Human Rights in 1948 expressed the shared expectation of the international community in its Article 4 that stated that "[n]o one shall be held in slavery or servitude; slavery and the slave trade shall be prohibited in all their forms." The prohibition is also found in article 8 of the ICCPR, article 6 of the ACHR, article 5 of the ACHPR, article 4 of the ECHR, and article 4 of the CHR of the

CIS. Although the CRC does not mention slavery explicitly, it prohibits all forms of exploitation (art. 36), sexual exploitation (art. 34), abduction and trafficking of children (art. 35), and economic exploitation of children (art. 32).

The Supplementary Convention on the Abolition of Slavery, the Slave Trade and Institutions and Practices Similar to Slavery of 1956 extended the prohibition of slavery to what were then contemporary forms of slavery.

Paragraph 1 of Article 8 of the ICCPR definitively prohibits slavery stating that "[n]o one shall be held in slavery" and that "slavery and the slave-trade in all their forms shall be prohibited." Paragraph 2 states further that "[n]o one shall be held in servitude." Prohibitions of slavery and similar activities are also found in article 6 of CEDAW and articles 34-36 of CRC. The provisions of the ICCPR make exception to compulsory civil or military duty, emergency work that may be required of an individual and reasonable work detail for prisoners.

In the later part of the 20th century the United Nations began to discuss contemporary forms of slavery including exploitation and inequalities between states, child labour, prostitution and other forms of sexual exploitation, child soldiers, debt bondage. The Working Group on Contemporary Forms of Slavery was formed and continues to report annually to the Sub-Commission on the Promotion and Protection of Human Rights.

CHAPTER ELEVEN
The Expression Rights

The expression rights are the human rights by which individuals can express their opinions and peacefully participate in the political life of their country. They are also rights over which states enjoy a more significant degree of discretion in deciding whether and how to impose limitations. The expression rights themselves often contain statements providing for a states' right to invoke some forms of limitations. State action must not, however, render the enjoyment of the right negligible or impossible.

11.1 Note on the General Test Applied to Determine a Violation of Expression Rights

These rights have been grouped together in part because the various human rights bodies have articulated a specific test for determining whether there has been a violation. The test is best stated by the European Court of Human Rights, although it is used by other international human rights bodies as well. The following are the questions that are asked when applying the test:

First, has there been an interference with a human right?
Second, was the interference based on law?
Third, was the interference based on a legitimate aim?
Fourth, was the interference necessary in a democratic society?

Most cases depend upon the answer to the last question. Thus, human rights bodies will often find an interference based on law and they will often find that the government has a legitimate aim, but, nevertheless, that the interference is not necessary in a democratic society.

11.2 Freedom of Thought, Conscience and Religion or Belief

Freedom of thought, conscience and religion or belief is protected in both regional and United Nations instruments. Article 18 of the ICCPR, article 9 of the ECHR, article 12 of the ACHR, article 8 of the ACHPR and article 10 of the CHR of the CIS provide for a broad spectrum of rights that are often described as thought, conscience and religion. For example, pacifism falls under the protection accorded by this right.

The European Court of Human Rights has described this freedom as "one of the most vital elements that go to make up the identity of believers and their conception of life, but...also a precious asset for atheists, agnostics, sceptics and the unconcerned." Religious belief has also been given protection, even against infringement through the exercise of other human rights. In *Otto-Preminger-Institut v. Austria*, Ser. A, No 295 (1994), it was given protection against encroachment by individuals seeking to exercise their freedom of expression by showing a film. The fact that the film offended the religious sentiments of Catholics was enough to provide the Austrian government legitimate reasons for seizing the film. In *Kokkinakis v. Greece*, ECtHR, Ser. A. No. 260-A (1993), the same Court considered a Greek law that made the proselytising of the Jehovah's Witnesses illegal to be a violation of article 9.

11.3 Right to Freedom of Expression and Opinion

The right to freedom of expression and opinion is found in article 19 of the ICCPR, article 13 of the ACHR, article 9 of the ACHPR, article 10 of the ECHR, article 11 of the CHR of the CIS, and article 13 of the CRC. The right is also reiterated in article 19 of the UDHR and article IV of the ADRDM. Article 14 of the ACHR also provides for a right to reply.

A classic case involving a violation of freedom of expression includes government action such as the prohibiting the publishing of dissenting views from those of the Government and the restriction of access to radio and television to opposition sympathizers. *World Organisation Against Torture, Lawyers' Committee for Human Rights, Union Interafricaine des Droits de l'Homme, Les Témoins de Jéhovah v. Zaire*, ACHPR, Comms. 25/89, 47/90, 56/91, 100/93, 9th An.Act.Rep., 18th Ordinary Sess., Praia, Cape Verde (October 1996).

Other cases in which violations of the freedom of expression have been found include prosecutions for criticizing Chancellor of Austria where the defendant is prohibited from raising the defense of the truth of published information, *Lingens v. Austria*, Ser. A, No. 103 (8 July 1986); a legal prohibition on a Parliamentarian writing an article critical of the government in a public magazine, *Castells v. Spain*, Ser. A, No. 236 (23 April 1992); and the publication of information that was already public contrary to a court order, *Sunday Times Case*, Ser. A., No. 30 (26 April 1979) and *Sunday Times v. United Kingdom ("Spycatcher Case")*, Ser. A, No. 217 (26 November 1991).

The cases before the European Court often elaborated the test they are applying to determine whether or not the right to freedom of expression has been violated. As a consequence the European Court has given a quite precise definition to what constitutes a violation of this right.

One of the leading cases dealing with the breadth of the right to freedom of expression is *Handyside v. UK*, ECtHR, Ser. A, No. 24 (7 December 1976), in which the distribution of a schoolbook containing sex education was stopped by the British government. The publishers challenged this action as a violation of article 10, but the case came before the Court only after the books had been confiscated and burned. The Court decided that no breach of article 10 has been established applying a broad doctrine of margin of appreciation. As a result, the *Handyside Case* is often cited as the basis of the doctrine of margin of appreciation. This doctrine is indicated by the Court's finding that the government of the United Kingdom is the appropriate body to determine what might be contrary to the public morals of its citizens.

The types of expression that are protected have usually been interpreted broadly, although the state's discretion to limit expression will also be broader when the value of the expression is not considered socially valuable. Commercial speech, for example, may be limited by states to a greater extent than political speech. It is important to remember, however, that all forms of expression are protected by the human right to freedom of expression. For example, pornographic material may be protected by the right to freedom of expression. For example, in *Müller and others v. Switzerland*, ECtHR, Ser. A, No. 133 (1988), the government confiscated paintings that the government considered to be immoral because they concerned sexual acts of bestiality and was found to have violated Article 10 of the ECHR. The *Otto-Preminger Case* described in the previous section and the *Olmeda Bustos, et al., v. Chile ("The Last Temptation of Christ")*, IAmCtHR, Ser. C, No 73 (5 February 2001), are examples of different views on the relative value of expression that is essentially artistic in nature.

With the exception of prior restraint in article 13 of the ACHR, every human rights treaty allows limitations of the freedom of expression. For example, peaceful protests against militarism may be legitimately limited for concerns of national security and a government enjoys a broad grant of discretion in deciding what constitutes a concern of national security. *Arrowsmith v. United Kingdom*, Comm. Report of 12 October 1978, 19 *D.R.* (20).

Sometimes limitations on this right have been the result of a decision that no exercise of the right is taking place. For example, in *Gleisenopp and Kosiek v. Germany*, Appl. No. 9704/82 (28 August 1986), when two civil servants who were refused employment as civil servants because of their political views, the European Court of Human Rights dealt with the case as one concerning the right to access to public employment. The right to access of employment as a civil servant is not explicitly protected in the ECHR, but it is protected by both article 21(2) of the UDHR, which arguably probably reflects customary international law, and article 25(c) of the ICCPR, a treaty that Germany had ratified.

Engel v. Netherlands, ECtHR, Ser. A, No. 22 (8 June 1976), presented a problem of a different but related nature. In this case, a member of the Dutch military is exercising his freedom of expression to protest against the government's policy of increased militarization. The Court found the restrictions allowed because of the necessity of maintaining order within the military. But in *Piermont v. France*, ECtHR, Ser. A, No. 314 (27 April 1995), the same Court limited the state's discretion over its immigration laws, holding that a deportation motivated by political grounds may violate the freedom of expression.

Governments often argue that the freedom of expression can and must be limited when it interferes with the ability of a country to develop economically and socially. As a result, the weight given to the right to freedom of expression in different cases and at different times has been somewhat inconsistent. On the one hand, for example, the freedom of journalists has been protected, *De Becker v. Belgium*, Ser. B, No. 2 (1960) (lifetime ban on a journalist for publishing in contravention of law was held to be unreasonable and disproportionate); while on the other hand, artistic expression and commercial speech have been less protected. There are also significant differences between the holdings of different human rights bodies.

In *Olmedo Bustos et el. vs. Chile ("The Last Temptation of Christ")*, IAmCtHR, Ser. C, No. 73 (5 February 2001), involving the showing of a film that the government claimed was blasphemous and thus violated the right of religion of others, the Inter-American Court held that Chile had violated Article 13 of the ACHR by prohibiting the showing of the film. However, in the *Otto-Preminger Case* mentioned above that was based on similar facts, the European Court of Human Rights found the Austria government's prohibition of the showing of a film justified for the protection of others' human rights.

The right to freedom of expression is also expressly limited in some treaties by provision prohibiting certain kinds of expression. Article 20 of the ICCPR, for example, specifically prohibits "[a]ny advocacy of national, racial or religious hatred that constitutes incitement to discrimination, hostility or violence, by requiring governments to enact laws prohibiting these activities." This prohibition extends to any advocacy of hatred that constitutes incitement to discrimination, hostility or violence, whether such propaganda or advocacy has aims that are internal or external to the State concerned.

The obligations imposed on the state under this article are two-fold. First, states must prohibit advocacy of hatred by any natural or legal person. And second, the states "themselves must refrain from any such propaganda or advocacy." As with the other obligations in the convention, the obligations under article 20 are obligations of result, which means that the state must not merely enact laws, but must ensure their equal and effective application.

Some human rights treaties also provide specific obligations that the state must fulfill by providing individuals under its jurisdiction information about human rights. For example, the article 25 of the ACHPR clearly provides an obligation of human rights education on states.

The significance of the right to freedom of expression is also indicated by the existence of a United Nations and several regional special rapporteurs on the right to freedom of expression. These rapporteurs visit countries and report on how the right is respected or violated in these countries in regular written reports. The rapporteurs will also engage the governments they visit to discuss how the human right to freedom of expression can be better protected.

Finally, it is worth noting that a more recent phenomena related to the freedom of expression is the indirect government control of the media. For example, during its military campaigns in Afghanistan and Iraq the United States government controlled press reporting to the extent of actually targeting independent journalists. Such actions have the effect of stifling the human right to freedom of expression. In addition, the American media supported the American government's actions with propaganda that obscured the widely perceived illegality of the use of force by the United States government. Again, such actions, which are encouraged by the government, jeopardize the human right to freedom of expression, which includes the right to receive and transmit information.

11.4 Right to Association

The right to freedom of association is found in all the major international human rights instruments of a general nature, for example, article 22 of the ICCPR, article 10 of the ACHPR, article 16 of the ACHR, and article 11 of the ECHR, article 12 of the CHR of the CIS, and article 15 of the CRC. In the ECHR, article 11 contains both the right to freedom of association as well as the freedom of assembly. These two rights are closely connected to each other and to the freedom of expression. In some actions, such as public demonstrations, these three rights may converge to offer protection to certain actions. The right to freedom of association provides individuals the right to join with others to achieve their interests. The interests for which associations may be formed are limited in some circumstances. For example, article 29 of the ACHPR imposes some special responsibilities on individuals. Associations that are contrary to these responsibilities could be prohibited by the state. In addition, individuals may not form associations with the aim of committing acts of violence. Thus, even National Liberation Movements, that might be entitled to use force to achieve their goals under international law, may be banned by a state. Such associations are extra-legal and must find their justification in the struggle against state oppression that can no longer be fought by legal means. In such circumstances, human rights remain applicable, but extraordinary steps may be justified to secure them. Such circumstances are, however, very exceptional.

The right to freedom of association, like the other expression rights, is a right that can be limited in many circumstances for defined reasons that can be found in the articles defining the right. But while the state may limit this right, it may not extinguish it. The Nigerian government's attempt to control the Nigerian Bar Association, for example, was found to violate Nigerian lawyers' right to association. *Civil Liberties Organization in respect of the Nigerian Bar Association*, ACHPR, Comm. 101/93, 8th Ann.Act.Rep., 17th Ord. Sess., Lome, Togo (March 1995).

The right to association is a right that is often prized by members of political groups or trade unions, but it can be exercised by anyone, even members of the military. In *Engel v. Netherlands*, ECtHR, Ser A., No. 22 (8 June 1976) which has already been considered under the human right to freedom of expression above, it was also claimed that Mr. Engel and others had their right to association violated. The European Court did not agree the petitioners "were not punished by reason either of their membership of the VVDM or of their participation in its activities, including preparation and publication of the journal Alarm...[but] that the Supreme Military court punished them... only because it considered that they had made use of their freedom of expression with a view to undermining military discipline."

The freedom of association is a broad right that is relevant to a wide variety of actions carried out by individuals in concert with other individuals. There is, however, no duty on individuals to join associations or for private associations to admit certain individuals into their ranks, although there may be prohibitions against discrimination on certain grounds such as race or ethnicity.

The freedom of association is also protected in several treaties of the International Labour Organization that protect the rights of workers to organize. These treaties were the first human rights treaties to deal with the freedom of association, although they confined themselves to the exercise of this right by trade unions. These treaties and their wide acceptance leads to the inclusion that the freedom of association applies to trade unions even when it is not explicitly stated such as in the ACHPR. The success of the ILO can be largely attributed to its tripartite structure in which delegations include the representatives of employers and workers as well as governments. The protection of the human right to freedom of association through the ILO suggests means by which governments and representatives of other organs of society might cooperate to achieve the better protection of human rights.

11.5 Right to Assembly

Another right of political expression is the right to freedom of assembly. This freedom is essentially the freedom to cooperate with others in peaceful undertakings. It differs from freedom of expression in that it relates to action—public meetings and demonstrations—rather than merely speech. Like the freedom of expression, however, it must be exercised peacefully to be protected. The human right to freedom of assembly is provided for in article 21 of the ICCPR, article 11 of the ACHPR, article 15 of the ACHR, article 11 of the ECHR, article 12 of the CHR of the CIS, article 15 of the CRC.

Like the rights to freedom of association and expression, the right to assemble is an essential part of other expression rights such as the right to demonstrate. People may express themselves by peacefully demonstrating for or against policies that are of concern to them. In *Auli Kivenmaa v. Finland*, UN HRC, Comm. No. 412/1990 (7 March 1990), a group of citizens of Finland showed their opposition to state policies in a peaceful manner. The Human Rights Committee found that Finland had interfered with the right to assemble of these Fins, but the Committee also had to consider if such interference was justified. The Committee found that a requirement to notify the police of an intended demonstration in a public place six hours before its commencement may be compatible with the permitted limitations laid down in Article 21 of the Covenant, but that a gathering of several individuals at the site of the welcoming ceremonies for a foreign head of State on an official visit, publicly announced in advance by the State party authorities, cannot be regarded as a demonstration. Thus, the Finnish authorities attempt to regulate the gathering violated the right to assemble of the individuals involved.

In *Ezelin v. France*, ECtHR, App. No. 11800/85 (26 April 1991), Mr. Ezelin, a lawyer, had been disciplined by the Bar Association for being involved in a demonstration in which he neither supported nor objected to some vandalism that was apparently carried out by some of the demonstrators. Although the vandalism was proven, it was not proven that Mr. Ezelin had any knowledge of it or could have prevented it. In examining the complaint the Court relied on Mr. Ezelin's right to demonstrate to find that the disciplinary measures violated his human rights as protected by the ECHR.

The right to freedom of assembly has also been considered by the regional human rights bodies. The European Court of Human Rights, for example, has developed some jurisprudence concerning this right. This Court has held the a judge's right to be a member of an organization that was considered incompatible with the judicial function by the Italian National Council of the Judiciary is protected by the right to assemble. *N.F. v. Italy*, ECtHR, App. No. 37119/97 (2 August 2001).

The expression rights, including the right to assemble with others in trade unions, are rights which states are often given a broad margin of appreciation in applying. *National Union of Belgian Police v. Belgium*, ECtHR, Ser. A, No. 19 (1975), is an example of the European Court of Human Rights' deference to the appreciation enjoyed by a state in deciding how a right may be exercised. In this case the National Union of Belgian Police complained about the Government's failure to recognize it as a body that it is required to consult on employee matters. The Court held that because the government's action did not directly restrict any police officer's right to join the union, it could not be found to have violated the right to freedom of assembly.

11.6 Freedom of Movement (Refugees, IDPs and Migrant Workers)

The right to freedom of movement is closely related to the expression rights because it is one of the means by which individuals may express their opinions. It is also important to human rights education and the defence of human rights as the ability of individuals to travel and to interact with each other is perhaps the best means to encourage better understanding of human rights. The freedom of movement may be both an exercise of one's own human rights as well as an activity that promotes others' human rights.

Everyone within the territory of a state enjoys the freedom of movement. This right is protected in article 13 of the UDHR, article 12 of the ICCPR, article 2 of the Fourth Protocol to the ECHR, article 22 of the ACHR, article 12 of the ACHPR and article 22 of the CHR of the CIS.

Many treaties protect more than the mere freedom of movement. For example, the collective expulsion of aliens is expressly prohibited by article 4 of the Fourth Protocol to the ECHR, article 25, paragraph 4, of the CHR of the CIS. The mass expulsion of aliens is expressly prohibited in article 12, paragraph 5 of the ACHPR. Article 13 of the ICCPR and article 5(f) of the ECHR also protect aliens against arbitrary expulsion. Article 13 of the ICCPR applies to any alien that is lawfully within a country. Whenever there is a dispute about the illegality of an alien's stay, the UN HRC has stated that "any decision on this point leading to his expulsion or deportation ought to be taken in accordance with article 13." A state must provide an alien "a decision in his [or her] own case and hence, article 13 would not be satisfied with laws or decisions providing for collective or mass expulsions." All these treaties prohibit discrimination between different categories of aliens.

Despite the entrenched right to freedom of movement, however, states continue to enjoy very broad discretion over immigration.

In *Piermont v. France*, ECtHR , Ser. A, No. 314 (27 April 1995), the French government was given broad discretion in deciding upon limitations that may be imposed upon the right to freedom of movement. Consequently, an expulsion order was considered to have removed the applicant's lawful right to freedom of movement.

Some regional organizations, agreements or traditions guarantee the movement of the nationals within a defined region consisting of a number of states. For example, within the Middle East many Arab countries have traditionally allowed the free movement of other Arab citizens across their borders. This informal practice based more in Islamic tradition then law has come under attack in recent years as wealthier Arab countries attempt to protect their riches. Nevertheless, some countries such as Saudi Arabia continue to allow a large number of foreign workers into their country for discretionary periods of time. In Africa and the Americas, several trade zones have been established where the free movement of people takes place. African countries currently host more refugees and internally displaced persons than any other region in the world. Should the states hosting these people who are fleeing from persecution or other calamities be compensated by the richer developed countries? This argument is often made, but also often rejected by the more wealthy developed countries that do not wish to share their wealth and instead opt to prevent refugees from reaching their borders.

11.6.1 Asylum and Refugees

The right to asylum has been guaranteed in several instruments of modern international human rights law. The most widely cited evidence of this right is article 14 of the Universal Declaration of Human Rights, but the right is also found in article 12(3) of the ACHPR and article 22(7) of the ACHR. It is notably absent from the ICCPR and the ICESCR as well as the ECHR. In each case, the right is subject to the laws of the state in which the refugee finds him or herself. In the ACHPR the right is to "seek and obtain" asylum, while the right is stated as "to seek and be granted" asylum. There is probably little difference in this wording particularly in light of the fact that both African and South American countries have accepted wide definitions of asylum. The right to asylum or the protection of refugees is also provided for, or at least referred to, in a host of other treaties. Most notable among these treaties is the 1951 Convention Relating to the Status of Refugees that was adopted under the auspices of the United Nations. While this treaty does not contain a right to asylum, it does contain a clause on non-refoulement, which amount to the same thing because it prohibits a state from returning a refugee to a state in which he or she fears persecution. Other treaties dealing specifically with asylum are the Convention on the Specific Aspects of Refugee Problems in Africa, which includes in its definition of a refugee those fleeing from persecution as well as from "occupation, foreign domination or events seriously disturbing public order;" the Caracas Convention on Territorial Asylum, and the Caracas Convention on Diplomatic Asylum. There are also provisions of other treaties that protect some refugee rights, such as article 22 of the CRC whereby states undertake to give refugee children special protection, but not to accord them refugee status in the first place. And finally, there have been many resolutions and declarations calling upon states to protect refugees' rights. Among the most prominent are the Cartagena Declaration on Refugees and the UN Declaration on Territorial Asylum.

The first refugee treaties and protection mechanisms were adopted under the auspices of the League of Nations. After the Second World War, in 1946, the International Refugee Organization was formed, but by 1949 this organization was converted into a programme of the United Nations that became known as the Office of the High Commissioner for Refugees. Today this office has the main international responsibility for protecting refugees, although it increasingly violates the trust of refugees in favour of states' interests. A striking example has been documented in a petition to the African Commission on Human and Peoples' Rights in which the UNHCR colluded with the government of Sudan to withdraw refugee status from already recognized Ethiopian refugees living in Sudan and to force them back to Ethiopia. Although UNHCR admitted that some of its actions were improper, it refused to correct them.

Both the Statute of the High Commissioner for Refugees and the 1951 Convention Relating to the Status of Refugees define a refugee as person outside his or her country of nationality or habitual residence and unable or unwilling to return to, or to seek the protection of, this country due to a well-founded fear of persecution "for reasons of race, religion, nationality or political opinion."

The expulsion of large groups of people has several times been the subject of communications to the African Commission on Human and Peoples' Rights as the following communication indicates. In *Organization Mondiale Contra la Torture, Ass. Int'l des Jurists Democrates, Commission Internationale des Jurists (C.I.J.), and Union Interafricaine des Droits de l'Homme v. Rwanda*, ACommHPR, Comms. 27/89, 46/91, 49/91 and 99/93, 10th Ann. Act. Rep., 20th Ord. Sess., (October 1996), Rwanda threatened to expel large groups of Burundi nationals who had been refugees in Rwanda for many years. Although the Rwandan government attempted to justify its action as required by national security concerns, the Commission found that the expulsions were due to the nationality of the individuals involved and thus violated the prohibition of mass deportations found in article 12(3) of the ACHPR.

The ACHR and the ACHPR both guarantee the right to asylum. Both treaties, however, condition the right of asylum on provisions of national law. For example, the ACHPR states that "[e]very individual shall have the right, when persecuted, to seek and obtain asylum in other countries in accordance with the laws of those countries and international conventions." One of the international conventions referred to is undoubtedly the Convention Relating to the Status of Refugees, which the overwhelming majority of countries in the world have ratified. While this convention does not explicitly require that states grant individuals asylum article 32 prohibits a state from expelling a person who has a well founded fear of persecution for reasons of "race, religion, nationality, membership of a particular social group or political opinion" in the country to which he or she might be sent. In the African context the Convention Governing the Specific Aspects of Refugee Problems in Africa broadens the grounds for asylum by extending them to persons who "owing to external aggression, occupation, foreign domination or events seriously disturbing public order in either part or the whole of his country of origin or nationality, is compelled to leave his place of habitual residence in order to seek refugee in another place outside his country of origin or nationality."

Asylum law is one of the main areas for domestic human or civil rights lawyers in developed countries. Unfortunately, in developing countries, where the overwhelming majority of refugees are found, asylum seekers are usually not legally represented. Sometimes UNHCR – the United Nations body mandated to protect refugees has even refused to allow refugees to be legally represented or to protect them itself. The UNHCR has often interpreted its mandate as promoting the interests of wealthy states to prevent migrants from reaching their countries instead of to protect the interests of refugees by defending their right to flee persecution, war, or famine against states that seek to deny refuge. The problem UNHCR faces as an intergovernmental programme under the auspices of the United Nations is that the wealthy states pay for its work, while it is usually the interests of individuals from poorer states that require protection.

11.6.2 IDPs (Internally Displaced Persons)

Internally displaced person (IDP) is a term used to describe an individual who has been forced to relocate within his or her own country due to war, violence, natural disaster, government action or government toleration of action contrary to her or his human rights. In the legal literature, one will find many different definitions of IDPs. Even within the United Nations, there are varying definitions. What is clear is that the designation of an individual or group of individuals as IDPs is not a derogatory designation, nor does it automatically point the finger at any government or group of people as the violators of human rights. In fact, it is a designation of vulnerability, and thus recognition of the necessity of assisting these people.

There is no specific international convention protecting IDPs as there is for children, women and refugees. Instead, general international human rights law applies to IDPs because these persons are under the jurisdiction of their governments.

Some of the most important human rights are the right to life, which is violated by the displacement of people into situations without the basic necessities of life; the right to choose one's place of residence, which is violated by the forcing of people to flee their homes; cruel, inhuman, and degrading treatment, which is violated by the forcing of people to flee their homes to areas where they lack the necessities of human living conditions; and the right to property, which is violated when a person's property is damaged or destroyed without adequate compensation. In numerous social economic rights of internally displaced persons are often threatened by the conditions into which families are thrust by the action attributable to a government such as actions depriving persons of a minimum standard of living, adequate health care, educational opportunities and adequate housing.

In addition to these legally binding articles of international law, there are a set of 'Guiding Principles' that have been proffered by Dr. Francis Deng, who was the UN Secretary-General's Special Representative on IDPs. These Principles have been adopted by the United Nations in 1998. The 'Guiding Principles' echo existing international human rights law with special reference to IDPs, but they are not themselves binding legal obligations. The guiding principles have received broad support from governments.

11.6.3 Migrant Workers

The rights of workers have always been a concern of international human rights law and these rights are protected in numerous international treaties and other non-binding instruments. As globalization enabled and often-required workers to cross national borders the rights of migrant workers have gained increasing international attention.

In 2003 the Convention on the Protection of All Migrant Workers and Members of Their Families (MWC) entered into force. Generally, a migrant worker is defined as any "person who is to be engaged, is engaged or has been engaged in a remunerated activity in a State of which he or she is not a national." Treaty is meant to apply to persons who are not otherwise protected such as refugees and stateless persons for which there are separate treaties. Thus, the treaty excludes refugees, stateless person, students, investors, offshore oil rig workers, diplomats and other foreign government or international organization employees. While the rights protected by the treaty are not significantly different from rights already protected in more general human rights treaties, there are some significant additions and some differences in how the rights are expressed. For example, protection against the acts of private actors has been made clearer so that article 16 paragraph 2 reads: "[m]igrant workers and members of their families shall be entitled to effective protection by the State against violence, physical injury, threats and intimidation, whether by public officials or by private individuals, groups or institutions." Another example is the right to consular assistance that has been made explicit in article 16, paragraph 7 in the case of arrest and in article 23 more broadly. Other rights have been added for example the right of a convicted criminal that "[h]umanitarian considerations related to the status of a migrant worker, in particular with respect to his or her right of residence or work, should be taken into account in imposing a sentence for a criminal offence committed by a migrant worker or a member of his or her family." In addition, the right of all migrant workers to be able to transfer their earnings and personal effects back to their own country. As indicated in the title of the treaty the rights of the families of migrant workers are protected as well with a labyrinth of rights in articles 36 through 63. Finally, articles 64 through 71 provide for a number of provisions that, for example, restrict one state's ability to recruit another state's nationals for employment abroad and require states to take into account the consequences of a workers migration for the communities concerned.

Despite its focus on migrants as a group, it is important to realize that the treaty protects individual rights. According to article 77, therefore, only individuals or their authorized representatives can bring complaints, thus not groups. Furthermore, the rights in the MWC only apply to the conditions of migrant workers in a country and thus the Convention "shall be interpreted as implying the regularization of the situation of migrant workers or members of their families who are non-documented or in an irregular situation or any right to such regularization of their situation." This means that as long as a foreigner is working in a country that has ratified the Convention he or she has the rights specified in the Convention, but this person may still be deported or removed if he or she has not entered the country legally.

For several years prior to the entry into force of this treaty, there already existed a United Nations Special Rapporteur on Migrant Workers Rights and a Working Group. The work of these bodies will eventually be done by the Committee for the Protection of the Rights of All Migrant Workers and Members of Their Families that will be entitled to receive and express views upon states initial and periodic reports and inter-state and individual communications.

On 17 September 2003, the Inter-American Court of Human Rights issued an *Advisory Opinion on the Legal Status and Rights of Undocumented Migrants* in which it held that undocumented migrants had human rights that all states were required to respect. Among the rights found to exist was the right of equal treatment or the principle of non-discrimination found, among other places in articles 2(1) of the ICCPR, article 3 of the ACHR, and article

17 of the ADRDM. This right, according to the Court, had achieved the status of a norm *jus cogens*, which all states were legally bound to respect, and was a right *erga omnes*, in which all states had an interest in ensuring. This Advisory Opinion is a significant step forward for the rights of migrants and puts the Inter-American Court at the forefront of developments of this law.

CHAPTER TWELVE
Property, Minorities, Democracy, Privacy, Children

12.1 Right to Property

The right to property is one of the more controversial human rights both in terms of its very existence and its interpretation. The controversy about the existence of a right to property was already apparent during the drafting of the two Covenants in the 1950s and 1960s when proposals to include an article protecting the right to property were rejected and did not even reach a vote. The objections emanated largely from socialist and communist countries in which the right to private property was contrary to their basic principle of communal property. The intricacies of interpreting the right are best displayed by the jurisprudence of the European Court of Human Rights where this right has been extensively, but perhaps not consistently, interpreted.

Although the right to property does not appear in either of the two covenants from 1966, it does appear in Article 17 of the UDHR; article 14 of the ACHPR; article 21 of the ACHR; article 22 of the CHR of the CIS and article 1 of Protocol I of the ECHR, the latter being where the jurisprudence has been most developed.

The European human rights bodies have held that the right to property is not absolute and that it allows for limitations of a wider nature than other human rights. Although there are many cases in which the right to property is found to be protected, there are also many in which no violation has been found. This reflects in part the more flexible nature of this right and the significant margin of appreciation states may enjoy in limiting the exercise of this right. The margin of appreciation was most prominently expressed by the European Court of human rights in *Handyside v. United Kingdom*, ECtHR, Ser. A, No. 24 (7 December 1976). Although other human rights bodies have adopted similar approaches some (such as the UN Human Rights Committee) have expressly rejected the broad approach of the European Court.

In *Holy Monasteries v. Greece*, ECommHR, App. Nos. 13092/87 & 13984/88 (9 December 1994), several monasteries in Greece complained that a Greek law that effectively transferred monastic land to the state was an arbitrary deprivation of property in breach of the right to property under Article 1 of Protocol No. 1 of the ECHR. The Commission held, unanimously, that the Greek laws concerning the management and administration of the property of the monasteries did not violate the applicants' right to property, explaining in detail how the broad breadth of the state's discretion in deciding what is in the public interest. A similar challenge was made to the appropriateness of compensation in *Lithgow and Others v. United Kingdom*, ECtHR, Ser. A, No. 102 (8 July 1986), but this also failed because the government was held to have discretion in determining what compensation its nationals are entitled to receive. In this case the applicants' property had been nationalized to build an airport. They were given basic compensation that was established by law, but did not reflect what they believed to be the current market value of their property. The applicants claimed a violation of Article 1 of Protocol No. 1 of the ECHR. While finding that inadequate compensation might sometimes constitute a violation of the right to property, the Court held that in this case the government did not overstep its discretion in deciding what constituted appropriate compensation.

The European human rights bodies have found there to be limits on a state's discretion. In the case of *Sporrong and Lonnroth v. Sweden*, ECtHR, Ser. A, No. 52 (23 September 1982), for example, the Commission found a violation of the right to property where a Swedish law kept property under the threat of expropriation for an extended period of time.

12.2 Minority Rights

Although minorities have often been of major concern to the international community, this concern has not always translated into instruments protecting minority rights. Among the major human rights instruments, only article 27 of the ICCPR contains a provision explicitly protecting minorities. Nevertheless, in many ways the protection of minorities has been a greater priority of the international community than the actual development of international human rights law in general. The connection between minorities and human rights precedes the numerous modern human rights treaties of the last fifty years and goes back at least to the First World War. After the First World War, provisions were included in the Treaty of Versailles in 1919 that vested the League of Nations with a responsibility for ensuring the protection of minorities. Auxiliary to the Treaty of Versailles was a series of bilateral and multilateral treaties providing protections for particular minorities and sometimes even providing specific mechanisms to adjudicate upon claims concerning the rights of minorities. These treaties had the goal of "eliminating a dangerous source of aggression, recrimination and dispute" and were designed to "prevent racial and religious hatreds from having free play." They were the policy instruments by which the League of Nations could secure for certain elements incorporated in a State, the population of which differs from them in race, language or religion, the possibility of living peacefully alongside that population and cooperating amicably with it, while at the same time preserving the characteristics which distinguish them from the majority.

This diverse and abundant corpus of treaty law became known simply as the "minority treaties." In light of the minority treaties concluded between the 1919 and 1940, one can conclude that the legal protections of the rights of minorities actually preceded the legal protections of every individual's basic rights in the international human rights treaties that came after the Second World War.

This privileged position did not survive the end of the Second World War. With the creation of the United Nations, the legal protection of every individual's human rights became a goal and ultimately a reality. Although attempts to incorporate human rights provisions into both the United Nations Charter and Universal Declaration of Human Rights failed, a Sub-Commission on the Prevention of Discrimination and the Protection of Minorities was formed and long line of human rights provisions and practices began. Although renamed the Sub-Commission for the Protection and Promotion of Human Rights it has continued to play a leading role in developing the contemporary regime of international law protecting minorities.

Since 1949, the Sub-Commission has considered the plight of minorities, placing on its agenda that year the item entitled "Definition and classification of minorities." It was also the Sub-Commission which proposed and initially drafted article 27 of the ICCPR. Since 1949, the Sub-Commission has also submitted a long line of draft resolutions to the Commission on Human Rights and initiated several reports on minorities. In 1977, Francesco Capotorti, as Special Rapporteur on minority rights submitted a report on the definition of minorities defining them as a "group numerically inferior to the rest of the population of a State, in a non-dominate position" and possessing ethnic, religious and linguistic characteristics that differ from the rest of the population. He also found that they should show a "sense of soli-darity, directed towards preserving their culture, traditions, religion or lan-guage." And he interpreted article 27 of the ICCPR as requiring a member of a minority to be a national of the State in which he or she is claiming minor-ity rights. In 1978, the Republic of Yugoslavia submitted a draft declaration on the rights of minorities. In consequence of the Yugoslavian proposal, Mr. Jules Dechênes, a member of the Sub-Commission, was requested to pre-pare a report on a draft declaration and an open-ended working group was formed under the auspices of the Commission on Human Rights. In 1985, Mr. Jules Dechênes submitted his report. The most controversial part of this report was the definition of a minority. Adopting the definition of Mr. Capotorti, the report further elaborated on the collective motivation neces-sary to identify a minority by adding the requirement of, "if only implicitly ... a collective will to survive and whose aim is to achieve equality with the majority in fact and in law." In 1987, Claire Palley presented a report on "possible ways and means to facilitate the peaceful and constructive resolu-tion of situations involving racial, national, religious and linguistic minori-ties." In 1989, Asbjørn Eide was appointed the Sub-Commission's Special Rapporteur on national experience in the protection of minorities. Mr. Eide became the chairman-rapporteur of the Working Group on Minorities that was formed in 1994. This Work Group meets annually and evaluates the protection of minorities in different states. In addition, in 1995 it proposed a study evaluating the provisions relating to the protection of minorities in national constitutions.

The work of the Sub-Commission has centred on the definition of a mi-nority and the evaluation of state practice concerning minorities. Steps to create legally binding instruments for the protection of minorities have not been successful because some states remained tied to the tradition of requir-ing assimilation of minorities and other states fail to see this as a priority. Nevertheless, the work of the Sub-Commission has kept the issue of mi-norities on the United Nations' agenda and is likely to ultimately lead to the adoption of a binding instrument as governments become more aware of the importance of minorities in contemporary society.

According to article 27 of the ICCPR ethnic, religious and linguistic minori-ties have the right to enjoy their own culture, to profess and practice their religion and to use their own language. The provision thus provides extra protection above, but they are limited in two aspects. First only minorities whose common characteristic is ethnicity, religion and language qualify for protection under article 27. Political, economic or social minorities are not protected as such, but of course, the non-discrimination provisions apply to them as well. Second, the protections are accorded only to specific rights, namely, to enjoy their own culture, to profess and practice their religion and to use their own language. In the few individual communications and the general comment where the Human Rights Committee has article 27, several points have emerged.

The Committee has made it clear that article 27 does not provide for a right to self-determination in the sense that minorities have a right to sucede from the state in which they are situated. In fact, the Committee has made it clear that even as concerns the right to self-determination in article 1 of the International Covenant of Civil and Political Rights, minorities, if they qualify as peoples, are not usually entitled to sucede from the state in which they find themselves. The right to sucede, according to the Committee, only becomes part of the right to self-determination when it is the only means for a people to exercise a reasonable degree of autonomy to which they are entitled under this right. This will usually be the case only when there are gross violations of the human rights of a minority and when the minority possesses the qualities of statehood, including the ability to ensure human rights. The Committee has also found that the right to "enjoy their own culture" includes the right to work in professions or trades that are related to that culture. In other words, culture includes economic and social dimensions, including the right to work. For this to be the case, however, one must show that the right to work in a specific profession or trade is intimately connected to the culture.

As concerns the right to use their own language, the Committee has held that this does not mean the right to use one's own language in all circumstances. For example, a nation's courts may prescribe a single common language as official. In such cases, the procedural guarantees included under a right to a fair trial will require that the government provide appropriate translators in criminal cases.

Finally, the Committee has interpreted article 27 to apply to minorities whether or not they are nationals of the state in which they are found. In paragraph 5.1 of its General Comment 23, the Committee states that the "terms used in article 27 indicate that the persons designed to be protected are those who belong to a group and who share in a common culture, a religion and/or a language ... [t]hose terms also indicate that the individuals designed to be protected need not be citizens of the State party." This emphasises the fact that the Covenant requires states to ensure human rights to all individuals within a state's jurisdiction, except when rights are expressly reserved for citizens. Thus, the Committee concludes unambiguously that a "State party may not, therefore, restrict the rights under article 27 to its citizens alone," which derogates from the traditional belief that minorities had to be nationals of a state. This reading makes more sense in light of the object and purpose of the ICCPR, which is to provide the best protection possible. Nevertheless, several United Nations reports and some European instruments have restricted minority rights to individuals who are both members of a minority and nationals of the state concerned. This interpretation places too much emphasis on the state of protection and too little emphasis on the rights of the individual. While only article 27 provides a clear statement of minority rights and is therefore the central international human rights legal provision on this topic, other instruments do have a direct bearing on minority rights. The Convention on the Prevention and Punishment of the Crime of Genocide from 1948, prohibits the killing or undertaking of measures with the intention to destroy, in whole or in part, members of a national, ethnic, racial or religious group. The Convention on the Elimination of All Forms of Racial Discrimination from 1965, the Convention on the Rights of the Child from 1989 and the UNESCO Convention against Discrimination in Education from 1960 all provide for protections of rights that are of particular importance to minorities.

Perhaps the most substantive step towards ensuring the rights of minorities, although still at a political level, is the creation of the office of the High Commissioner on National Minorities with the Organization for Security and Co-operation in Europe. The OSCE Minorities Commissioner has a broad mandate and undertakes a broad array of tasks on his own initiative. In Europe, there is the European Framework Convention for the Protection of National Minorities and the European Charter for Regional Minorities. The Framework Convention provides numerous minority rights; it allows states to determine which groups are minorities. France has determined that there are no minorities in the country and Germany that there are only two. This Convention is unlikely to add much to the protection of minorities in Europe because of the problems involving the definition of a minority. The Language Charter elaborates already existing rights to use one's own language that are found in article 27 of the International Covenant of Civil and Political Rights and in many provisions scattered among different human rights treaties that protect the freedom of expression.

The treaty provisions mentioned above are also evidence of customary international law that can be identified by the many references to minority rights in international declarations. These declarations include the Concluding Documents of the Conference on Security and Co-operation in Europe (CSCE, later to become the OSCE) from the Vienna meeting in 1989, the Copenhagen meeting in 1990 and the Geneva Meeting of Experts in 1991; the Charter of Paris (the so called 'Stability Pact') signed by the CSCE in Paris in 1990; and perhaps most importantly, the Declaration on the Rights of Persons Belonging to National or Ethnic, Religious and Linguistic Minorities adopted by the UN General Assembly in 1992.

All of these instruments indicate that there are at least three principles that have reached the level of customary international law. The first is that minorities have a right to exist. The second is that minorities have a right to profess, practice or otherwise enjoy at least a minimum level of cultural rights. And the third is that minorities have a right to participate in decision-making processes relevant to them. These minimum rights are balanced between the general rules of international human rights law emanating from treaties and customary law and the legitimate requirements of public order that are claimed by states. Thus while governments cannot provide minorities with less rights than every other person in that country, the government may only have to provide minorities with additional or special protections when this does not threaten the public order of the state. The rules of customary international law concerning the protection of minorities are still in flux; nevertheless, some basic principles can be discerned. This foundation is reflected by the three rules to which reference has just been made. While this foundation can be developed, attempting to establish a too elaborate a regime of protection maybe neither practical or valuable if it only leads to unfulfilled promises.

Finally, it must also be remembered that human rights also require human responsibilities. Thus for examples there may be cases where minorities persecute members of an ethnic, religious or racial majority. In these types of cases the members of majorities are entitled to the protection of their human rights even if it limits the action of minorities and the persecution of the majority will constitute a violation of international human rights law.

The protection of minorities continues to be a complex question under international human rights law. Increasingly, it is related to conflict, sometimes even armed conflict. In countries like Sudan, protecting the rights of the minorities from the South of the country has spawned the world's longest and most deadly civil war starting even before Sudan became an independent state. The importance attributed to minority questions during, and immediately after, the creation of the League of Nations has not been repeated in the context of the United Nations, although there is increasing reason to believe greater emphasis on minority rights is necessary to ensure international as well as national peace and security.

12.3 The Right to Participate in Government

The right to participate in one's government can be found in article 25 of the ICCPR, article 23 of the ACHR, article 13 of the ACHPR, and article 29 of the CHR of the CIS. Article 3 of Protocol No. 1 to the ECHR requires states to hold "free elections at reasonable intervals by secret ballot." The articles in the ACHPR, ACHR and CIS treaties protect a broad right to participate that includes access to public service and property, while the First Protocol to the ECHR only instructs states to hold elections.

The right to participate in one's government is often the framework for the realization of human rights for large groups of people or populations because it can create an environment in which individuals can express value preferences about the policies of their state. There is a commonly held belief that democratically chosen governments will generally make policies that have a better chance of providing for individuals' human rights than other forms of government, however, it is also true that all democracies also have human rights problems and regularly violate human rights. The problem is not one of achieving perfection, but of finding the best possible means of mediating between the rights and interests of all citizens in a society. Providing all citizens the right to participate in their own government is the first step in making the decision making process broader and fairer.

The European Union (EU) has expressed its faith in participatory government by requiring all states seeking recognition by the EU to agree to "respect for the provisions of the Charter of the United Nations and the commitments subscribed to in the Final Act of Helsinki and in the Charter of Paris, especially with regard to the rule of law, democracy and human rights." Although a state may superficially satisfy the EU criteria, their failure to do so in substance may well have consequences even when the state has been recognised. The current Draft European Union Treaty defines democratic participation generally as the right of all citizens to vote and stand for office, but does not exclude other forms of participation.

The goal of participatory government is recognised as a human right in international instruments starting with the Universal Declaration of Human Rights. Again, the emphasis is on the right of every individual in society to take part in their government. The concept of participation differs in the Draft European Union Treaty and the UDHR. Is it appropriate to focus one's right to participate in the government of their country or should (do) we have this right more broadly as concerns international governance? Read article 21 of the UDHR found in the back of the Coursebook. How might this article be extended to global governance?

This aspirational statement has been reiterated in a legally binding human rights treaty in almost identical terms. This repetition and the fact that it was not controversial in the drafting of either instrument indicate that there is an overwhelming international consensus concerning the right to democratic participation. The most widely accepted legal definition of this consensus is found in article 25 of the ICCPR.

The right to participate in government has been the subject of UN General Assembly resolutions as well as the work of the OSCE's Office for Democratic Institutions and Human Rights. It is also a priority concern of the Office of the UN High Commissioner for Human Rights because of the belief that democracy and participation in government will led to the greater protection of human rights. As stated above, however, the evidence of this is mixed. On 29 December 2003, the Inter-American Commission of Human Rights decided *Statehood Solidarity Committee v. US* (Case 11.204, Rep. No. 98/103) in which it held that individuals were denied the right to participate in their government under article XX of the ADRDM by laws that denied the residents of the District of Colombia representation in the United States Congress.

The right to participate in government or the right to democracy does not presume a certain form of government. Instead it allows a nation to decide on how its people will govern themselves. For example, in the case of *Marie-Hélène Gillot et al. v. France*, UN HRC, Comm. No 932/2000, UN Doc. CCPR/C/75/D/932/2000 (26 July 2002) the UN Human Rights Committee decided that the people of New Caledonia could decide upon a certain form of government even if everyone in the country did not agree and even if some people living in the country were excluded from participation,

Specific governments have also made claims in their basic laws and in regional agreements. For example, the Tunisian Constitution stipulates in Article 3 that sovereignty belongs to the people, in article 18 that the people exercise their sovereignty through their representatives, in article 39 that the president of the country shall be elected, and in articles 19 and 39 that suffrage shall be universal, free, direct and secret. Other Islamic countries have expressed their support for the "right to participate, directly or indirectly in the administration of [one's] country's public affairs." The concept of the *ijma* (consensus) of the *umma* (the people) was rooted in foundation of the Islamic state from the time of the Prophet Mohammed in the 7th century. Today the modern Islamic state often includes the concept of consensus rule by the people and regular consultation of the people.

Often statements calling for democracy have emanated from the people of a state or states. A noteworthy example is the statement of the non-governmental Regional Council on Human Rights that states in Article IV:

> 1. It is the duty of government to respect and promote the right of the people freely to participate directly at all levels of social, political and economic decision making, to ensure that the people are provided with the information needed to make informed decisions, and to encourage the formation, and respect the autonomy, of authentic popular or grassroots organizations or movements at local, regional and national levels, rather than creating or supporting its own organizations. Government may not directly or indirectly, compel the people to join any organization.

The consensual definition of democracy, as can be seen from the few examples expressed above, is not one that prejudges the means and form in which it is expressed. All that is required is that individuals are able to participate as decision makers in their own government. Thus, when governments and politicians claim that a certain form of democracy is necessary, they are not dealing with the consensually accepted definition of democracy or the human right to democratic participation, they are usually trying to achieve their own political ends.

There are many ways that a state may allow its nationals to participate in government. One way may be to allow a broad range of referendums on policy questions relating to the well-being and security of the state. Other states may reserve these questions for elite decision makers only allowing the population the ability to vote for these decision makers or to object to their decisions after the fact. The crucial point is not the form that democracy takes but its participatory aspects. The element of participation is missing in a state that holds periodic free elections, but less than half the population turns out to vote. It is missing in a state that prevents any form of peaceful dissent to government policy. In addition, it is also missing in a state that holds elections, but offers voters only one candidate or several candidates with only one policy line. Democracy means participation and diversity and its crucial active ingredient is choice. When participation, diversity, and consequently choice are lacking, then democracy is also lacking.

Democracy is a substantial asset in a country committed to protecting human rights because it allows the people of that country to decide whether the government is doing a good job. When a democratic government is not doing a good job, it may be changed. An undemocratic government that is insulated from the popular voice of its people can violate human rights without fear of condemnation from its people and can thus continue to govern even when its people do not want it to govern. Democratic participation or democracy in the form that it has been agreed upon by the majority of governments around the world in international human rights instruments is a major factor in ensuring respect of all human rights.

12.4 Right to Privacy and Family Life

Although two separate rights, the right to privacy and family life are considered together because of their close relationship in practice. Of the two rights, the human right to private life is somewhat controversial. While it is protected in article 17 of the ICCPR, article 8 of the ECHR, article 11 of the ACHR, article 9 of the CHR of the CIS, and article 16 of the CRC, it is not protected in the ACHPR. It is restated, however, in both article 12 of the UDHR and article V of the ADRDM.

The right to privacy and family life has been most comprehensively dealt with by the European Court of Human Rights. Privacy for example has been interpreted by this body as extending to such diverse activities as wiretaps and consensual sex. In *Malone v. UK*, Ser. B, No. 67 (1983-85), secret wiretaps were considered to violate the petitioners' right to privacy and in *Dudgeon v. UK*, Ser. A, No. 52 (1981), consensual sex between consenting adult homosexuals was considered to be protected by the right to privacy. In *Silver v. United Kingdom*, 5 *EHRR* 347 (1983) when prison authorities opened the letters of prisoners, the government argued that their censorship was necessary to protect public order and ensure order within the prison. The European Court, however, found that this violated the human rights of the prisoners. In *Klass and Others v. Germany*, Ser. A, No. 28, 2 *EHRR* 214 (1978), the European Court of Human Rights held that although telephone conversations were covered as private communications, there was no violation where the state could show it had an important interest. In *Klass*, the state argued security concerns involving alleged terrorists were at stake.

And in *Golder* an interference with communications between a detainee and his lawyer was found to constitute a violation of the right to privacy. *Golder v. United Kingdom*, EurCtHR, Ser. A, No. 18 (21 February 1975) and *Puzinas v. Lithuania*, ECHR, 13 *HRCD* 247 (2002). Not only is an individual's right to communicate with his or her lawyer an important human right and part of the right to privacy, but so too is a lawyer's right to keep confidential communications with clients. *Niemietz v. Germany*, Judgment of the European Court of Human Rights (6 December 1992).

The right to privacy also applies to consensual sexual relations. The notable cases have come from the European Court of Human Rights starting with *Dudgeon v. United Kingdom*, ECtHR, Ser. A, No. 45, 4 EHRR 149 (1981), in which the Court held that tolerance and broad-mindedness were hallmarks of democratic society in Europe and thus found homosexual activities between adult men in private to be protected by the right to privacy. *Also see Toonen v. Australia*, UN HRC, Comm. No. 488/1992, UN Doc. CCPR/C/50/D/488 (1992).

If the right to privacy applies to consenting sex between two adults, , does this mean that it also includes the right to have one's own physical gender preferences and changes recognized by law? According to the European Court of Human Rights it does "[s]ince there are no significant factors of public interest to weigh against the interest of this individual applicant in obtaining legal recognition of her gender re-assignment." *Goodwin v. UK*, ECtHR, Appl. No. 28957/95 (11 July 2002).

Do you think a human rights body examining a case from Libya would reach the same conclusion? Why or why not? Can the conclusion of the court in Goodwin be reconciled with more conservative ideology?

* * *

The right to family is protected in article 18 of the ACHPR, article 11 of the ACHR, article 8 of the ECHR, article 9 of the CHR of the CIS and article 16 of the CRC. It is also protected in article 12 of the UDHR and article V of ADRDM. Often these are the same articles as protect the right to privacy. The concept of family life is broader than merely husband and wife and parent and child. It includes the right to live with another siblings or grandparents and grandchildren. Individuals in a consensual relationship may also have a right to family life, although the petitioner will have the burden of proving that a relationship qualifying as family life exists. This right is also protected both in substance and in procedure. In other words, one cannot be denied their right to family life by an unduly long procedure for determining whether or not this right exists. Nevertheless, this is exactly what the government purported to do in *H. v. UK*, ECtHR, Appl. No. 00009580/81 (8 July 1987). The European Court of Human Rights however found the United Kingdom government to have violated article 8 by its action holding that "an effective respect for the applicant's family life required that that question be determined solely in the light of all relevant considerations and not by the mere effluxion of time."

Sometimes the right to family rights is indirectly raised as a subsidiary claim to a procedural right. In *Airey v. Ireland*, ECtHR, Ser. A, No. 32 (9 October 1979), the complainant argued that denying her legal aid for divorce proceedings prevented her from getting a divorce and consequently from properly registering a child she had with a new partner. The European Court agreed finding that the link between the denial of legal aid and the harm suffered was sufficient. In *Kroon and others v. Netherlands*, ECtHR, Ser. A, No. 297-A (27 October 1994), a similar question arose whereby a man and a women who had lived together out of wedlock had four children, but Dutch law refused to allow the children to be registered to them both if they did not marry. The European Court held that ""respect" for "family life" requires that biological and social reality prevail over a legal presumption which, as in the present case, flies in the face of both established fact and the wishes of those concerned without actually benefiting anyone. Accordingly, the Court concludes that, even having regard to the margin of appreciation left to the State, Netherlands has failed to secure to the applicants the "respect" for their family life to which they are entitled under the Convention. There has accordingly been a violation of Article 8 [of the ECHR]."

The right to privacy is sometimes a controversial right because it may pit individual rights against communal rights. How should this balance be draw? Is a government deserving of a greater margin of appreciation when it is acting to protect the rights of others to know information of relevance to the functioning for society? What information is relevant to the functioning of society?

12.5 Special Protections for Children

Some individuals in society need special protection. The reasons for these special protections may be the inherent or assumed vulnerability of the person in the group (children), past discrimination (women), or the traditional value of the group to society (families). Children are among those who have received the greatest attention in recent years. Some human rights treaties provide for special protections for children and the CRC is entirely devoted to protection of children's rights. The following articles are examples of those in general human rights treaties that provide children with special protection: article 24 of the ICCPR, article 19 of the ACHR, article 18(3) of the ACHPR, and articles 16(3) and 17 of the CHR of the CIS. There are also European and African treaties particularly protecting children's rights.

Children have been provided special protection under international law because of their status as minors. The pre-eminent text providing these protections is the Convention on the Child. The CRC is the most ratified human rights treaty in the world. Its fifty-four articles provide protection for more than forty non-derogable rights. The treaty also creates a Committee on the Rights of the Child, which supervises its implementation. Although this Committee does not entertain individual complaints, it does periodically review states reports and has the unusual (and expressed) power of being able to "encourage international cooperation" by transmitting its comments and requests for assistance to international organizations. The CRC is not the only instrument that provided special protections to children. Article 24 of the ICCPR provides for the special protection for a child because of his or her "status as a minor." The UN Human Rights Committee has stated that "[c]onsequently, the implementation of this provision entails the adoption of special measures to protect children, in addition to the measures that States are required to take under article 2 to ensure that everyone enjoys the rights provided for in the Covenant." In specifying what these special measures might be, the Committee has stated that:

> [i]n most cases...the measures to be adopted are not specified in the Covenant and it is for each State to determine them in the light of the protection needs of children in its territory and within its jurisdiction. The Committee notes in this regard that such measures, although intended primarily to ensure children fully enjoy the other rights enunciated in the Covenant, may also be economic, social and cultural. For example, every possible economic and social measure should be taken to reduce infant mortality and to eradicate malnutrition among children and to prevent them from being subjected to acts of violence and cruel and inhumane treatment or from being exploited by means of forced labour or prostitution, or by their use in the illicit trafficking of narcotic drugs, or by any other means.

Article 24 of the ICCPR also provides children with an expressed right to acquire a nationality. This right is often a vital step in securing protections of a child's most basic rights. As was discussed in Chapter One (Section 1.1) states have been and continue to be the starting point for the protection of an individual's human rights. As children hold within their youth our common future, the protection of children has been of special concern to governments in recent years. The question of the protection of children and children's rights have, therefore, been dealt with both in treaties and in the opinions of international human rights bodies. Most frequently, it has been the Committee on the Rights of the Child that has elaborated children's rights in its general comments and its comments on state's reports. Sometimes, however, other international human rights bodies have contributed their opinions.

In 2002, the Inter-American Court of Human Rights was asked to give an advisory opinion on the obligations states had concerning children. The request came from the Inter-American Commission because some states appeared to be allowing themselves too much discretion and were treating children like adults for some purposes. The Court's Advisory Opinion is one of the most comprehensive legal considerations of children's rights and the responsibilities of states towards children and families. It holds that children's rights expressed in the Convention on the Rights of the Child have become customary international law and in most cases *jus cogens*. *Legal Status and Human Rights of the Child*, IAmCtHR, Advisory Opinion OC-17/2002 (28 August 2002).

The economic and social rights of children are protected in paragraph 3 of article 10 of the ICESCR. In addition, in the regional contexts of Africa and Europe, states have promulgated further instruments protecting children. The African Charter on the Rights and Welfare of the Child essentially reiterates the rights in the CRC but with particular attention to African values of family, community and nation. This treaty also creates a Committee of Experts with the important authority to receive individual complaints (art., 44) and to initiate investigations. In contrast, European Convention on the Exercise of Children's Rights from 1996 aims primarily to better ensure the implementation of many of the rights in the CRC by providing for the representation of children in domestic proceedings. Both the African and the European treaties protecting children provide for the protection of all persons under 18 year-of-age and do not allow states the freedom to raise this age as the CRC does.

The protection of children also requires that families and women be protected. Article 10 of the ICESCR, for example, provides for special protections for families, mothers and children. It echoes protections especially provided for in the Convention on the Rights of the Child and the Convention on the Elimination of All Forms of Discrimination against Women. Three paragraphs in article 10 of the ICESCR provide protections for family, mothers and children. It should be noted that different levels of protection are suggested in each. Paragraph 1 concerning the protection to be accorded families is very general and leaves much discretion in the hands of the state. The right to protection of family life is also provided for in article 23 of the ICCPR and by the provisions on privacy in the ECHR. The ICCPR and ECHR provide more specific protections. The right to special protection of mothers in the ICCPR is a right they have "during a reasonable period before and after childbirth." Achieving the protection and equality of women may require special action in some cases. Affirmative action may be one alternative form of action which is foreseen in some international treaties protecting women. A more extensive list of women's rights are protected in the Convention on the Political Rights of Women, the Inter-American Convention on the Granting of Political Rights to Women, and the Convention on the Elimination of All Forms of Discrimination against Women (CEDAW). Despite the lengthy list of protections in CEDAW, women continue to suffer discrimination. Even within the United Nations, there is a great disparity between the number of men and women in senior positions; something the United Nations has been trying to address for years with little success.

The United Nations, it is important to note, is bound to respect human rights by article 55 of the Charter of the United Nations. There is also article 8 in the Charter that states that the "United Nations shall place no restrictions on the eligibility of men and women to participate in any capacity and under conditions of equality in its principal and subsidiary organs." If women are so under-represented in the United Nations, is this article being adequately applied? Is affirmative action needed within the United Nations to ensure women are as equally represented as men? Since the Beijing Conference on Women was held under the auspices of the United Nations in 1995, this world organization has often been seen as the lead international organization for securing women's rights. The United Nations has bodies such as the Commission on the Status of Women, which like the Commission on Human Rights was created by ECOSOC in its early years to further the human rights of women, and offices such as the Office for the Advancement of Women within the United Nations and the Office of the Under-Secretary General for Women. The advancements the United Nations have made, however, have been woefully insufficient. If the United Nations cannot set a good example for the international community can its member states be expected to act to eliminate discrimination against women?

Also protected in several international instruments are families. Most notably the African Charter of Human and Peoples' Rights protects the family as "the natural unit and basis of society" and "the custodian of morals and traditional values recognized by the community." These paragraphs also call upon states to "take care" of the family's "physical and moral health" and to "assist" the family. In articles 27 and 29, individuals' duties towards the family are stated. The importance of the family is recognized universally in article 16(3) of the UDHR. Articles 24 and 25 of the ICCPR reiterate this concern while additionally providing for the right of men and women of marriageable age to form a family and for special protections of children within families. The protection of the families of migrant workers is also recognized by the International Convention on the Protection of the Rights of All Migrant Workers and Members of Their Families.

CHAPTER THIRTEEN
Groups, Development, Peace, Environment, and Individual Responsibility

13.1 Self-Determination

The first human right protected in the two covenants from 1966 is the right to self-determination. This right is stated in identical terms in Article 1 of both covenants and has occupied a prominent place in the realm of general international law since the early days of the United Nations. It is also recognized in article 20 of the ACHPR, where its importance cannot be overemphasized considering how African states struggled to free themselves from colonization in the 20th Century.

This right is also mentioned in the Charter of the United Nations, although Judge Higgins has pointed out that

> In 1946 the focus was on the rights and obligations of sovereign member states. It was not yet fashionable to think about the rights of those not yet independent. There were, certainly, recognized duties that colonial powers had towards the peoples they governed. But at that time that did not clearly include any duty to grant independence. The common assumption that the UN Charter underwrites self-determination in the current sense of the term is in fact a retrospective rewriting of history. Rosalyn Higgins, *Problems and Process: International Law and How We Use It* 111 (1994).

Be this as it may, the Charter refers to the right and this reference has reappeared in contemporary expressions and interpretations with regularity. It is also true that the Charter does little to define this right. Perhaps the most elaborated expression of this is in the context of colonial territories and the statement concerning these territories that is contained in Article 73 of the Charter. This article indirectly defines self-determination in vague terms as "self-government" taking "due account of the political aspirations of the peoples" and assisting "them in the progressive development of their free political institutions, according to the particular circumstances of each territory and its peoples and their varying stages of development." Article 76 of the Charter further links the right of self-determination to "independence as may be appropriate to the circumstances of each territory and its peoples and the freely expressed wishes of the peoples concerned." Other references to self-determination appear in article 55 where it is a qualifier for economic and social development and in article 1, paragraph 2 where it is expressed as a purpose of the United Nations. These provisions were only the beginning of the development of the right.

During the debates on the UDHR and the Covenant, the right became an important moral and political issue. It was particularly of interest to the increasing number of peoples who finally saw the chance to rise out from under the oppression of colonialism and to participate as sovereign states in world society. The expression of self-determination in the context of colonialism was expressed in United Nations General Assembly (UNGA) Resolution 1514—the Declaration on Granting Independence to Colonial Countries and Peoples—as well as UNGA Resolution 1541(XV) adopted a few days later. These resolutions recognised the right of self-determination as a right of peoples who are subject to colonial rule to decide on their own form of government. A slightly more general recognition can be found in UNGA Resolution 2625, the Declaration on Principles of International Law concerning Friendly Relations and Co-operation among States in accordance with the Charter of the United Nations. In UNGA Resolution 3301 on the Basic Principles of the Legal Status of Combatants Struggling against Colonial and Alien Domination and Racists Regimes (UN Doc. A/9120 (1973)) the United Nations General Assembly recognizes the struggle for self-determination as legitimate and fully in accordance with international law. The right has also been reiterated in the resolutions of the Commission on Human Rights.

In 1966, the two Covenants stated the right to self-determination in broad terms in identical articles 1. Article 1 of the ICCPR has been interpreted in a General Comment of UN the Human Rights Committee. The General Comment distinguishes the right from the rights of minorities, but does not provide a precise definition of the right to self-determination. The Committee has been willing to deal with a communication under the Optional Protocol when the alleged victim is properly authorized to represent a people whose right to self-determination is being denied. However, in the *Lubicon Lake Band v. Canada*, UN HRC, Comm. No. 78/1980 (29 July 1984), it became clear that this is not the case. In this case, neither the right to represent the people nor was the status of the Lubicon Lake Band as a peoples, questioned. The main question was whether Article 1 could be the subject of an individual communication under the Optional Protocol. The Committee decided that "the Covenant recognizes and protects in most resolute terms a people's right to self-determination and its right to dispose of its natural resources, as an essential condition for effective guarantees and observance of individual human rights and for the promotion and strengthening of those rights. However, the Committee observed that the author, as an individual, could not claim under the Optional Protocol to be a victim of a violation of the right of self-determination enshrined in Article 1 of the Covenant, which deals with rights conferred upon peoples, as such."

It is important to recognize the distinction between the right of self-determination in article 1 and the rights of members of a minority in article 27 of the Covenant. The Committee has gone to great lengths to separate these two rights. The important procedural point is that while minority rights are individual rights that can be the subject of a communication under the Optional Protocol, the right to self-determination is a collective right and cannot be the subject of a communication.

13.2 The Right to Development

The right to development is discussed separately from other human rights because it is a comprehensive human right whose understanding requires an understanding of the complex political debate that has been waged around its existence, definition and implementation. At the onset, however, it can be stated that there is no doubt that the human right to development exists. Despite reservations to the contrary, it is clear that there is a consensus in the international community that the right to development is a legal right. This consensus, as we will seem, has been reiterated repeatedly.

There has been much scepticism about the right to development. At a 1987 conference on human rights and development in Netherlands, K.K. Prach of Sudan expressed the concern that human rights and development can hardly be considered when even the essentials of coexistence between human groups cannot be settled. Others have admitted its existence only as a derivative right. For example, F.V. Garcia-Amador in his book *Law of International Development. A New Dimension of International Economic Law* from 1990 argues that the new law of development as a human right is a derivative of the right to development and the duty to cooperate for development, both of which are state rights or obligations. The human right to development is not state-centric, but depends on the participation of individuals within the state. An expression of this definition is the statement by Ved P. Nanda at the 1990 Global Consultation on the Right to Development where he defined the right as that "of every individual and of all peoples to participate in, contribute to, and enjoy economic, social, cultural and political development." From these conceptual statements about the right to development it can be seen that while the right may have been born in the wake of the new economic order, which was an attempt by under-developed or developing countries to gain a greater degree of empowerment in international society, it has matured into a right of each and every individual not only to have their country develop, but also to participate in and share in the benefits of that development.

The legal history of this maturity can be traced through various legal instruments, resolutions and declarations. A starting point may be articles 55 and 56 of the Charter of the United Nations. In Chapter IX, which is entitled International Economic and Social Co-operation, Article 55 prescribes that with a view to the creation of conditions of stability and well-being that are necessary for peaceful and friendly relations among nations and based on the principle of equal rights and self-determination of peoples, the United Nations shall promote higher standards of living, full employment, and conditions of economic and social progress and development, solutions to international economic, social and health problems, and human rights. In the next article states pledge themselves to take joint and separate action in co-operation with the United Nations Organization for the achievement of the purposes set forth in article 55. These two articles express the right to development in somewhat state-centric sense while nevertheless setting the basis for realizing it as an individual right by connecting it to human rights.

In the years following the creation of the United Nations, however, it was the State-centric view that prevailed. United Nations General Assembly Resolution 1161(XII) from 1957 expressed the view that balanced economic development would contribute to human rights. In the 1968 Teheran World Conference on Human Rights, in its Resolution XVII, the Conference accepted a more balanced concept of development in expressing the belief that economic and social rights were linked to civil and political rights and called for international cooperation. The resolution noted that "the vast majority of mankind continues to live in poverty, suffer from squalor, disease, and illiteracy and thus leads a subhuman existence, constituting in itself a denial of human dignity" and that there was an "ever-widening gap between the standards of living in the economically developed and developing countries" and that the "universal enjoyment of human rights and fundamental freedoms would remain a pious hope unless the international community succeeds in narrowing this gap."

The history of the right to development is long and complicated. At its initial stages the right to development emanated from the rights that states claimed. Particularly developing countries were seeking a more equitable distribution of the world's wealth from the developed countries that had exploited developing countries under colonial regimes. This 'right to development', however, was not the same as the human right to development. The human right to development is the right of an individual to participate in his or her country's development. It is like all human rights a right against one's own state and not directly against other states. It is a right over which there is much controversy, but also a right that has had a long and sustained historical development.

An arbitrary starting point from which to observe this development might be the 1969 United Nations Declaration on Social Progress and Development that was adopted by the General Assembly. Article 1 of this declaration stated that every individual has the right to benefit and contribute to social progress. Article 2 further stated that "social progress and development shall be founded on respect for the dignity and value of the human person and shall ensure the promotion of human rights and social justice." The declaration defines social progress and development as continuous rise in material and spiritual standards of living of all with respect for and in compliance with human rights, especially the right to work, food, a minimum standard of living, health, education, and social services. Between 1970 and 1973, there were several declarations that reiterated a broad right of individuals to share in prosperity. Among the most well known are those entered into by the non-aligned countries at Lusaka (1970) and Algiers (1973). These declarations led to ECOSOC Resolution 1746 (LIV) of 16 May 1973 which was the first of a long line of United Nations resolutions specifically calling for active participation by the entire population in a country's development.

At the same time, the governments of developing countries were pushing their bid for a greater share of the world's wealth through the Declaration on the Establishment of a New International Economic Order and the Charter of Economic Rights and Duties of States, both adopted by the UN General Assembly in 1974. These instruments were based on the ideas of equity, common interest and interdependence as basis for the right of countries to development. At the end of 1974 an important step was taken in assisting developing countries in securing the means for development when the Universal Declaration on the Eradication of Hunger and Malnutrition was adopted by World Food Conference on 16 November 1974 and endorsed by United Nations General Assembly on 17 December 1974 in Resolution 3348 (XXIX). In the preamble to this declaration, developing countries accept primary responsibility for development. These instruments were the setting in which the two covenants entered into force two years later.

The two covenants contain several rights that form the basis of the human right to development. These rights cumulatively evidence an agreement about the right of every individual to participate in his or her country's development. When the International Development Strategy for the Third United Nations Development Decade was adopted in 1980, it declared the ultimate aim of development to be the well-being of the entire population and the fair distribution of benefits. Other human rights instruments also began to include provisions on development. Often the references, however, have been indirect or seem to describe development as a social condition. For example, Article 3 of the Convention on the Elimination of All Forms of Discrimination Against Women requires states to take all appropriate steps to ensure development of women.

It was only in 1986 with the adoption of the Declaration on the Right to Development by the United Nations General Assembly that a large international consensus of the international community declared development unequivocally to be a human right. This instrument recognizes both the human right to development and the right of states to development. It has also been repeatedly confirmed by the overwhelming majority of states in the international community.

Since 1986, the Global Consultation on the Right to Development that took place in Geneva in 1990 concentrated on the principle of popular participation and Article 10 of 1993 Vienna Declaration of the World Human Rights Conference that the international community "reaffirms the right to development ... as a universal and inalienable right and an integral part of fundamental human rights." The subsequent 1995 Copenhagen Declaration on Social Development, the 1995 Beijing Declaration on Women's Rights and the 1996 Istanbul Declaration on the Human Settlements, all contain similar reaffirmations of the right to development.

At the turn of the century the United Nations adopted the Millennium Development Goals. These goals call on all countries of the world to contribute to achieving eight social and economic objectives by 2015. Although described as development goals they are all goals that are required to be achieved by international human rights such as the right to life, health care, and education.

13.3 Right to Peace

One of the most controversial human rights is the right to peace. Nevertheless, the representatives of almost every country in the world have repeatedly stressed that the right to peace is a concrete and meaningful goal of the international community. They have expressed themselves in oral and written statements, international instruments and the writings of individuals in the international community. In doing so they have expressed their belief that peace is necessary for the survival and development of the human race. While this right is found in the ACHPR in article 23, it is perhaps most importantly expressed in the Charter of the United Nations.

The Charter exclaims that the United Nations is created to "save succeeding generations from the scourge of war" and "for these ends to unite our strength to maintain international peace and security." The preamble from which the passages are taken is full of statements encouraging the achievement of common interests. This message is again emphasized in Chapter I, Article 1, paragraph 1 that states that it is a purpose of the organization to "maintain international peace and security" by taking "effective collective measures" and by bringing about the adjustment of international disputes by peaceful means. Article 55 adds to this responsibility minimum conditions for the "peaceful and friendly relations among states" that include the realization of fundamental human rights. And by article 56 states "pledge themselves to take joint and separate action in co-operation" with the United Nations to achieve respect for the values expressed in article 55. In these articles, the Charter of the United Nations expresses the collective expectations of world society to a peaceful environment. The consensus of states expressed in the Charter has been reiterated and elaborated in successive United Nations resolutions.

The practice by which this has happened in the framework of the United Nations is evidenced by a succession of resolutions and declarations. The Declaration on the Preparation of Societies for Life in Peace, adopted by the General Assembly in Resolution 33/73 of 15 December 1978 reaffirms in principle 1 of part I, that "[e]very nation and every human being, regardless of race, conscience, language or sex, has the inherent right to life in peace." Furthermore, "[r]espect for that right, as well as for other human rights, is in the common interest of all mankind and an indispensable condition of advancement of all nations, large and small in all fields." The Declaration on the Right of Peoples to Peace, approved by the General Assembly in Resolution 39/11 on 12 November 1984 proclaims, "that life without war serves as the primary international prerequisite for the material well-being, development and progress of countries, and for the full implementation of the rights and fundamental freedoms proclaimed by the United Nations." With these words, the human right to peace is elevated to the status of a right *prima intra patris* as far as its attainment is "the primary international prerequisite" for the full implementation of other human rights. Often women have been at the forefront of consideration of the human right to peace.

In 1980, state representatives adopted a number of conclusions and recommendations agreeing that "human rights, peace and development are interrelated and that the fostering of one promotes the enhancement of the others." The *Report of the Seminar on the Relations that Exist between Human Rights, Peace and Development* further concluded that "[t]he maintenance of international peace and security for all peoples and individuals is vital for social and economic progress and for the full realization of human rights and vice a versa" and that "the advancement of development is related to the promotion of peace."

The General Assembly has attempted to provide some clarification in instruments such as the Declaration on Principles of International Law concerning Friendly Relations and Cooperation among States in accordance with the Charter of the United Nations, which was adopted by the General Assembly in Resolution 2625(XXV) on 24 October 1970. The third preambular paragraph of this resolution stresses "the importance of maintaining and strengthening international peace founded upon freedom, equality, justice and respect for human rights." Thus, this declaration explicitly states that peace is the aggregate of freedom, equality, justice and respect for human rights. In 1984, the General Assembly adopted the Declaration on the Right of Peoples to Peace. This declaration expressly refers to the right to peace as a right of people's.

Whatever the difficulties with the right to peace as a human right of individuals or people, it is clear that it is an aspiration of a majority of the individuals alive today. This alone may be a good enough reason for governments to respect it.

Of particular relevance in the information age of globalization and rapidly developing technology is the United Nations Declaration on the Use of Scientific and Technological Progress in the Interests of Peace and for the Benefit of Mankind, General Assembly Resolution 3384(XXX) (10 November 1975). It should be remembered, however, that this declaration was adopted in 1975. Since then the world has undergone immense changes in the field of technology development.

13.4 Right to an Adequate Environment

One of the most important contemporary issues is the environment. If the current generation does not preserve their environment, the quality of life for future generations may be destroyed or severely degraded. This is a problem that affects both developed and developing countries. Developed countries often suffer from the exhaustion of their natural resources because of the high rate at which they have industrialized. Developing countries, while often preserving their resources somewhat better, often suffer from damage that is done to the environment through inappropriate means of resource exploitation and through natural or man-made disasters. Africa alone is the site of numerous wars that have destroyed many countries' natural and human resources.

The right to an adequate environment is explicitly recognized in article 24 of the ACHPR, article 11 of the San Salvador Protocol to the ACHR, and article 24(2)(c) of the CRC. It is also in the Constitution of more than fifty countries.

Even where it is not directly justiciable, international human rights tribunals have been willing to hear arguments concerning the environment.

In this way, in both the European context as well as the Inter-American context the right to an adequate environment has been recognized as a human right. In the case of *Lopez Ostra v. Spain*, Appl. No. 16798/90, 20 *European Human Rights Reports* 277 (Judgment of 4 December 1994), the European Court of Human Rights held that an individual who suffered damages from pollution emitted by a government subsidized waste treatment plant located on municipal property, had a right to compensation for interference with the human right to family life (art. 8, ECHR). However, the Court rejected a claim that the right to humane treatment was also violated. The Inter-American Commission of Human Rights has turned to the right to life to reach similar conclusions. In the *Yanomami People v. Brazil*, Case No. 7615, Reports of the Inter-American Court of Human Rights 24, OEA/ser.L/V/II.66, doc. 10 rev.1 (1985) the Inter-American Commission reached the conclusion that the ecological destruction of the Yanomami lands violated the right to life in the ACHR (art. 4).

Although Zarsky has suggested that the link between human rights and the environment is a "chaotic and contested terrain," it has also been viewed by international human rights bodies as an unambiguous human right. The African Commission has been most prominent in making this clear. In *Social and Economic Rights Action Center and the Center for Economic and Social Rights v. Nigeria*, ACHPR, Comm. 155/96, 31st Ord. Sess. (13-27 October 2001), it found that the right to development of peoples had been violated.

The right to an adequate environment has been the subject of numerous universal and regional initiatives. The following bodies have all dealt with environmental issues in the very recent past: internationally: the International Labour Organization, the Human Rights Commission, the Human Rights Committee, the United Nations Environmental Programme, the Commission on Sustainable Development, the High Commissioner for Human Rights, the Law of the Sea Tribunal, the World Conservation Union, the World Bank (especially its Inspection Panel), and various United Nations Working Groups and Rapporteurs; regionally, the Rhine Commission, the International Joint Commission, the Inter-American Commission on Human Rights, the Inter-American Court of Human Rights, the African Commission on Human Rights, the Organization for Security and Cooperation in Europe, the Inter-American Development Bank Inspection Panel, the Asian Development Bank Inspection Panel and the North American Commission on Environmental Cooperation. Each of these bodies has confirmed that there is a human right to a clean and/or healthy environment, even if their understanding of this right has not always been similar.

The human right to an environment has also stood in close relation to other rights especially those related to the protection of indigenous peoples. Although the United Nations has maintained a Working Group on

Indigenous Peoples for many years and although a Draft Declaration on the Rights of Indigenous Peoples is being negotiated, special protections for indigenous people have not been developed beyond these areas of discussion. One of the primary exceptions has been in the area of environmental rights. In this area international bodies as diverse as the World Bank's Inspection Panel and the African Commission on Human and Peoples' Rights have found that indigenous people have rights to a protected and healthy environment.

The *Chad/Cameroon Oil and Pipeline Project* involved a complicated lending arrangement whereby the World Bank would provide Chad, Cameroon, Exxon-Mobil, Chevron and Petronas financing to exploit oil in southern Chad. The arrangements were found to be in violation of the World Bank's Operational Policies concerning the protection of the environment by the Inspection Panel's, whose does not extend to considering human rights *per se*. Had the Inspection Panel been able to consider the human rights obligations of Chad and Cameroon, as the African Commission is entitled to do, it is likely, that violations of the right to environment of the indigenous populations would have been found. In this case only the government, but also private oil companies were involved in the violations that took place. In fact, the Shell Oil Company was one of the major investors in both situations. Do such non-state actors have responsibilities for international human rights law? [In 2006, the World Bank finally suspended lending, but for Chad's failure to meet the condition of the loan.]

The human right to a healthy or adequate environment is also intricately related to the right to development because sustainable development is unlikely without preserving a healthy environment. Is it possible to protect the environment when the global community promotes its exploitation for the sake of economic growth? An often cited reply is that there is no hard evidence that the environment is being destroyed. Although that is not always true—for example, we know of the dangers of air pollution and damage to the ozone layer—even if the evidence is only circumstantial is that not enough of a reason to require governments to act responsibly? The international community expressed its belief that we should act to prevent harm in the Rio Declaration in what has come to be known as the precautionary principle. This principle states in relevant part that "[w]here there are threats of serious or irreversible damage, lack of full scientific certainty shall not be used as a reason for postponing cost-effective measures to prevent environmental degradation."

13.5 Group Rights

Human rights were generally rights of individuals, nevertheless, some human rights may accrue to groups of individuals. While this subject usually gets slight attention in human rights textbooks, it is often the subject of international human rights law that is of primary concern to countries who do not share western liberal understandings about society that are concentrated on the individual. The societies that generally, view the community, the state or some other collectivity as more important than the individual are numerous. In fact, they are much more numerous than societies that have adopted the liberal western concentration on the individual as the centre of human rights. They include China, India, Iran, and most of Southeast Asia, Africa and some South American countries. One of the first expressions of the recognition of group rights is the Algiers Declaration of 1978 that clearly recognized the existence of human rights belonging to groups. But since then there have been many such statements and some treaties that recognize group human rights.

Groups' rights, like individual rights, provide groups protections primarily from the state. They concentrate attention on the belief that a crucial problem confronting modern society is the optimalization of the individual as part of society.

Identifying group rights requires first identifying a relevant group. Among groups that have been identified by the international community at large or by regional organizations are minorities, indigenous peoples, women, children, refugees, stateless people, people with disabilities, and, more recently, people in particularly deprived socio-economic conditions.

13.5.1 Claiming Groups' International Human Rights

Sometimes groups may claim a multitude of rights that are also enjoyed by individuals. Until recently some writers questioned the ability of groups to claim human rights before international tribunals. However, in 2002 the African Commission of Human and Peoples' Rights decided unambiguously that the human rights in the ACHPR could be claimed by groups, in this case the *Social and Economic Rights Action Center and the Center for Economic and Social Rights v. Nigeria*, ACHPR, Comm. 155/96, 30th Ord. Sess., Banjul, Gambia (October 2001). The Commission dealt with many rights especially social and economic rights in the group context. This case is perhaps the leading case on groups' rights and unequivocally established their legitimacy. It may also be a case that is unique to the African context because of the rights provided for in the African Charter on Human and Peoples' Rights. Although the *Nigerian Case* provides strong support for group rights, the debate over these rights will undoubtedly continue to be waged.

13.6 Individual Criminal Responsibility and International Humanitarian Law

Of increasing importance is the link between international human rights law and international humanitarian law. The major treaties on international humanitarian law include the four Geneva Conventions — particularly the fourth protecting civilians in wartime and their two protocols—one applying to international armed conflicts and the other to non-international armed conflicts. Both human rights and international humanitarian law have to deal with similar acts of violence by state actors against individuals. Furthermore, the two spheres of law have often overlapped. For example, the African Commission on Human and Peoples' Rights has held that human rights continue to apply without derogation and in full force during armed conflicts. The Inter-American Commission on Human Rights has also decided that international humanitarian law should play a very prominent role in interpreting how international human rights law applies. In a case involving an attempted coup in Argentina, the Inter-American Commission held that it should use international humanitarian law to determine how human rights like the right to life should be interpreted. *Juan Carlos Abella v. Argentina*, Case No. 11,137, Annual Report 1997, OAS Doc. OAE/Ser.L/ V/II.98, Doc. 7 rev. (13 April 1998).

There can be little doubt that there exists a close relationship between international human rights law (IHRL) and international humanitarian law (IHL). The main sources of international humanitarian law, like those of international human rights law, are customary international law and treaties. There is also a similarity in the purposes of IHL and IHRL. These common goals include that of installing some humanity in an often-inhumane world. From the 1864 Geneva Convention concerning IHL that was brought about with Henri Dunant's encouragement, to more modern instruments limiting the use of landmines, much of IHL has been directed at protecting the individual human being. The protections of individuals range from the basic protections of medical personnel and wounded in the 1864 Geneva Convention to the more elaborate provisions of the 1949 Geneva Conventions and their Protocols which secure individuals respect for their persons, honour, family rights, religious convictions, manners, customs and property; prohibit discrimination; prohibit violence against civilians; prohibit reprisals against civilians; prohibit collective penalties; and prohibit hostage taking. All of these rights have their parallels in universal and regional human rights treaties. For example, the rights to privacy and private life; the rights to religious and cultural freedom; the right to property; the prohibition of discrimination; and the prohibition of torture, cruel, inhuman and degrading treatment are all part of IHRL. Although none of the instruments state the right in exactly the same language, the protections they offer are very similar in their general nature as well as in their specific protection.

Despite the similarities, there are also differences. IHL usually will be applied in the context of armed conflicts, while IHRL usually will have most relevance in times of peace. This is confirmed by practice and stark realities. The first instruments of IHL were written and ratified while war was still a legitimate tool of international affairs between states. It was not until the Kellogg-Briand Pact in 1928 that war was even theoretically condemned as illegal. Nevertheless, even today, states continue to use war as a means of foreign policy and in violation of international law. Thus, IHL was created in the hope of adapting the situation to the more humane tendencies of human beings. It is this aspect of IHL that the International Court of Justice referred to in its Advisory Opinion on the *Legality of the Threat or Use of Nuclear Weapons*, 1996 I.C.J. *Reports* 225 at 240, para. 25. and to which the Inter-American Commission of Human Rights was referring in its finding in *Abella v. Argentina* when each body found that it should have recourse to IHL in order to consider killings taking place in a situation of armed conflict. In other words, each of these bodies was intelligently using all the sources at its disposal to determine the meaning of the applicable law. It is wrong to conclude that they were applying every source to which they referred. While the ICJ could indeed apply all the sources of international law falling under article 38(1) of its statute, the Inter-American Commission could only apply the instruments of the Organization of American States or to which the states before it were parties. This was made clear when the Court considered the preliminary objections of the government of Columbia in the *Las Palmeras Case*, Judgment on Preliminary Objections of February 4, 2000, IACtHR, Ser. C, No. 67 (2000), holding that "[t]he fact that States members of the Organization of American States must observe the Geneva Conventions in good faith and adapt their domestic legislation to comply with those instruments does not give the Commission competence to infer State responsibility based on them."

Just as IHL law applies in times of war, IHRL usually applies in time of peace. IHRL, however, may be derogated from during an armed conflict, unlike IHL which is non-derogable. The right of derogation is provided for in specific articles of some human rights conventions. These articles require that a state wishing to derogate from its human rights obligations provide notice in writing of its derogation, including the reason, the provisions being suspended, and the date when the suspension would be terminated. While this right exists, it has been rarely used. Thus, despite there having been well over a hundred wars since 1945, many between states who are parties to IHRL treaties, there have only been a handful of examples of derogations. In addition, some claims that a national emergency exists, like that of the *Greek Colonels' Case* concerning the military junta that took power by a *coup d'etat* in Greece in 1967, have been rejected as invalid. Additionally, there are some important exceptions to instruments that allow the right of derogation. One of the most prominent is the African Charter of Human and Peoples' Rights. In the case of *Commission Nationale des Droits de l'Homme et des Libertés v. Chad*, Communication 74/92, AHG/Res. 250 (XXXII) (10 July 1996), decided just two days after the ICJ decision in the *Nuclear Weapons Case*, ICJ Reports No. 95 (1996), its was held that all the rights in the ACHPR are non-derogable. Thus, avoiding the application of human rights by derogations is impossible for the fifty-three states that have ratified this treaty. Another instrument prohibiting derogation from any of the human rights therein is the Convention on the Rights of the Child, which is ratified by 191 states—more than any other convention of either IHL or IHRL. The CRC contains thirty-nine articles providing for the human rights of children. A substantial number of international human rights provisions therefore deny states the right to derogate from them.

A second exception is the many non-derogable rights. Among these is the right to life in the ICCPR. The ICJ recognized the non-derogable nature of this right in the *Nuclear Weapons Case* stating that "[i]n principle, the right not to be deprived of one's life applies also in hostilities." Other non-derogable rights include the prohibition of torture, freedom from slavery, freedom of religion and conscience, the right to equality before the law, the right not to be convicted of a crime that was made a crime *ex post facto*, the right not to be imprisoned for a contractual breach, the rights of the family, the right to a name, the right to a nationality, the right to participate in government and the rights of children.

Even where IHL applies there is often a Martens clause that expressly preserves the application of other laws, including IHRL. This clause first appeared in the 1907 Hague Convention, but has since reappeared in most IHL treaties thereafter. In Protocol I from 1977 the clause reads:

In cases not covered by this Protocol or by other international agreements, civilians and combatants remain under the protection and authority of the principles of international law derived from established custom, from the principles of humanity and from the dictates of public conscience.

This clause echoes a general principle of international law that holds that a rule of international law continues to apply unless a later rule of law expressly derogates from it. In so far as treaties are concerned—the source of most IHRL—this rule is confirmed by the Vienna Convention on the Law of Treaties in articles providing for the binding force of treaty obligations and the rule stating that other existing international legal obligations are not effected when a state withdraws from a treaty. Because of the above principles and provisions, IHRL has been applied in cases of armed conflict, while IHL on very rare occasions applies in times of peace.

As a practical matter, there are many thousands of cases more brought before tribunals that must apply specific rules of IHRL, than there are cases brought before tribunals that may apply IHL. Human rights are usually applied by international human rights bodies with mandates limited to certain treaties. These bodies must apply IHRL. Thus, the Human Rights Committee, the IHRL body created under the ICCPR, must apply the ICCPR and cannot decide to apply even general principles of public international law instead. Thus, if a case concerning the threat or use of nuclear weapons arises before the HRC, this body will be forced to apply the ICCPR. Even if it examines other sources of law for assistance, the HRC will have to decide whether the right to life in article 6 of the ICCPR is violated. Confronted with a practical, not theoretical case, such as the ICJ was in 1996, the HRC could not decide to turn to IHL to interpret article 6 of the ICCPR, at least not with the same degree of discretion with which the ICJ did. Instead, it is suggested, the HRC would first have to examine article 6, its drafting history, its own comments and expressions of views and other similar evidence first. Only when this provided no way forward, could the HRC turn to IHL or as an assistance—as the Inter-American Commission did—for interpretation. Any other decision-making strategy, it is suggested, would be contrary to the HRC mandate under the ICCPR. This mandate, in the case of individual communications, is defined by article 1 of the Optional Protocol to the ICCPR that limits these communications to those concerning violations of the ICCPR. Similar limitations appear in article 44 of the ACHR and article 25 of the ECHR.

Determining whether international humanitarian law should play a role in evaluating a situation requires asking questions about (1) whether or not there is an armed conflict, (2) whether or not combatants are involved, and (3) whether or not the armed conflict is international or non-international. A *conditio sine qua non* for either applying international humanitarian law or using this corpus of law for interpretation is the positive determination that an armed conflict exists.

Another issue involves the application of IHL and IHRL to soldiers acting under the auspices of the United Nations. Although at one point, claims were made that these laws do not apply to UN peacekeepers, the Secretary-General has issued a directive which puts this myth to rest and states that peacekeepers under UN authority are bound by all relevant international law.

At a more general level international humanitarian law or international criminal law bodies such as the International Criminal Tribunals for the Former Yugoslavia (ICTFY) and Rwanda (ICTR), have applied an approach very much related to international human rights law. For example, in the *Tadiç Case* the Tribunal for the Former Yugoslavia held that in international law "[a] State-sovereignty-oriented approach has been gradually supplanted by a human-being-oriented approach." The ICTFY has also found that threats of rape constituted torture *Prosecutor v. Anto Furundzija*, Case No. IT-95-17/1-T, Judgment, 10 December 1998 and the two tribunals are the only contemporary international human rights bodies to have convicted persons of the crimes of genocide, *Prosecutor v. Krstic ("Srebrenica-Drina Corps")*, Case No. IT-98-33, ICTFY Trial Chamber, Judgment of 2 August 2001 and *Prosecutor v. Clément Kayishema*, Case No. ICTR-95-1-T, ICTR Trial Chamber, Judgment of 21 May 1999.

Although individual responsibility for human rights is currently one of the most popular topics among international lawyers, a topic has been on the agenda of international lawyers for some time. Already in 1937, an attempt was made to create an international court to try persons committing acts of terrorism and other grave breaches of international law. However, this attempt failed as only India signed this convention and no state ratified it. This and other previous attempts to create international criminal courts have failed because there was a lack of consensus in defining what constitutes an offense for which there may be individual responsibility under international law and states were reluctant to surrender a part of their sovereignty — the unfettered ability to try individuals within their jurisdiction — that is necessary for the creation of an effective system of international justice.

After World War II another attempt was made in Nüremberg and Tokyo to create international courts to try individuals. The Nüremberg Tribunal was a creation of the victorious allied states, while the Tokyo Tribunal was a creation of a single American Army general acting on behalf of the allies. Both these attempts had mixed success. On the one-hand, they prosecuted and sentenced several war criminals, while on the other hand they were influenced by the vengeance of the victors. They were also problematic because individuals were tried for crimes that were not crimes at the time they were committed and carried no individual responsibility at the time they were committed. One of the Tokyo Tribunal judges, Professor Röllings, later confessed that this had been contrary to the principles of international law protecting individuals. Nevertheless, the Nüremberg principles have been influential and were the basis of a General Assembly Resolution that called for them to be circulated to states as the basis of a Draft Code of Offenses Against the Peace and Security of Mankind.

Finally, while international criminal responsibility of the individual may be a means of protecting an individual from abuses of his or her human rights, it is not the traditional means of protecting human rights — which is usually through one's own state or through an international human rights body to which the state has consented. For this reason there is still much confusion and disagreement about how such a system functions and how it should be classified under public international law. In this book, the emphasis is not on conceptualization, but on decision-making and the substantive protection of the values of human dignity. From this perspective, the advent of an international court that can decide upon an individuals responsibility for actions that infringe upon other individual's human rights is an important consideration in the formulation of policies and decisions towards achieving the values of human dignity.

In 1994, the UN General Assembly began work on an International Criminal Court. By 1998, an international conference was held in Rome, Italy that drafted the statute for an International Criminal Court. On 1 July 2002, this Statute entered into force and by the end of 2003, it was ratified by about 100 states.

The ICC Statute is 128 articles long and provides for the punishment of individuals committing the international crimes of genocide (art. 6), crimes against humanity (art. 7), war crimes (art. 8), and aggression—although the latter is not yet defined.

After the ICC Statute entered into force in 2003, the judges and prosecutor began their work. Unfortunately, some states remain opposed to cooperation with the Court. Most prominent among these states is the United States which has not only refused to ratify the Rome Statute, but has attempted to procure by coercion agreements from other states that prohibit these states from handing Americans over to the Court. If such obstruction continues to plague the ICC it must be wondered if it will not merely be used as an instrument for oppressing weak states and their nationals, instead of as an instrument of justice. To ensure that the ICC promotes international law the most powerful states must also be subject to its jurisdiction. This is especially the case as citizens of non-state parties, especially soldiers, are among those who violate the law most frequently and most seriously. Indeed, American President George W. Bush and Israeli Premier Ariel Sharon have both been guilty of acts that warrant investigation.

CHAPTER FOURTEEN
Strategies for Protecting Human Rights

Protecting human rights in practice requires a human rights defender be able to work with different types of actors and in different situations. It also requires an understanding of one's social and political environment. This chapter starts with comments on social justice—the relationship between individuals and their social and political environment.

14.1 Social Justice

Human rights in much of the world—for the overwhelming majority of the people in the world—are intricately linked to social justice issues such as debt relief, terms of trade, terms of loans, economic exploitation, etc. Often these issues arise in ways that affect the human rights of vulnerable people in relations between developed countries and developing countries. This means that respect for human rights for many people depends as much on what goes on outside of their country as inside of it. While this by no means excuses the government of any country from its legal obligations to respect the human rights of individuals under its jurisdiction, it does point towards the duties of other countries for human rights outside their own borders and additional rights and responsibilities for human rights defenders.

At the turn of the century, approximately half the world's population lived on less than two Euros per day, and many on less than a dollar a day. This means that approximately three billion people were unable to afford the basic necessities of life such as adequate food, housing, clothing, the right to work and adequate work conditions, the rights to health and education, and the right to an adequate standard of living. As the 21st Century dawned, this group was growing larger and the gap between them and the richest people in the world was growing wider. Even during the economic downturn at the start of the twenty first century, the rich grew richer as a group and the poor grew poorer. The social justice movement was established to combat this discrepancy.

The social justice movement is crucial to moving human rights forward in these two directions. First, this movement has argued that the violations of the basic human rights of many poor people are caused as much by rich countries and their policies as by the corruption and inhumane practices of many developing countries. While initially the blame was directed at the world's financial institutions, after America's attacks on Afghanistan and Iraq in the early part of the 21st century, much of the focus has been shifted to the United States. Even American writers have argued how the United States of America and its rich industrialized allies have conspired to exploit much of the world's people causing severe impoverishment and thereby shouldering the blame — despite the American government's failure to acknowledge this — for much of the world's ills. Second, by concentrating on non-state actors, including individuals acting in community with other individuals, the social justice movement has moved the responsibility for social change onto the shoulders of every individual in accordance with his or her abilities. This has meant — to the social justice movement — that everyone can and must play a role in trying to secure the basic human rights of every vulnerable person around the world. While this role is, of course, limited by one's abilities it is never the less urged to the best of each person's abilities. This provides an even greater motivation for individuals then does mere rights — it is social responsibility. It means that not only do individuals have a right to help other individuals achieve respect for their human rights, but a duty to do so.

In these two ways the social justice movement is affecting a transformation of human rights from the western paradigm of "may" and the focus on individualism to the developing world's values of the individual as a communal being and "must" as far as concerns efforts to protect basic human rights.

The social justice movement has backed this theory with action in the form of demonstrations, teaching, writing and practice. The last has been the least prominent because of the obstacles that the movement has faced in trying to break down traditional barriers — such as individuals greed, capitalism, and elite-selfish or misguided institutionalism that has maintained structures of oppression. Nevertheless, the small gains that have been made can be seen. For example, 50 Years are Enough — a movement taking aim at the world's financial institutions, especially the World Bank and IMF — has forced the World Bank to accept greater responsibility for human rights. The work ahead, however, is tremendous. Cooperation between human rights defenders using the law you have learned in this book and the social justice movement — whose members range from anarchists to open-minded professionals, can play a major role in promoting the very compatible agendas.

14.2 Actors and Actions

International human rights law is not static. It is a concept that evolves with time and must reflect the changing values of the people who need it most. To evolve and to have meaning to individual human rights depends on action by different actors. These actors include states, but also individuals. Furthermore, each of these actors and their actions can be disaggregated. When considering the actions of states it is important to disaggregated them into the individuals who are acting on behalf of or under the control of the state. When considering individuals it is important to understand in what capacity the individual is acting. And when considering actions one must attribute them to specific actors in order to apportion responsibility.

The living nature of the law is most traditionally reflected in the practice of states. States are the actors which develop the law most directly by establishing new human rights treaties. The Statute of the International Criminal Court is one such treaty that has developed international human rights law by providing for individual responsibility for violations of human rights as is indicated in Chapter 13. Developments in law, however, may not always have a positive effect on human rights. For example, at the ASEAN meeting held in July 1997 several Asian countries — including China, Malaysia and Indonesia — proposed the re-evaluation of international human rights law. Some countries, including the United States, opposed this as an attempt to avoid existing obligations. Other countries, including the United Kingdom, France and Netherlands, reacted by encouraging the development and inclusion of new principles into the realm of the law. At a theoretical level it is also often the developments driven by states that have the greatest impact. In the area of Islamic studies or the Islamization of knowledge, for example, where states have adopted particular positions taking into account the contribution of Islamic values, challenges have been brought to the older and more traditional understanding of the human values underlying international human rights law.

States are, however, not the only actors. Increasingly, elites no longer legitimately speak for their constituents or a majority of the international community of individuals, unless they speak and act with sensitivity to international human rights law. Human rights defenders and advocates can now rely on international human rights law to gain leverage against leaders who do not respect this law. Moreover, the future of international human rights law is increasingly influenced by the perspectives of individuals. Of particular relevance have been the views of individuals that reflect the values and concerns of the most impoverished and vulnerable people in the world. It is likely that many of the leading human rights advocates of the 21st century will have to understand the values and problems of the most vulnerable in world society — which make up the majority of the world's population — in order to be viewed as legitimate human rights defenders. Today most western, especially American, human rights defenders lack this perspective.

Non-state actors — individuals and NGOs — are increasingly pressuring elites to concede more authority to private individuals and groups. Rather than fighting these non-state actors, elites who either control states or work through states, often attempt to co-opt them. They have developed strategies for re-asserting their authority through the means of private enterprise and sometimes even using force when no-state actors have challenged their authority. One such effort is the Global Compact between civil society, transnational corporations, and IGOs, which has to date led to little noticeable improvement in the protection of human rights.

Nevertheless, even private enterprise is now being challenged by the claims and demands of those who have remained excluded from the process and by those whose values are not reflected in the process. The difference between these claims and those mentioned in the preceeding paragraph is that by and large — although not exclusively — individuals in developed countries are willing to accept the existing norms of international human rights law as adequately reflecting their values. To this extent, they have concentrated on implementation rather than re-evaluation of the norms. Strategies for implementation have become more and more complex. At one extreme, they are often beyond the comprehension of all but the leading practitioners, and at the other, they are so simple that they have become part of everyday life. In the latter case, they may even lose their attraction, as appears to have happened to the right to vote in several developed countries where potential voters complain that their choices are so limited as to be illusionary.

It is also important to understand that the protection of human rights is a serious responsibility. Those individuals who honestly strive to ensure the protection of human rights are acting for the benefit of society as a whole and they are acting to preserve the most fundamental basic values of human dignity. Without these people, our societies would be doomed to failure because no country fully ensures the protection of human rights. Failure means that people will be condemned to inhumane treatment. Have you ever seen a baby dying because she lacks health care, a person who has been killed after prolonged torture, a woman who has been brutally raped, a refugee who has lost all his or her family members, or a person who wants to change his or her religion but who is forbidden from doing so? Oppressed and mistreated people are the victims of violations of human rights. If you are among such people, know such people, or care about people in general, you will probably realize the importance of protecting their human rights.

Human rights are also as important to the state or the government as they are to individuals. No government can claim to be legitimate today if it violates human rights. No government can defend itself from outside sanctions, from the wrath of is own people, and from the criticism of other states when it repeatedly flouts international human rights law. Even states that appear to be friendly will always be willing to change their minds to protect their self-interests when they are asked to react to a state that violates human rights. Democracy is one means of safeguarding against a bad human rights record but it is not sufficient, mere propaganda without substantive change just adds to the problem. Democracy is valuable because when a government is not doing a good job in securing the basic rights and responsibilities of its people, the people will change them. Without this threat, a government may become self-confident and it may trample its citizens' human rights. However, even democracy must be accompanied by a government's commitment to ensuring human rights, a government's willingness to invest in protecting human rights, a government's willingness to change to ensure the protection of human rights, the investigation of violations, the punishment of violators and the compensation of persons injured by a violation. It certainly takes a courageous, honest and sincere government to admit violations and to ensure they are not repeated as much as it takes a weak, uncaring and dishonest government to continue to violate its peoples' human rights. Ultimately, it may be the mere threat that is posed by the realisation that abuse of human rights has been the single most common reason from revolutions and civil war, that will encourage governments to respect human rights when all else fails.

The effectiveness of human rights strategies can be measured by their ability to achieve respect for human rights with the least possible amount of coercion. This definition of effectiveness balances concerns of public order with those of individual freedom. The effectiveness of human rights strategies thus depends on both individuals and society. In some societies, the use of force or coercion may be the means by which public order is maintained. In democratic societies, however, the optimal balance should be found in policies that maintain public order with the minimum necessary amount of coercion while providing for the widest possible enjoyment of the human rights. Such an optimalization does not lend itself to measurement because it depends on too many variables for which we have not yet developed competent means of measurement. For example, we do not know how many people are enjoying or being denied the right to freedom of expression in any country. Usually only simple descriptions of what it means to enjoy the freedom of expression are possible. Nevertheless, if we examine the claims for respect for their human rights that individuals make in courts of law and the outcomes of these processes that uphold or deny these claims, we can arrive at a basic understanding of the effectiveness of these mechanisms. The standards of evaluation used by courts are prior claims, demands, and expectations, as well as the decisions that have been made concerning them.

14.3 Promoting Education

Human rights education has been an international concern for both governmental and non-governmental actors in the human rights community for several decades. This is not surprising given that human rights are relatively new to international affairs and most international human rights treaties are less than fifty years old. Neither is it surprising that human rights education has been as much a concern of primary schools as it has been of universities. This is because the values behind international human rights law are among the most basic tenants of social education being linked to our religions, our philosophy, and our understanding of humanity.

The United Nations has often been at the forefront of education in the field of international human rights law. The Office of the High Commissioner for Human Rights has provided funding and training to governments, and occasionally support to non-governmental organizations. The decade from 1995 to 2004 was declared The Decade of Human Rights Education. During this decade a series of regional meetings were held to promote human rights education in the Middle East, Africa and Asia. UNESCO also established a series of UNESCO chairs, which initially received funding from UNESCO, but gradually were devolved into a loosely connected network or independently funded initiatives.

The concern for human rights education is widespread. For years, Amnesty International has produced materials for human rights education at the elementary and secondary school levels. The rapidly increasing number of students in human rights courses in universities around the world attests to the increased attention for human rights in law faculties. The American Bar Association's Central European and Eurasian Law Initiative (CEELI) has also provided support for the training of judges, lawyers, and occasionally law students in international human rights law. Additionally, the increasing number of human rights cases being brought before international bodies has prompted increased attention to this field of law. In other areas, the increasing relevance of human rights for political and social policy making processes encourages the study of human rights.

Often human rights is taught as an interdisciplinary course whereby students study law, sociology, philosophy, social action and other areas as part of a course entitled human rights. In these cases human rights is identified with protection of basic human values rather than the technicalities of law. Human rights are often viewed as one means by which the goal of protecting basic human values can be realized. One area of higher education and research where the values of human rights are expressed but not always by name is development economics. Often the values that development economists try to introduce into their analyses and prescriptions for policy makers are based on the assumption of consensually accepted international human rights norms.

Because 'human rights' is a concept that became fashionable after it was expressed in international declarations and treaties, human rights education often focuses on the law. Sometimes this takes the form of classes in international human rights law. Since law is usually studied at the university level, it is in university law faculties around the world where one can see the increased attention being given to international human rights law. In specialized courses in other faculties, human rights law may also be integrated into the curriculum. For example, courses in public health, economics, international relations, political science, business administration, social science, education, development, *et cetera*, all have human rights law components. Moreover, there are examples of university level courses in all of these disciplines that have been taught from a human rights perspective.

Setting the curriculum for a human rights course is an undertaking that greatly influences how well individuals will come to know and respect human rights. At primary and secondary levels, the indoctrination of students with an understanding of human rights might merely mean teaching them the virtue of shared human values. At the level of higher education, successful human rights education means teaching individuals the following:

(1) What their rights are.
(2) How they may protect their rights.
(3) How they may contribute to developing their rights.
(4) And how they may contribute to assisting in the protection of other's rights.

This teaching is probably most effective when it includes (a) involvement in real cases; (b) contacts with real victims; and (c) the urging of students to the limits of critical thinking—that is criticism of existing social processes that allow violations of human rights to exist as well as those which can end these violations.

Human rights education is also a right, not only as part of the right of freedom of expression, but sometimes also in its own right. The right to human rights education can be derived from Art. 26 of the UDHR that states: "[e]veryone has the right to education ... [and that this e]ducation shall be directed to the full and fundamental freedoms ...". In 1994, the United Nations General Assembly when proclaiming The Decade for Human Rights Education and Plan of Action for the Decade for Human Rights Education 1995-2004 emphasizes that: "... human rights education shall be defined as training, dissemination and information efforts aimed at the building of a universal culture of human rights through the imparting of knowledge and skills and the moulding of attitudes and directed to: (a) The strengthening of respect for human rights and fundamental freedoms; (b) The full development of the human personality and the sense of its dignity; (c) The promotion of understanding, tolerance, gender equality and friendship among all nations, indigenous peoples and racial, national, ethnic, religious and linguistic groups...." These manifestations indicate a commitment to human rights education, but one that has not always been met in practice.

14.4 Working with Governments

Cooperation with governments is as much a part of encouraging respect for human rights as is confrontation. Moreover, cooperation is preferable because it has lower social costs and its results are likely to last longer. The path of cooperation is especially relevant to human rights bodies that are closely connected to the government such as parliamentary human rights committees and other national human rights institutions. For example, one of the most important and constructive activities of national human rights institutions is providing advice to their government. Such advice may be informal or formal. In both cases, it should be based on a preliminary phase involving the exchange of ideas with both human rights experts and with the individuals whose rights are being affected.

Where human rights experts are not readily available within a country – something that is increasingly unusual–the United Nations' Office of the High Commissioner for Human Rights (OHCHR) provides Advisory and Technical Services. These services can often be accessed free by countries that show a willingness to cooperate with the OHCHR. Several IGOs including UNHCR, UNICEF, the European Union and the OSCE, also include human rights advice and cooperation within their mandates of assistance to emerging democracies.

Broad based participation, at least at the preliminary phase of advice and cooperation, is essential, although often over-looked. Experts in human rights sometimes tend to think that they know what is best for the population they are trying to help. One reason that they rely on to justify their belief is the inalienability of human rights. The point of participation is not to determine what human rights are—something that is indeed determined by a universal consensus—but how they can be best implemented and respected.

14.5 Investigating and Reporting on Human Rights Abuses

Investigating human rights abuses may be a risky and expensive undertaking. The motivation for taking such risks and incurring the expense may be found in the protection that may be provided for possible future victims or the redress that past victims may receive.

An important task of many human rights organizations is their ability to investigate violations of individual's human rights. The *Handbook for National Human Rights Institutions* lists the following four vital characteristics for successful investigation: (1) adequate legal capacity; (2) organizational competence; (3) a defined and appropriate set of priorities; and (4) the political will to pursue the work.

Reports on the situation of human rights around the world are today issued by numerous NGOs. Even small NGOs can often play an important part in reporting human rights abuses if they concentrate on areas that are not reported by other organizations. Reporting is one of the most important functions of non-state actors and it is a function that can best be undertaken by non-state actors because of their greater independence.

Reporting on human rights is especially important in areas and at times when such information may not be readily available. This is especially the case in armed conflicts or areas where violence is likely to interfere with traditional means of human rights data collection such as armed conflicts. As states rarely exercise they prerogative of derogating from human rights instruments in modern armed conflicts it is essential that brave individuals monitor the violations of international human rights and international humanitarian law.

14.6 Domestic Courts

Domestic courts are vital to protecting human rights. These courts often ensure greater respect for human rights merely because the decisions they take are backed by the implementation authority of the state in which the court sits.

Often domestic courts are the best places to ensure human rights. While there are few forums where social and economic rights can be claimed and even fewer international forums for claiming these rights in Asia, some domestic courts have taken the lead in providing remedies for violations of human rights. The decision of the Indian Supreme Court in the case of *Olga Tellis v. Bombay Municipal Corporation* in 1985 is a rare example of a court effectively protecting a social and economic right, the right to housing. In this case, the petitioner claimed that their right to life under article 21 of the Indian Constitution was violated by the state's failure to provide adequate housing. The Supreme Court held that „the right to life which is conferred by Art. 21 includes the right to livelihood and ... that it is established that if the petitioners are evicted from their dwellings, they will be deprived of their livelihood."

In the United States, civil and political rights, especially the right to freedom of expression, have been significantly developed. In other words, domestic courts have often proven to be better protectors of human right than even international human rights bodies.

Finally, recourse to domestic courts is often a necessary constituent of the requirement that individuals exhaust domestic remedies before appealing to international tribunals. Thus a lawyer who applies international law in a domestic court is strengthening his or her chance that a negative decision will be condemned by an international tribunal.

Despite the few bright spots indicated above, most judges — even the most senior judges — in most countries remain woefully uneducated about human rights.

14.7 International Human Rights Mechanisms

Too often too little attention is placed on the role that international mechanisms for the protection of human rights can play in ensuring human rights in concrete situations. An effort has also been made to illustrate their relevance to specific human rights situations. The success of these mechanisms requires at least two more activities. First, human rights lawyers and practitioners, whether lawyers or not, must use and encourage the use of international mechanisms. In many countries that have recently become parties to, for example, the Optional Protocol of the ICCPR, relatively little use has been made of the individual communications procedure. At the same time, NGOs in these countries continue to document and victims continue to complain about human rights violations. Where domestic NGOs or individuals within a country are not able to bring claims themselves or have been intimidated from doing so, foreign NGOs and human rights practitioners can bring claims. One does not have to be a lawyer qualified in the country in which a human rights violation is alleged to represent the victim of a violation. One does not even have to be a lawyer. Of course, one should be knowledgeable about the relevant international human rights law and must have a signed (but not notarized) power of representation from the victim of the human rights violation in order to pursue their case. Unfortunately, there is often apathy and lack of commitment among NGOs and lawyers who do not want to take a case unless it is 'profitable' to them. Such practices do little to promote human rights.

Second, human rights activists, practitioners, and indeed, every individual can and should urge their respective governments or any government to which they can address themselves to ensure the financial viability and integrity of international human rights mechanisms. In recent years, governments have spent near to nothing on international human rights mechanisms. Several countries still do not provide the United Nations with their assessed annual contribution. The United States has not done so because it claims the United Nations does not 'do enough'. The hypocrisy of this claim is seen when it is set against the fact that it is failure to provide adequate resources to 'do enough' that has been the primary handicap of the United Nations human rights efforts. Furthermore, when the United States has organized supposedly 'leaner and meaner' human rights efforts, for example the OSCE mission in Bosnia and Hercegovina that was organized by the Washington office of the OSCE and was very much under the control of the United States government, the missions have been much more ineffective than comparable United Nations missions. While many states have listened to their constituents to agree to create the international mechanisms few have really supported these institutions' work in the field of human rights.

Although, like domestic legal procedures, human rights usually become the concern of international mechanisms after a violation has taken place; provisions for interim measures do exist. However, these provisions have not always been respected by states in practice, although they have been held to be binding by some international bodies such as the European Court of Human Rights.

Procedurally international human rights bodies will usually attempt to assist individual petitioners because they recognize that individuals are in a weaker position than a state. This may, for example, entail that a burden of proof that may normally be the responsibility of the petitioner must be shared by the state.

The judicial decisions of international human rights bodies have had a mixed record of effectiveness. Although the European Commission's requests concerning interim measures were not always effective, the European Court of Human Rights has received much more respect from national authorities. In general, it may be said that a decision of the European Court of Human Rights is as effective as that of the highest judicial body in any European state. The decisions of the Inter-American Court of Human Rights have been less effective. Some of its decisions have been ignored and the state members of the Organization of American States, for whom it relies for its authority, have often failed to support the Court with appropriate action against states that do not comply with its judgments. Despite this pessimistic state of affairs, there are signs that the American states will rally behind the Court. One such sign is the increase in resources that the Court has been granted. Nevertheless, whether this support will remain consistent enough to provide for the real effectiveness of the Court's judgments has yet to be seen. Furthermore, in comparison to its European counterpart, the Inter-American Court has decided many fewer cases and thus the instances of non-compliance with its judgments are more apparent. The Inter-American Commission has also enjoyed mixed success. While states party to the American Convention on Human Rights appear to respect its decisions, non-states party over whom it exercises a general jurisdiction do not often respect its decisions. In Africa, the African Commission on Human and Peoples' Rights has a mixed record that depends on the efforts of single Commissioners. The new African Court (not yet in force) may bring a change, because unlike the African Commission, its decisions will be legally binding on states. The United Nations' mechanisms are also of mixed value, often depending on the political weight and initiative of particular members. Despite these inconsistencies, these international mechanisms remain an important part of any overall strategy merely because sometimes they do work quite efficiently.

In addition you must always determine whether there has been a violation of a protected human right. Chapters 8 through 13 have been devoted to helping you understand how to do this. It requires studying the treaties and jurisprudence. What treaties has the country in question ratified? What rights are protected in these treaties?

After you have done this you must determine the procedural requirements. You must ask yourself such questions as: What possibilities exist in the treaties a state has ratified for individual complaints? What rights are protected in these treaties? What are the requirements of admissibility where individual complaints are allowed (this requires consulting the rules, statute and often the jurisprudence of the body to which you are considering filing a petition or communication)? Admissibility will often — but not always — be considered before the merits of your communication are considered. Especially Chapters 5 and 6 of this book and the checklist that follows the glossary of terms provide you some general guidance as to the functioning of these procedures. These requirements include that domestic remedies have been exhausted and a person filing the communication have adequate standing.

Using international law to protect human rights requires mixing legal procedure, a substantive knowledge of the law, and politics together to protect individuals inalienable human rights. It is not an easy task, but if you are successful both you and those around you will reap substantial rewards.

GLOSSARY

&

CHECKLIST FOR
SUBMITTING PETITIONS TO
INTERNATIONAL HUMAN RIGHTS BODIES

Glossary

Accession acceptance of a **treaty** by a state that did not participate in the negotiations or drafting of the treaty and after the time specified for **ratification**.

Admissibility refers to the initial stage of proceedings in a human rights **case** before an **international human rights body** during which the body will decide of the petitioner has satisfied all the formal conditions for bringing a **case**, such as the requirement of **exhaustion of domestic remedies**.

Advisory opinion is a formal opinion expressed by a body legally entitled to give such opinions that, although not strictly legally binding, is an authoritative interpretation of a point of law. Usually **courts** issue advisory opinions at the request of states or other international bodies.

Affirmative action refers to the practice of a state that causes disadvantage to an otherwise protected person for the legitimate objective of remedying past discrimination against a person from another group. Affirmative action must be narrowly tailored and limited temporarily to accomplishing a reversal of the past discrimination.

Aggression refers to the use of force in **violation** of **international law**. Although defined in the UN Resolution on Aggression, it has yet to be defined in the Statute of the International Criminal Court.

Allegation refers to a claim made — but not yet proven — that one's **human rights** have been violated.

Amicus curiae means 'friend of the court' and refers to interventions in a court, usually by a written brief, to support one party in a **case** even though the case does not directly involve the intervenor. An *amicus curiae* brief can provide an **international human rights body** deciding a case addition information that is not otherwise contained in the parties' briefs. **Applicant** is a person or persons who are petitioning an **international human rights body** for redress in the case of a **violation** of **human rights** when domestic remedies have failed.

Attribution is a requirement of **state responsibility** and means that an act can be traced back to an actor acting on behalf of the allegedly responsible state.

Breach of an international obligation means **violation** of an **international legal obligation** based on **customary international law** or a **treaty**.

Bretton Woods Institutions refers to the International Financial Institutions of the International Monetary Fund (IMF) and World Bank.

Brief is a term referring to a formal pleading to an **international human rights body** or notes written about a case summarizing its **facts**, the **issue(s)**, the **decision** of the body, the **reasons for the decision** and perhaps the **arguments** of each party and the author's own **comments**.

Cairo Declaration and Programme for Action refers to a document affirming women's reproductive rights that was adopted by consensus at the 1994 International Conference on Population and Development in Cairo.

Case refers to a formal legal case or a set of events giving rise to an **issue** of legal relevance.

Charter is another word for **treaty**. The word *Charter* is often used when the treaty creates an **international organization**.

Civil and political rights refer to rights that are related to the realm of civil and political activities of individuals. They are sometimes referred to a 'negative rights' because they usually — but not always — require a state to refrain from action instead of take action. They have usually included the right to life, the prohibition of torture, the rights of expression, etc.
Comments are the remarks made by the writer of a note on a **decision** of an **international human rights body**.

Commission is an international human rights body that reviews cases, although usually without making a legally binding decision, but rather making a recommendation to the state concerned. Some Commissions do, however, view their recommendations as becoming legally binding after they have been agreed to by other bodies. This is the case with the African Commission on Human and Peoples' Rights that views its decisions as legally binding after they have been adopted and published by the Assembly of Heads of Governments and States of the African Union.

Committee is an international human rights body that reviews cases, although usually without making a legally binding decision, but rather making a recommendation to the state concerned. The decisions of some UN Committees are considered binding by some states.

Communication is how some human rights bodies (for example, the UN system treaty bodies and the African Commission on Human and Peoples' Rights) refer to a **petition** to the **international human rights body** on behalf of an individual or individuals whose human rights have been violated.

CONGOs refers to co-opted **non-governmental organizations** (NGOs), which are NGOs created by states to defend a specific state's or states' position.

Convention is another word for **treaty**.

Court is an international human rights body that reviews cases making a legally binding decision and sometimes providing non-binding but very authoritative advisory opinions.

Customary international law is law formed by the *opinio juris* and practice of states. Both these characteristics exercise by an overwhelming majority of states must confirm a rule of customary international law. Sometimes, however, a rule may be confirmed in a regional context by a regional majority. In its Advisory Opinion in the case *Concerning the Legality of Nuclear Weapons* (1996) the International Court of Justice indicated that sometimes a minority of effected states might prevent a rule of customary international law from forming. This proposition is controversial and perhaps the application of the **persistent objector rule** would have been more appropriate.

Decision refers to both legally binding and not clearly legally binding conclusions and views of an **international human rights body**.

Declaration is a word referring to an act by states that is not in itself legally binding. The Universal Declaration of Human Rights is, for example, not in itself legally binding under **international law**, although many of its provisions may reflect **customary international law** and some even **jus cogens**.

Declarations are statements made by states at the time of ratifying a **treaty** that indicate that the state interprets an obligation in a treaty in certain manner. For example, some states have stated that they do not believe a treaty obligation applies to a territory they may govern overseas.

Declaratory relief refers to a written decision of a **court** or other authoritative body establishing a **violation** of human rights.

Derogation is an act by a state declaring it cannot or will not abide by its international obligations under specific provisions of a human rights **treaty** invoking the provisions of that treaty that allow a state to derogate.

Domestic law is the law within a state, created by the state's authorities, under the state's constitution, but never allowed to be in conflict with **international law**. *Also see* **national law**.

Economic and social rights are human rights that relate to the economic and social sphere of human behaviour. They have usually included the rights to work, health care, education, etc.
Entry into Force is the date on which a **treaty** becomes fully legally binding on states that have ratified it.

Equality refers to the right of every individual to be treated similar to other individuals in relation to his or her basic human rights. Sometimes achieving equality will require the state take action to even a playing field that has not been even (for example, **affirmative action**), although the state is not under an obligation to eliminate all forms of discrimination.

Equality of Arms is a basic principle of due process entitling an individual litigant to equal rights before a court of law. This enables the litigant to present his or her case fully.

Erga omnes refers to a legal obligation that creates an interest in all states (and perhaps non-state actors) for ensuring its respect.

Exhaustion of domestic remedies refers to the requirement for a petitioner to an **international human rights body** to have tried all reasonable and accessible domestic procedures to resolve his or her case. Remedies that are not adequate or will cause undue delay do not have to be exhausted.

Fact-finding is action that may be carried out by a human rights mechanism to determine the facts in a particular case. It may include on-site visits, enlisting experts, taking evidence, etc.

Facts are the actual actions, omissions or manifestations of opinion by states or individuals acting on behalf of states or on their own behalf. The facts of a case are a description of events that led to the case being brought.

Female genital mutilation (FGM) or **female circumcision** is a harmful practice carried out on women by which parts of their genitals or surrounding body parts are removed. It has been considered both a violation of the human right to health and the prohibition of cruel and inhuman treatment.

General principles of law are a source of **international law** that includes the rules of law that are common to most major legal systems in the world.

Generations of rights refers to the various academic classifications of rights that were prominent during the latter part of the 20th century. Civil and political rights were usually called 'First Generation Human Rights' and economic and social rights were considered 'Second Generation Human Rights.' There were also sometimes reference to third and fourth generation rights, which included peoples' rights and group rights.

High Commissioner on Human Rights of the United Nations is the focal point for human rights activities in the United Nations and is an Under-Secretary General. Since the post was created, the High Commissioners have been Mr. Ayala Lasso 1994-1997, Mrs. Mary Robinson 1997-2002, Mr. Sergio Veriera de Mello 2002-2003, Mr. Bertrand Ramcharan (acting) 2003-2005, and Mrs. Louise Arbour 2005-Present. There is also a Commissioner for Human Rights under the auspices of the Council of Europe.

Horizontal working or **horizontality** means the application of a human rights treaty to relations in which the human rights violator is a private actor, although the obligation to protect the victim of the abuse will still be on the state.

Human rights are the rights that every individual holds by virtue of their being a human being. They are defined differently depending on one's perspective and definitional tools.

Impunity is the ability of human rights violators to remain outside the law and to avoid punishment for their human rights violations. In principle, no person should enjoy impunity for his or her violations of **international law** and amnesties that lead to impunity are contrary to **international human rights law**.

Inter-governmental organization is similar to an **international organization** because it is created by states, but it may not be a formal legal person under international law.

International Bill of Human Rights refers to the three instruments that are the foundation of the international protection of **human rights**, namely, the Universal Declaration of Human Rights, the International Covenant of Civil and Political Rights, and the International Covenant of Economic, Social and Cultural Rights.

International human rights are that have been agreed upon by consensus among states and individuals everywhere. Of course, determining this consensus may be difficult.

International human rights law is the corpus of human rights agreed to by states in treaties or by their overwhelming consensus on a principle of customary international human rights law.

International human rights bodies usually refer to commissions, courts and other tribunals created by states in a treaty that protects human rights or created by another body that has a responsibility for protecting human rights. They usually review state reports and often accept individual or state petitions against states that have violated an individual's or sometimes a group's human rights.

International human rights mechanisms include **international human rights bodies**, but are a broader category of institutions that include special rapporteurs and other bodies that promote human rights based on authority granted them by states.

International law is law formed at a level above the national level between states and binding on all states irrespective of domestic law. To an international lawyer there can be no justification for a **violation** of international law based on **domestic law**.

International legal obligation refers to the obligation of a state under international law.

International organization is a legal person under international law created by states. The United Nations, the Council of Europe, the African Union and the African Commission on Human and Peoples' Rights, the Organization of American States and the Inter-American Court of Human Rights, the International Labour Organization, the World Health Organization, and the Pan-American Health Organization are all international organizations created by states to protect human rights.

Interpretation refers to the act of determining the meaning of a **treaty** provision or a provision of **customary international law**. International human rights courts, commissions, and committees interpret human rights treaties.

Issue refers to legal issue. This is a question or statement hat must be decided in a case.

Judgment is a **legally binding decision** of a **court**.

Jus cogens is a rule of **customary international law** that has gained such widespread acceptance that it cannot be derogated from at any time and in any manner whatsoever.

Legally binding decision refers to a **decision**, usually of a court, that must be implemented by the state concerned otherwise an additional **violation** of **international law** occurs.

Legitimate aim is the term used to refer to a state's legitimate interest in suspending human rights in very specific instances. Legitimate aims — such as public health, public moral, the rights of others, *et cetera* — are often stated in treaty articles providing for **human rights** and their **limitation** for specific reasons.

Limitation refers to a lawful act by a state applying **international human rights law** in a restrictive manner that is expressly allowed by a human rights **treaty** and thus legal.

Litigation is the process of bringing a case before an **international human rights body**.

Mandate refers to the basic responsibility of an organization or post. The mandate of an **international organization** like the United Nations is this body's heart and soul and should be the main terms of reference for the work of the UN.

Margin of Appreciation refers to the discretion that **international human rights bodies** sometimes allow states in deciding how to respect or suspend human rights.

National human rights institutions are human rights organizations created by state to assist them in an honest manner in protecting human rights. They are encouraged by the United Nations Office of the **High Commissioner on Human Rights**.

National law is the law within a state, created by the state's authorities, under the state's constitution, but never allowed to be in conflict with **international law**. When a national law is in conflict with **international law** is must not be applied otherwise a violation of international law takes place.

Ne bis in idem is a Latin maxim describing the basic principle of **international human rights law** that an individual cannot be tried twice for the same crime.

Non-governmental organizations (NGOs) are organizations formed under the domestic law of a particular state, but not by a state. In the field of **international human rights law** these actors often play an important role in ensuring states protect individual's human rights by lobbying states and sometimes bringing cases to **international human rights bodies** on behalf of individuals. *Also see* **CONGOs**.

Non-state actors include non-governmental organizations, individuals, private companies, corporations and other actors not created by states or not state themselves. Usually quasi-states such as the Vatican or Holy See are not included as non-state actors.

Nullum crimen sine lege is Latin maxim that describes the principle of international human rights law that prohibits the retroactive application of criminal law.

Petition is a generic term used to refer to communications and other initial and subsequent written filings with an **international human rights body** on behalf of individuals.

Persistent objector rule is a principle of **international law** whereby a state may prevent itself from being bound by a rule of **customary international law** if it objects to that rule from the very start and continuously.

Proportionality refers to the test used by **international human rights bodies** to determine whether a state's limits on an individual's human rights were necessary in a democratic society.

Protocols are treaties that are attached to other treaties and thereby amend or add to the original treaty.

Ratification is the usual process by which a state becomes a legally bound party to a **treaty**. This process often involves domestic action by different branches of government confirming the signature of the head of state or state representative who initially signed the **treaty**.

Reasons for the decision refer to the explanation given by an **international human rights body** for its **decision** in a particular case.

Recommendation is a (generally) non-binding decision by an international body. It is similar to a **resolution**.

Redress refers to a remedy for the violations of one's rights and may include monetary damages, a change of law, reinstatement, **declaratory relief**, etc.

Reparations refer to damages for a violation of one's human rights.

Reservations are acts done at the time of signing a **treaty** whereby a state, as allowed by the terms of the treaty, states that it will not or cannot honour an obligation under the treaty and is thereby exonerated from that legal obligation.

Resolution is an official act of an international body that is (generally) non-binding. It is similar to a **recommendation**.

Revolution is the rejection of a state of law because of the failings of that system it perpetuates and the replacing of that state of law with a more just state. For example, many individuals in developing countries and among the world's 3.2 billion impoverished people have called for a revolution against the oppression of the elites and American imperialism.

Signature is the act of a state official that binds his country to a **treaty** to the extent that the state must not take any action that makes the accomplish of obligations agreed to in the **treaty** impossible and obliges the state to strive to ratify the **treaty** within a reasonable time period.

State party refers to a state that has ratified a specific **treaty**.

State responsibility is the liability of state for its **violation** of an international obligation under either a **treaty** or **customary international law** that is attributable to the state.

Subsidiarity is a principle by which **international human rights bodies** defer to national forums to deal with questions of human rights. Only after the exhaustion of domestic remedies will the body accept to review a **case**.

Treaty is a written agreement between states that has been signed and ratified. When a state signs a treaty, it undertakes not to act to defeat the object and the purpose of the treaty. When a state ratifies a treaty it is fully bound by the treaty, except to the extent it has made **reservations** or **declarations**.

Understandings are statements made by states at the time they ratify a treaty indicating their interpretation of a specific provision of the **treaty**.

Violation refers to the failure of a state to do or refrain from doing something that is required by **international law**. *Also see* **breach**.

General Checklist for Submitting Petitions

✓ Has there been a violation of a human right? (Review the facts.)

✓ Is the violation attributable to a state? (Review the actors.)

✓ What treaties has the state ratified and do any of them protect the right? (Review the treaties carefully as well as a state's ratification record and its reservations, understandings, and declarations.)

✓ Do any of the treaties provide for individual petition procedures? (Read any relevant statutes, rules or regulations of any body that can accept petitions to be sure.)

✓ What are the conditions for making a petition? (Check the treaty, rules or statute carefully.)

✓ Have domestic remedies been exhausted? (Check the domestic procedure, and, if in doubt, the decisions of the relevant international human rights body.)

✓ What evidence of the violation do you have? (Check facts, witnesses, media, medical reports, etc.)

✓ What are the temporal requirements for filing a petition or is the violation ongoing? (Usually a petition must be filed within six months of the exhaustion of domestic remedies.)

✓ What are the acceptable languages for a petition and can you draft a petition in one of the languages? (If not, get help.)

✓ To which address must you send the petition? (Also confirm your petition can be sent securely. Email is often acceptable.)

SELECTED
INTERNATIONAL HUMAN
RIGHTS INSTRUMENTS

Charter of the United Nations

Entered into force 26 June 1945.

CHAPTER I: PURPOSES AND PRINCIPLES

...

Article 1

The Purposes of the United Nations are:

1. To maintain international peace and security, and to that end: to take effective collective measures for the prevention and removal of threats to the peace, and for the suppression of acts of aggression or other breaches of the peace, and to bring about by peaceful means, and in conformity with the principles of justice and international law, adjustment or settlement of international disputes or situations which might lead to a breach of the peace;

2. To develop friendly relations among nations based on respect for the principle of equal rights and self-determination of peoples, and to take other appropriate measures to strengthen universal peace;

3. To achieve international co-operation in solving international problems of an economic, social, cultural, or humanitarian character, and in promoting and encouraging respect for human rights and for fundamental freedoms for all without distinction as to race, sex, language, or religion; and

4. To be a centre for harmonizing the actions of nations in the attainment of these common ends.

Article 2

The Organization and its Members, in pursuit of the Purposes stated in Article 1, shall act in accordance with the following Principles.

1. The Organization is based on the principle of the sovereign equality of all its Members.

2. All Members, in order to ensure to all of them the rights and benefits resulting from membership, shall fulfil in good faith the obligations assumed by them in accordance with the present Charter.

3. All Members shall settle their international disputes by peaceful means in such a manner that international peace and security, and justice, are not endangered.

4. All Members shall refrain in their international relations from the threat or use of force against the territorial integrity or political independence of any state, or in any other manner inconsistent with the Purposes of the United Nations.

5. All Members shall give the United Nations every assistance in any action it takes in accordance with the present Charter, and shall refrain from giving assistance to any state against which the United Nations is taking preventive or enforcement action.

6. The Organization shall ensure that states which are not Members of the United Nations act in accordance with these Principles so far as may be necessary for the maintenance of international peace and security.

7. Nothing contained in the present Charter shall authorize the United Nations to intervene in matters which are essentially within the domestic jurisdiction of any state or shall require the Members to submit such matters to settlement under the present Charter; but this principle shall not prejudice the application of enforcement measures under Chapter VII.

. . .

CHAPTER V: THE SECURITY COUNCIL

FUNCTIONS AND POWERS

Article 24

1. In order to ensure prompt and effective action by the United Nations, its Members confer on the Security Council primary responsibility for the maintenance of international peace and security, and agree that in carrying out its duties under this responsibility the Security Council acts on their behalf.

2. In discharging these duties the Security Council shall act in accordance with the Purposes and Principles of the United Nations. The specific powers granted to the Security Council for the discharge of these duties are laid down in Chapters VI, VII, VIII, and XII.

3. The Security Council shall submit annual and, when necessary, special reports to the General Assembly for its consideration.

Article 25

The Members of the United Nations agree to accept and carry out the decisions of the Security Council in accordance with the present Charter.

...

CHAPTER IX: INTERNATIONAL ECONOMIC AND SOCIAL CO-OPERATION

Article 55

With a view to the creation of conditions of stability and well-being which are necessary for peaceful and friendly relations among nations based on respect for the principle of equal rights and self-determination of peoples, the United Nations shall promote:

a. higher standards of living, full employment, and conditions of economic and social progress and development;

b. solutions of international economic, social, health, and related problems; and international cultural and educational cooperation; and

c. universal respect for, and observance of, human rights and fundamental freedoms for all without distinction as to race, sex, language, or religion.

Article 56

All Members pledge themselves to take joint and separate action in co-operation with the Organization for the achievement of the purposes set forth in Article 55.

...

Universal Declaration of Human Rights
Adopted by UN General Assembly Resolution 217A (III) of 10 December 1948.

[1]Whereas recognition of the inherent dignity and of the equal and inalienable rights of all members of the human family is the foundation of freedom, justice and peace in the world,

[2]Whereas disregard and contempt for human rights have resulted in barbarous acts which have outraged the conscience of mankind, and the advent of a world in which human beings shall enjoy freedom of speech and belief and freedom from fear and want has been proclaimed as the highest aspiration of the common people,

[3]Whereas it is essential, if man is not to be compelled to have recourse, as a last resort, to rebellion against tyranny and oppression, that human rights should be protected by the rule of law,

[4]Whereas it is essential to promote the development of friendly relations between nations,

[5]Whereas the peoples of the United Nations have in the Charter reaffirmed their faith in fundamental human rights, in the dignity and worth of the human person and in the equal rights of men and women and have determined to promote social progress and better standards of life in larger freedom,

[6]Whereas Member States have pledged themselves to achieve, in cooperation with the United Nations, the promotion of universal respect for and observance of human rights and fundamental freedoms,

[7]Whereas a common understanding of these rights and freedoms is of the greatest importance for the full realization of this pledge,

Now, therefore,

The General Assembly

[8]Proclaims this Universal Declaration of Human Rights as a common standard of achievement for all peoples and all nations, to the end that every individual and every organ of society, keeping this Declaration constantly in mind, shall strive by teaching and education to promote respect for these rights and freedoms and by progressive measures, national and international, to secure their universal and effective recognition and observance, both among the peoples of Member States themselves and among the peoples of territories under their jurisdiction.

Article 1

All human beings are born free and equal in dignity and rights. They are endowed with reason and conscience and should act towards one another in a spirit of brotherhood.

Article 2

Everyone is entitled to all the rights and freedoms set forth in this Declaration, without distinction of any kind, such as race, color, sex, language, religion, political or other opinion, national or social origin, property, birth or other status.

Furthermore, no distinction shall be made on the basis of the political, jurisdictional or international status of the country or territory to which a person belongs, whether it be independent, trust, non-self-governing or under any other limitation of sovereignty.

Article 3

Everyone has the right to life, liberty and security of person.

Article 4

No one shall be held in slavery or servitude; slavery and the slave trade shall be prohibited in all their forms.

Article 5

No one shall be subjected to torture or to cruel, inhuman or degrading treatment or punishment.

Article 6

Everyone has the right to recognition everywhere as a person before the law.

Article 7

All are equal before the law and are entitled without any discrimination to equal protection of the law. All are entitled to equal protection against any discrimination in violation of the Declaration and against any incitement to such discrimination.

Article 8

Everyone has the right to an effective remedy by the competent national tribunals for acts violating the fundamental rights granted him by the constitution or by law.

Article 9

No one shall be subjected to arbitrary arrest, detention or exile.

Article 10

Everyone is entitled in full equality to a fair and public hearing by an independent and impartial tribunal, in the determination of his rights and obligations and of any criminal charge against him.

Article 11

1. Everyone charged with a penal offence has the right to be presumed innocent until proved guilty according to law in a public trial at which he has had all the guarantees necessary for his defence.

2. No one shall be held guilty of any penal offence on account of any act or omission which did not constitute a penal offence, under national or international law, at the time it was committed. Nor shall a heavier penalty be imposed than the one that was applicable at the time the penal offence was committed.

Article 12

No one shall be subjected to arbitrary interference with his privacy, family, home or correspondence, nor to attacks upon his honour and reputation. Everyone has the right to the protection of the law against such interference or attacks.

Article 13

1. Everyone has the right to freedom of movement and residence within the borders of each state.

2. Everyone has the right to leave any country, including his own, and to return to his country.

Article 14

1. Everyone has the right to seek and to enjoy in other countries asylum from persecution.

2. This right may not be invoked in the case of prosecutions genuinely arising from non-political crimes or from acts contrary to the purposes and principles of the United Nations.

Article 15

1. Everyone has the right to a nationality.

2. No one shall be arbitrarily deprived of his nationality nor denied the right to change his nationality.

Article 16

1. Men and women of full age, without any limitation due to race, nationality or religion, have the right to marry and to found a family. They are entitled to equal rights as to marriage, during marriage and at its dissolution.

2. Marriage shall be entered into only with the free and full consent of the intending spouses.

3. The family is the natural and fundamental group unit of society and is entitled to protection by society and the State.

Article 17

1. Everyone has the right to own property alone as well as in association with others.

2. No one shall be arbitrarily deprived of his property.

Article 18

Everyone has the right to freedom of thought, conscience and religion; this right includes freedom to change his religion or belief, and freedom, either alone or in community with others and in public or private, to manifest his religion or belief in teaching, practice, worship and observance.

Article 19

Everyone has the right to freedom of opinion and expression: this right includes freedom to hold opinions without interference and to seek, receive and impart information and ideas through any media and regardless of frontiers.

Article 20

1. Everyone has the right to freedom of peaceful assembly and association.

2. No one may be compelled to belong to an association.

Article 21

1. Everyone has the right to take part in the government of his country, directly or through freely chosen representatives.

2. Everyone has the right of equal access to public service in his country.

3. The will of the people shall be the basis of the authority of government; this will shall be expressed in periodic and genuine elections which shall be by universal and equal suffrage and shall be held by secret vote or by equivalent free voting procedures.

Article 22

Everyone, as a member of society, has the right to social security and is entitled to realization, through national effort and international co-operation and in accordance with the organization and resources of each State, of the economic, social and cultural rights indispensable for his dignity and the free development of his personality.

Article 23

1. Everyone has the right to work, to free choice of employment, to just and favourable conditions of work and to protection against unemployment.

2. Everyone, without any discrimination, has the right to equal pay for equal work.

3. Everyone who works has the right to just and favourable remuneration ensuring for himself and his family an existence worthy of human dignity, and supplemented, if necessary, by other means of social protection.

4. Everyone has the right to form and to join trade unions for the protection of his interests.

Article 24

Everyone has the right to rest and leisure, including reasonable limitation of working hours and periodic holidays with pay.

Article 25

1. Everyone has the right to a standard of living adequate for the health and well-being of himself and of his family, including food, clothing, housing and medical care and necessary social services, and the right to security in the event of unemployment, sickness, disability, widowhood, old age or other lack of livelihood in circumstances beyond his control.

2. Motherhood and childhood are entitled to special care and assistance. All children, whether born in or out of wedlock, shall enjoy the same social protection.

Article 26

1. Everyone has the right to education. Education shall be free, at least in the elementary and fundamental stages. Elementary education shall be compulsory. Technical and professional education shall be made generally available and higher education shall be equally accessible to all on the basis of merit.

2. Education shall be directed to the full development of the human personality and to the strengthening of respect for human rights and fundamental freedoms. It shall promote understanding, tolerance and friendship among all nations, racial or religious groups, and shall further the activities of the United Nations for the maintenance of peace.

3. Parents have a prior right to choose the kind of education that shall be given to their children.

Article 27

1. Everyone has the right freely to participate in the cultural life of the community, to enjoy the arts and to share in scientific advancement and its benefits.

2. Everyone has the right to the protection of the moral and material interests resulting from any scientific, literary or artistic production of which he is the author.

Article 28

Everyone is entitled to a social and international order in which the rights and freedoms set forth in this Declaration can be fully realized.

Article 29

1. Everyone has duties to the community in which alone the free and full development of his personality is possible.

2. In the exercise of his rights and freedoms, everyone shall be subject only to such limitations as are determined by law solely for the purpose of securing due recognition and respect for the rights and freedoms of others and of meeting the just requirements of mortality, public order and the general welfare in a democratic society.

3. These rights and freedoms may in no case be exercised contrary to the purposes and principles of the United Nations.

Article 30

Nothing in this Declaration may be interpreted as implying for any State, group or person any right to engage in any activity or to perform any act aimed at the destruction of any of the rights and freedoms set forth herein.

International Covenant on Civil and Political Rights

UNTS No. 14532, vol. 993 (1976), entered into force 23 March 1976.

PREAMBLE

The States parties to the present Covenant,

[1]Considering that, in accordance with the principles proclaimed in the Charter of the United Nations, recognition of the inherent dignity and of the equal and inalienable rights of all members of the human family is the foundation of freedom, justice and peace in the world,

[2]Recognizing that these rights derive from the inherent dignity of the human person,

[3]Recognizing that, in accordance with the Universal Declaration of Human Rights, the ideal of free human beings enjoying civil and political freedom and freedom from fear and want can only be achieved if conditions are created whereby everyone may enjoy his civil and political rights, as well as his economic, social and cultural rights,

[4]Considering the obligation of States under the Charter of the United Nations to promote universal respect for, and observance of, human rights and freedoms,

[5]Realizing that the individual, having duties to other individuals and to the community to which he belongs is under a responsibility to strive for the promotion and observance of the rights recognized in the present Covenant, agree upon the following articles:

PART I

Article 1

1. All peoples have the right of self-determination. By virtue of that right they freely determine their political status and freely pursue their economic, social and cultural development.

2. All peoples may, for their own ends, freely dispose of their natural wealth and resources without prejudice to any obligations arising out of international economic co-operation, based upon the principle of mutual benefit, and international law. In no case may a people be deprived of its own means of subsistence.

3. The States parties to the present Covenant, including those having responsibility for the administration of Non-Self-Governing and Trust Territories, shall promote the realization of the right of self-determination, and shall respect that right, in conformity with the provisions of the Charter of the United Nations.

PART II

Article 2

1. Each State Party to the present Covenant undertakes to respect and to ensure to all individuals within its territory and subject to its jurisdiction the rights recognized in the present Covenant, without distinction of any kind, such as race, colour, sex, language, religion, political or other opinion, national or social origin, property, birth or other status.

2. Where not already provided for by existing legislative or other measures, each State Party to the present Covenant undertakes to take the necessary steps, in accordance with its constitutional processes and with the provisions of the present Covenant, to adopt such legislative or other measures as may be necessary to give effect to the rights recognized in the present Covenant.

3. Each State Party to the present Covenant undertakes:

(a) To ensure that any person whose rights or freedoms as herein recognized are violated shall have an effective remedy, notwithstanding that the violation has been committed by persons acting in an official capacity;

(b) To ensure that any person claiming such a remedy shall have his right thereto determined by competent judicial, administrative or legislative authorities, or by any other competent authority provided for by the legal system of the State, and to develop the possibilities of judicial remedy;

(c) To ensure that the competent authorities shall enforce such remedies when granted.

Article 3

The States parties to the present Covenant undertake to ensure the equal right of men and women to the enjoyment of all civil and political rights set forth in the present Covenant.

Article 4

1. In time of public emergency which threatens the life of the nation and the existence of which is officially proclaimed, the States parties to the present Covenant may take measures derogating from their obligations under the present Covenant to the extent strictly required by the exigencies of the situation, provided that such measures are not inconsistent with their other obligations under international law and do not involve discrimination solely on the ground of race, colour, sex, language, religion or social origin.

2. No derogation from articles 6, 7, 8 (paragraphs 1 and 2), 11, 15, 16 and 18 may be made under this provision.

3. Any State Party to the present Covenant availing itself of the right of derogation shall immediately inform the other States parties to the present Covenant, through the intermediary of the Secretary-General of the United Nations, of the provisions from which it has derogated and of the reasons by which it was actuated. A further communication shall be made, through the same intermediary, on the date on which it terminates such derogation.

Article 5

1. Nothing in the present Covenant may be interpreted as implying for any State, group or person any right to engage in any activity or perform any act aimed at the destruction of any of the rights and freedoms recognized herein or at their limitation to a greater extent than is provided for in the present Covenant.

2. There shall be no restriction upon or derogation from any of the fundamental human rights recognized or existing in any State Party to the present Covenant pursuant to law, conventions, regulations or custom on the pretext that the present Covenant does not recognize such rights or that it recognizes them to a lesser extent.

PART III

Article 6

1. Every human being has the inherent right to life. This right shall be protected by law. No one shall be arbitrarily deprived of his life.

2. In countries which have not abolished the death penalty, sentence of death may be imposed only for the most serious crimes in accordance with the law in force at the time of the commission of the crime and not contrary to the provisions of the present Covenant and to the Convention on the Prevention and Punishment of the Crime of Genocide. This penalty can only be carried out pursuant to a final judgment rendered by a competent court.

3. When deprivation of life constitutes the crime of genocide, it is understood that nothing in this article shall authorize any State Party to the present Covenant to derogate in any way from any obligation assumed under the provisions of the Convention on the Prevention and Punishment of the Crime of Genocide.

4. Anyone sentenced to death shall have the right to seek pardon or commutation of the sentence. Amnesty, pardon or commutation of the sentence of death may be granted in all cases.

5. Sentence of death shall not be imposed for crimes committed by persons below eighteen years of age and shall not be carried out on pregnant women.

6. Nothing in this article shall be invoked to delay or to prevent the abolition of capital punishment by any State Party to the present Covenant.

Article 7

No one shall be subjected to torture or to cruel, inhuman or degrading treatment or punishment. In particular, no one shall be subjected without his free consent to medical or scientific experimentation.

Article 8

1. No one shall be held in slavery; slavery and the slave-trade in all their forms shall be prohibited.

2. No one shall be held in servitude.

3. (a) No one shall be required to perform forced or compulsory labour;

(b) Paragraph 3 (a) shall not be held to preclude, in countries where imprisonment with hard labour may be imposed as a punishment for a crime, the performance of hard labour in pursuance of a sentence to such punishment by a competent court;

(c) For the purpose of this paragraph the term "forced or compulsory labour" shall not include:

(i) Any work or service, not referred to in subparagraph (b), normally required of a person who is under detention in consequence of a lawful order of a court, or of a person during conditional release from such detention;

(ii) Any service of a military character and, in countries where conscientious objection is recognized, any national service required by law of conscientious objectors;

(iii) Any service exacted in cases of emergency or calamity threatening the life or well-being of the community;

(iv) Any work or service which forms part of normal civil obligations.

Article 9

1. Everyone has the right to liberty and security of person. No one shall be subjected to arbitrary arrest or detention. No one shall be deprived of his liberty except on such grounds and in accordance with such procedure as are established by law.

2. Anyone who is arrested shall be informed, at the time of arrest, of the reasons for his arrest and shall be promptly informed of any charges against him.

3. Anyone arrested or detained on a criminal charge shall be brought promptly before a judge or other officer authorized by law to exercise judicial power and shall be entitled to trial within a reasonable time or to release. It shall not be the general rule that persons awaiting trial shall be detained in custody, but release may be subject to guarantees to appear for trial, at any other stage of the judicial proceedings, and, should occasion arise, for execution of the judgment.

4. Anyone who is deprived of his liberty by arrest or detention shall be entitled to take proceedings before a court, in order that that court may decide without delay on the lawfulness of his detention and order his release if the detention is not lawful.

5. Anyone who has been the victim of unlawful arrest or detention shall have an enforceable right to compensation.

Article 10

1. All persons deprived of their liberty shall be treated with humanity and with respect for the inherent dignity of the human person.

2. (a) Accused persons shall, save in exceptional circumstances, be segregated from convicted persons and shall be subject to separate treatment appropriate to their status as unconvicted persons;

(b) Accused juvenile persons shall be separated from adults and brought as speedily as possible for adjudication.

3. The penitentiary system shall comprise treatment of prisoners the essential aim of which shall be their reformation and social rehabilitation. Juvenile offenders shall be segregated from adults and be accorded treatment appropriate to their age and legal status.

Article 11

No one shall be imprisoned merely on the ground of inability to fulfil a contractual obligation.

Article 12

1. Everyone lawfully within the territory of a State shall, within that territory, have the right to liberty of movement and freedom to choose his residence.

2. Everyone shall be free to leave any country, including his own.

3. The above-mentioned rights shall not be subject to any restrictions except those which are provided by law, are necessary to protect national security, public order (*ordre public*), public health or morals or the rights and freedoms of others, and are consistent with the other rights recognized in the present Covenant.

4. No one shall be arbitrarily deprived of the right to enter his own country.

Article 13

An alien lawfully in the territory of a State Party to the present Covenant may be expelled therefrom only in pursuance of a decision reached in accordance with law and shall, except where compelling reasons of national security otherwise require, be allowed to submit the reasons against his expulsion and to have his case reviewed by, and be represented for the purpose before, the competent authority or a person or persons especially designated by the competent authority.

Article 14

1. All persons shall be equal before the courts and tribunals. In the determination of any criminal charge against him, or of his rights and obligations in a suit at law, everyone shall be entitled to a fair and public hearing by a competent, independent and impartial tribunal established by law. The press and the public may be excluded from all or part of a trial for reasons of morals, public order (*ordre public*) or national security in a democratic society, or when the interest of the private lives of the parties so requires, or to the extent strictly necessary in the opinion of the court in special circumstances where publicity would prejudice the interests of justice; but any judgment rendered in a criminal case or in a suit at law shall be made public except where the interest of juvenile persons otherwise requires or the proceedings concern matrimonial disputes or the guardianship of children.

2. Everyone charged with a criminal offence shall have the right to be presumed innocent until proved guilty according to law.

3. In the determination of any criminal charge against him, everyone shall be entitled to the following minimum guarantees, in full equality:

(a) To be informed promptly and in detail in a language which he understands of the nature and cause of the charge against him;

(b) To have adequate time and facilities for the preparation of his defence and to communicate with counsel of his own choosing;

(c) To be tried without undue delay;

(d) To be tried in his presence, and to defend himself in person or through legal assistance of his own choosing; to be informed, if he does not have legal assistance, of this right; and to have legal assistance assigned to him, in any case where the interests of justice so require, and without payment by him in any such case if he does not have sufficient means to pay for it;

(e) To examine, or have examined, the witnesses against him and to obtain the attendance and examination of witnesses on his behalf under the same conditions as witnesses against him;

(f) To have the free assistance of an interpreter if he cannot understand or speak the language used in court;

(g) Not to be compelled to testify against himself or to confess guilt.

4. In the case of juvenile persons, the procedure shall be such as will take account of their age and the desirability of promoting their rehabilitation.

5. Everyone convicted of a crime shall have the right to his conviction and sentence being reviewed by a higher tribunal according to law.

6. When a person has by a final decision been convicted of a criminal offence and when subsequently his conviction has been reversed or he has been pardoned on the ground that a new or newly discovered fact shows conclusively that there has been a miscarriage of justice, the person who has suffered punishment as a result of such conviction shall be compensated according to law, unless it is proved that the non-disclosure of the unknown fact in time is wholly or partly attributable to him.

7. No one shall be liable to be tried or punished again for an offence for which he has already been finally convicted or acquitted in accordance with the law and penal procedure of each country.

Article 15

1. No one shall be held guilty of any criminal offence on account of any act or omission which did not constitute a criminal offence, under national or international law, at the time when it was committed. Nor shall a heavier penalty be imposed than the one that was applicable at the time when the criminal offence was committed. If, subsequent to the commission of the offence, provision is made by law for the imposition of the lighter penalty, the offender shall benefit thereby.

2. Nothing in this article shall prejudice the trial and punishment of any person for any act or omission which, at the time when it was committed, was criminal according to the general principles of law recognized by the community of nations.

Article 16

Everyone shall have the right to recognition everywhere as a person before the law.

Article 17

1. No one shall be subjected to arbitrary or unlawful interference with his privacy, family, home or correspondence, nor to unlawful attacks on his honour and reputation.

2. Everyone has the right to the protection of the law against such interference or attacks.

Article 18

1. Everyone shall have the right to freedom of thought, conscience and religion. This right shall include freedom to have or to adopt a religion or belief of his choice, and freedom, either individually or in community with others and in public or private, to manifest his religion or belief in worship, observance, practice and teaching.

2. No one shall be subject to coercion which would impair his freedom to have or to adopt a religion or belief of his choice.

3. Freedom to manifest one's religion or beliefs may be subject only to such limitations as are prescribed by law and are necessary to protect public safety, order, health, or morals or the fundamental rights and freedoms of others.

4. The States parties to the present Covenant undertake to have respect for the liberty of parents and, when applicable, legal guardians to ensure the religious and moral education of their children in conformity with their own convictions.

Article 19

1. Everyone shall have the right to hold opinions without interference.

2. Everyone shall have the right to freedom of expression; this right shall include freedom to seek, receive and impart information and ideas of all kinds, regardless of frontiers, either orally, in writing or in print, in the form of art, or through any other media of his choice.

3. The exercise of the rights provided for in paragraph 2 of this article carries with it special duties and responsibilities. It may therefore be subject to certain restrictions, but these shall only be such as are provided by law and are necessary:

(a) For respect of the rights or reputations of others;

(b) For the protection of national security or of public order (*ordre public*), or of public health or morals.

Article 20

1. Any propaganda for war shall be prohibited by law.

2. Any advocacy of national, racial or religious hatred that constitutes incitement to discrimination, hostility or violence shall be prohibited by law.

Article 21

The right of peaceful assembly shall be recognized. No restrictions may be placed on the exercise of this right other than those imposed in conformity with the law and which are necessary in a democratic society in the interests of national security or public safety, public order (*ordre public*), the protection of public health or morals or the protection of the rights and freedoms of others.

Article 22

1. Everyone shall have the right to freedom of association with others, including the right to form and join trade unions for the protection of his interests.

2. No restrictions may be placed on the exercise of this right other than those which are prescribed by law and which are necessary in a democratic society in the interests of national security or public safety, public order (*ordre public*), the protection of public health or morals or the protection of the rights and freedoms of others. This article shall not prevent the imposition of lawful restrictions on members of the armed forces and of the police in their exercise of this right.

3. Nothing in this article shall authorize States parties to the International Labour Organisation Convention of 1948 concerning Freedom of Association and Protection of the Right to Organize to take legislative measures which would prejudice, or to apply the law in such a manner as to prejudice the guarantees provided for in that Convention.

Article 23

1. The family is the natural and fundamental group unit of society and is entitled to protection by society and the State.

2. The right of men and women of marriageable age to marry and to found a family shall be recognized.

3. No marriage shall be entered into without the free and full consent of the intending spouses.

4. States parties to the present Covenant shall take appropriate steps to ensure equality of rights and responsibilities of spouses as to marriage, during marriage and at its dissolution. In the case of dissolution, provision shall be made for the necessary protection of any children.

Article 24

1. Every child shall have, without any discrimination as to race, colour, sex, language, religion, national or social origin, property or birth, the right to such measures of protection as are required by his status as a minor, on the part of his family, society and the State.

2. Every child shall be registered immediately after birth and shall have a name.

3. Every child has the right to acquire a nationality.

Article 25

Every citizen shall have the right and the opportunity, without any of the distinctions mentioned in article 2 and without unreasonable restrictions:

(a) To take part in the conduct of public affairs, directly or through freely chosen representatives;

(b) To vote and to be elected at genuine periodic elections which shall be by universal and equal suffrage and shall be held by secret ballot, guaranteeing the free expression of the will of the electors;

(c) To have access, on general terms of equality, to public service in his country.

Article 26

All persons are equal before the law and are entitled without any discrimination to the equal protection of the law. In this respect, the law shall prohibit any discrimination and guarantee to all persons equal and effective protection against discrimination on any ground such as race, colour, sex, language, religion, political or other opinion, national or social origin, property, birth or other status.

Article 27

In those States in which ethnic, religious or linguistic minorities exist, persons belonging to such minorities shall not be denied the right, in community with the other members of their group, to enjoy their own culture, to profess and practise their own religion, or to use their own language.

PART IV

Article 28

1. There shall be established a Human Rights Committee (hereafter referred to in the present Covenant as the Committee). It shall consist of eighteen members and shall carry out the functions hereinafter provided.

2. The Committee shall be composed of nationals of the States parties to the present Covenant who shall be persons of high moral character and recognized competence in the field of human rights, consideration being given to the usefulness of the participation of some persons having legal experience.

3. The members of the Committee shall be elected and shall serve in their personal capacity.

Article 29

1. The members of the Committee shall be elected by secret ballot from a list of persons possessing the qualifications prescribed in article 28 and nominated for the purpose by the States parties to the present Covenant.

2. Each State Party to the present Covenant may nominate not more than two persons. These persons shall be nationals of the nominating State.

3. A person shall be eligible for renomination.

Article 30

1. The initial election shall be held no later than six months after the date of the entry into force of the present Covenant.

2. At least four months before the date of each election to the Committee, other than an election to fill a vacancy declared in accordance with article 34, the Secretary-General of the United Nations shall address a written invitation to the States parties to the present Covenant to submit their nominations for membership of the Committee within three months.

3. The Secretary-General of the United Nations shall prepare a list in alphabetical order of all the persons thus nominated, with an indication of the States parties which have nominated them, and shall submit it to the States parties to the present Covenant no later than one month before the date of each election.

4. Elections of the members of the Committee shall be held at a meeting of the States parties to the present Covenant convened by the Secretary-General of the United Nations at the Headquarters of the United Nations. At that meeting, for which two thirds of the States parties to the present Covenant shall constitute a quorum, the persons elected to the Committee shall be those nominees who obtain the largest number of votes and an absolute majority of the votes of the representatives of States parties present and voting.

Article 31

1. The Committee may not include more than one national of the same State.

2. In the election of the Committee, consideration shall be given to equitable geographical distribution of membership and to the representation of the different forms of civilization and of the principal legal systems.

Article 32

1. The members of the Committee shall be elected for a term of four years. They shall be eligible for re-election if renominated. However, the terms of nine of the members elected at the first election shall expire at the end of two years; immediately after the first election, the names of these nine members shall be chosen by lot by the Chairman of the meeting referred to in article 30, paragraph 4.

2. Elections at the expiry of office shall be held in accordance with the preceding articles of this part of the present Covenant.

Article 33

1. If, in the unanimous opinion of the other members, a member of the Committee has ceased to carry out his functions for any cause other than absence of a temporary character, the Chairman of the Committee shall notify the Secretary-General of the United Nations, who shall then declare the seat of that member to be vacant.

2. In the event of the death or the resignation of a member of the Committee, the Chairman shall immediately notify the Secretary-General of the United Nations, who shall declare the seat vacant from the date of death or the date on which the resignation takes effect.

Article 34

1. When a vacancy is declared in accordance with article 33 and if the term of office of the member to be replaced does not expire within six months of the declaration of the vacancy, the Secretary-General of the United Nations shall notify each of the States parties to the present Covenant, which may within two months submit nominations in accordance with article 29 for the purpose of filling the vacancy.

2. The Secretary-General of the United Nations shall prepare a list in alphabetical order of the persons thus nominated and shall submit it to the States parties to the present Covenant. The election to fill the vacancy shall then take place in accordance with the relevant provisions of this part of the present Covenant.

3. A member of the Committee elected to fill a vacancy declared in accordance with article 33 shall hold office for the remainder of the term of the member who vacated the seat on the Committee under the provisions of that article.

Article 35

The members of the Committee shall, with the approval of the General Assembly of the United Nations, receive emoluments from United Nations resources on such terms and conditions as the General Assembly may decide, having regard to the importance of the Committee's responsibilities.

Article 36

The Secretary-General of the United Nations shall provide the necessary staff and facilities for the effective performance of the functions of the Committee under the present Covenant.

Article 37

1. The Secretary-General of the United Nations shall convene the initial meeting of the Committee at the Headquarters of the United Nations.

2. After its initial meeting, the Committee shall meet at such times as shall be provided in its rules of procedure.

3. The Committee shall normally meet at the Headquarters of the United Nations or at the United Nations Office at Geneva.

Article 38

Every member of the Committee shall, before taking up his duties, make a solemn declaration in open committee that he will perform his functions impartially and conscientiously.

Article 39

1. The Committee shall elect its officers for a term of two years. They may be re-elected.

2. The Committee shall establish its own rules of procedure, but these rules shall provide, *inter alia*, that:

(a) Twelve members shall constitute a quorum;

(b) Decisions of the Committee shall be made by a majority vote of the members present.

Article 40

1. The States parties to the present Covenant undertake to submit reports on the measures they have adopted which give effect to the rights recognized herein and on the progress made in the enjoyment of those rights:

(a) Within one year of the entry into force of the present Covenant for the States parties concerned;

(b) Thereafter whenever the Committee so requests.

2. All reports shall be submitted to the Secretary-General of the United Nations, who shall transmit them to the Committee for consideration. Reports shall indicate the factors and difficulties, if any, affecting the implementation of the present Covenant.

3. The Secretary-General of the United Nations may, after consultation with the Committee, transmit to the specialized agencies concerned copies of such parts of the reports as may fall within their field of competence.

4. The Committee shall study the reports submitted by the States parties to the present Covenant. It shall transmit its reports, and such general comments as it may consider appropriate, to the States parties. The Committee may also transmit to the Economic and Social Council these comments along with the copies of the reports it has received from States parties to the present Covenant.

5. The States parties to the present Covenant may submit to the Committee observations on any comments that may be made in accordance with paragraph 4 of this article.

Article 41

1. A State Party to the present Covenant may at any time declare under this article that it recognizes the competence of the Committee to receive and consider communications to the effect that a State Party claims that another State Party is not fulfilling its obligations under the present Covenant. Communications under this article may be received and considered only if submitted by a State Party which has made a declaration recognizing in regard to itself the competence of the Committee. No communication shall be received by the Committee if it concerns a State Party which has not made such a declaration. Communications received under this article shall be dealt with in accordance with the following procedure:

(a) If a State Party to the present Covenant considers that another State Party is not giving effect to the provisions of the present Covenant, it may, by written communication, bring the matter to the attention of that State Party. Within three months after the receipt of the communication the receiving State shall afford the State which sent the communication an explanation, or any other statement in writing clarifying the matter which should include, to the extent possible and pertinent, reference to domestic procedures and remedies taken, pending, or available in the matter;

(b) If the matter is not adjusted to the satisfaction of both States Parties concerned within six months after the receipt by the receiving State of the initial communication, either State shall have the right to refer the matter to the Committee, by notice given to the Committee and to the other State;

(c) The Committee shall deal with a matter referred to it only after it has ascertained that all available domestic remedies have been invoked and exhausted in the matter, in conformity with the generally recognized principles of international law. This shall not be the rule where the application of the remedies is unreasonably prolonged;

(d) The Committee shall hold closed meetings when examining communications under this article;

(e) Subject to the provisions of subparagraph (c), the Committee shall make available its good offices to the States Parties concerned with a view to a friendly solution of the matter on the basis of respect for human rights and fundamental freedoms as recognized in the present Covenant;

(f) In any matter referred to it, the Committee may call upon the States Parties concerned, referred to in subparagraph (b), to supply any relevant information;

(g) The States Parties concerned, referred to in subparagraph (b), shall have the right to be represented when the matter is being considered in the Committee and to make submissions orally and/or in writing;

(h) The Committee shall, within twelve months after the date of receipt of notice under subparagraph (b), submit a report:

(i) If a solution within the terms of subparagraph (e) is reached, the Committee shall confine its report to a brief statement of the facts and of the solution reached;

(ii) If a solution within the terms of subparagraph (e) is not reached, the Committee shall confine its report to a brief statement of the facts; the written submissions and record of the oral submissions made by the States Parties concerned shall be attached to the report. In every matter, the report shall be communicated to the States Parties concerned.

2. The provisions of this article shall come into force when ten States Parties to the present Covenant have made declarations under paragraph I of this article. Such declarations shall be deposited by the States Parties with the Secretary-General of the United Nations, who shall transmit copies thereof to the other States Parties. A declaration may be withdrawn at any time by notification to the Secretary-General. Such a withdrawal shall not prejudice the consideration of any matter which is the subject of a communication already transmitted under this article; no further communication by any State Party shall be received after the notification of withdrawal of the declaration has been received by the Secretary-General, unless the State Party concerned has made a new declaration.

Article 42

1. (a) If a matter referred to the Committee in accordance with article 41 is not resolved to the satisfaction of the States Parties concerned, the Committee may, with the prior consent of the States Parties concerned, appoint an ad hoc Conciliation Commission (hereinafter referred to as the Commission). The good offices of the Commission shall be made available to the States Parties concerned with a view to an amicable solution of the matter on the basis of respect for the present Covenant;

(b) The Commission shall consist of five persons acceptable to the States Parties concerned. If the States Parties concerned fail to reach agreement within three months on all or part of the composition of the Commission, the members of the Commission concerning whom no agreement has been reached shall be elected by secret ballot by a two-thirds majority vote of the Committee from among its members.

2. The members of the Commission shall serve in their personal capacity. They shall not be nationals of the States Parties concerned, or of a State not Party to the present Covenant, or of a State Party which has not made a declaration under article 41.

3. The Commission shall elect its own Chairman and adopt its own rules of procedure.

4. The meetings of the Commission shall normally be held at the Headquarters of the United Nations or at the United Nations Office at Geneva. However, they may be held at such other convenient places as the Commission may determine in consultation with the Secretary-General of the United Nations and the States Parties concerned.

5. The secretariat provided in accordance with article 36 shall also service the commissions appointed under this article.

6. The information received and collated by the Committee shall be made available to the Commission and the Commission may call upon the States Parties concerned to supply any other relevant information.

7. When the Commission has fully considered the matter, but in any event not later than twelve months after having been seized of the matter, it shall submit to the Chairman of the Committee a report for communication to the States Parties concerned:

(a) If the Commission is unable to complete its consideration of the matter within twelve months, it shall confine its report to a brief statement of the status of its consideration of the matter;

(b) If an amicable solution to the matter on tie basis of respect for human rights as recognized in the present Covenant is reached, the Commission shall confine its report to a brief statement of the facts and of the solution reached;

(c) If a solution within the terms of subparagraph (b) is not reached, the Commission's report shall embody its findings on all questions of fact relevant to the issues between the States Parties concerned, and its views on the possibilities of an amicable solution of the matter. This report shall also contain the written submissions and a record of the oral submissions made by the States Parties concerned;

(d) If the Commission's report is submitted under subparagraph (c), the States Parties concerned shall, within three months of the receipt of the report, notify the Chairman of the Committee whether or not they accept the contents of the report of the Commission.

8. The provisions of this article are without prejudice to the responsibilities of the Committee under article 41.

9. The States Parties concerned shall share equally all the expenses of the members of the Commission in accordance with estimates to be provided by the Secretary-General of the United Nations.

10. The Secretary-General of the United Nations shall be empowered to pay the expenses of the members of the Commission, if necessary, before reimbursement by the States Parties concerned, in accordance with paragraph 9 of this article.

Article 43

The members of the Committee, and of the *ad hoc* conciliation commissions which may be appointed under article 42, shall be entitled to the facilities, privileges and immunities of experts on mission for the United Nations as laid down in the relevant sections of the Convention on the Privileges and Immunities of the United Nations.

Article 44

The provisions for the implementation of the present Covenant shall apply without prejudice to the procedures prescribed in the field of human rights by or under the constituent instruments and the conventions of the United Nations and of the specialized agencies and shall not prevent the States Parties to the present Covenant from having recourse to other procedures for settling a dispute in accordance with general or special international agreements in force between them.

Article 45

The Committee shall submit to the General Assembly of the United Nations, through the Economic and Social Council, an annual report on its activities.

PART V

Article 46

Nothing in the present Covenant shall be interpreted as impairing the provisions of the Charter of the United Nations and of the constitutions of the specialized agencies which define the respective responsibilities of the various organs of the United Nations and of the specialized agencies in regard to the matters dealt with in the present Covenant.

Article 47

Nothing in the present Covenant shall be interpreted as impairing the inherent right of all peoples to enjoy and utilize fully and freely their natural wealth and resources.

PART VI

Article 48

1. The present Covenant is open for signature by any State Member of the United Nations or member of any of its specialized agencies, by any State Party to the Statute of the International Court of Justice, and by any other State which has been invited by the General Assembly of the United Nations to become a Party to the present Covenant.

2. The present Covenant is subject to ratification. Instruments of ratification shall be deposited with the Secretary-General of the United Nations.

3. The present Covenant shall be open to accession by any State referred to in paragraph 1 of this article.

4. Accession shall be effected by the deposit of an instrument of accession with the Secretary-General of the United Nations.

5. The Secretary-General of the United Nations shall inform all States which have signed this Covenant or acceded to it of the deposit of each instrument of ratification or accession.

Article 49

1. The present Covenant shall enter into force three months after the date of the deposit with the Secretary-General of the United Nations of the thirty-fifth instrument of ratification or instrument of accession.

2. For each State ratifying the present Covenant or acceding to it after the deposit of the thirty-fifth instrument of ratification or instrument of accession, the present Covenant shall enter into force three months after the date of the deposit of its own instrument of ratification or instrument of accession.

Article 50

The provisions of the present Covenant shall extend to all parts of federal States without any limitations or exceptions.

Article 51

1. Any State Party to the present Covenant may propose an amendment and file it with the Secretary-General of the United Nations. The Secretary-General of the United Nations shall thereupon communicate any proposed amendments to the States Parties to the present Covenant with a request that they notify him whether they favour a conference of States Parties for the purpose of considering and voting upon the proposals. In the event that at least one third of the States Parties favours such a conference, the Secretary-General shall convene the conference under the auspices of the United Nations. Any amendment adopted by a majority of the States Parties present and voting at the conference shall be submitted to the General Assembly of the United Nations for approval.

2. Amendments shall come into force when they have been approved by the General Assembly of the United Nations and accepted by a two-thirds majority of the States Parties to the present Covenant in accordance with their respective constitutional processes. 3. When amendments come into force, they shall be binding on those States Parties which have accepted them, other States Parties still being bound by the provisions of the present Covenant and any earlier amendment which they have accepted.

Article 52

1. Irrespective of the notifications made under article 48, paragraph 5, the Secretary-General of the United Nations shall inform all States referred to in paragraph I of the same article of the following particulars:

(a) Signatures, ratifications and accessions under article 48;

(b) The date of the entry into force of the present Covenant under article 49 and the date of the entry into force of any amendments under article 51.

Article 53

1. The present Covenant, of which the Chinese, English, French, Russian and Spanish texts are equally authentic, shall be deposited in the archives of the United Nations.

2. The Secretary-General of the United Nations shall transmit certified copies of the present Covenant to all States referred to in article 48.

International Covenant on Economic, Social and Cultural Rights

UNTS No. 14532, vol. 993 (1976), entered into force 23 March 1976.

PREAMBLE

The States parties to the present Covenant,

[1]Considering that, in accordance with the principles proclaimed in the Charter of the United Nations, recognition of the inherent dignity and of the equal and inalienable rights of all members of the human family is the foundation of freedom, justice and peace in the world,

[2]Recognizing that these rights derive from the inherent dignity of the human person,

[3]Recognizing that, in accordance with the Universal Declaration of Human Rights, the ideal of free human beings enjoying freedom from fear and want can only be achieved if conditions are created whereby everyone may enjoy his economic, social and cultural rights, as well as his civil and political rights,

[4]Considering the obligation of States under the Charter of the United Nations to promote universal respect for, and observance of, human rights and freedoms,

[5]Realizing that the individual, having duties to other individuals and to the community to which he belongs, is under a responsibility to strive for the promotion and observance of the rights recognized in the present Covenant, agree upon the following articles:

PART I

Article 1

1. All peoples have the right of self-determination. By virtue of that right they freely determine their political status and freely pursue their economic, social and cultural development.

2. All peoples may, for their own ends, freely dispose of their natural wealth and resources without prejudice to any obligations arising out of international economic co-operation, based upon the principle of mutual benefit, and international law. In no case may a people be deprived of its own means of subsistence.

3. The States parties to the present Covenant, including those having responsibility for the administration of Non-Self-Governing and Trust Territories, shall promote the realization of the right of self-determination, and shall respect that right, in conformity with the provisions of the Charter of the United Nations.

Article 2

1. Each State Party to the present Covenant undertakes to take steps, individually and through international assistance and co-operation, especially economic and technical, to the maximum of available resources, with a view to achieving progressively the full realization of the rights recognized in the present Covenant by all appropriate means, including particularly the adoption of legislative.

2. The States parties to the present Covenant undertake to guarantee that the rights enunciated in the present Covenant will be exercised without discrimination of any kind as to race, colour, sex, language, religion, political or other opinion, national or social or other status.

3. Developing countries, with due regards to human rights and their national economy, may determine to what extent they would guarantee the economic rights recognized in the present Covenant to non-nationals.

PART II

Article 3

The States parties to the present Covenant undertake to ensure the equal right of men and women to the enjoyment of all economic, social and cultural rights set forth in the present Covenant.

Article 4

The States parties to the present Covenant recognize that, in the enjoyment of those rights provided by the State in conformity with the present Covenant, the State may subject such rights only to such limitations as are determined by law only in so far as this may be compatible with the nature of these rights and solely for the purpose of promoting the general welfare in a democratic society.

Article 5

1. Nothing in the present Covenant may be interpreted as implying for any State, group or person any right to engage in any activity or to perform any act aimed at the destruction of any of the rights or freedoms recognized herein, or at their limitation to a greater extent than is provided for in the present Covenant.

2. No restriction upon or derogation from any of the fundamental human rights recognized or existing in any country in virtue of law, conventions, regulations or custom shall be admitted on the pretext that the present Covenant does not recognize such rights or that it recognizes them to a lesser extent.

PART III

Article 6

1. The States parties to the present Covenant recognize the right to work, which includes the right of everyone to the opportunity to gain his living by work which he freely chooses or accepts, and will take appropriate steps to safeguard this right.

2. The steps to be taken by a State Party to the present Covenant to achieve the full realization of this right shall include technical and vocational guidance and training programmes, policies and techniques to achieve steady economic, social and cultural development and full and productive employment under conditions safeguarding fundamental political and economic freedoms to the individual.

Article 7

The States parties to the present Covenant recognize the right of everyone to the enjoyment of just and favourable conditions of work, which ensure, in particular:

(a) remuneration which provides all workers, as a minimum, with:

(i) fair wages and equal remuneration for work of equal value without distinction of any kind, in particular women being guaranteed conditions of work not inferior to those enjoyed by men, with equal pay for equal work;

(ii) a decent living for themselves and their families in accordance with the provisions of the present Covenant;

(b) safe and healthy working conditions;

(c) equal opportunity for everyone to be promoted in his employment to an appropriate higher level, subject to no considerations other than those of seniority and competence;

(d) rest, leisure and reasonable limitation of working hours and periodic holidays with pay, as well as remuneration for public holidays.

Article 8

1. The States parties to the present Covenant undertake to ensure:

(a) the right of everyone to form trade unions and join the trade union of his choice, subject only to the rules of the organization concerned, for the promotion and protection of his economic and social interests. No restrictions may be placed on the exercise of this right other than those prescribed by law and which are necessary in a democratic society in the interests of national security or public order or for the protection of the rights and freedoms of others;

(b) the right of trade unions to establish national federations or confederations and the right of the latter to form or join international trade-union organizations;

(c) the right of trade unions to function freely subject to no limitations other than those prescribed by law and which are necessary in a democratic society in the interests of national security or public order or for the protection of the rights and freedoms of others;

(d) the right to strike, provided that it is exercised in conformity with the laws of the particular country.

2. This article shall not prevent the imposition of lawful restrictions on the exercise of these rights by members of the armed forces or of the police or of the administration of the State.

3. Nothing in this article shall authorize States parties to the International Labour Organisation Convention of 1948 concerning Freedom of Association and Protection of the Right to Organize' to take legislative measures which would prejudice, or apply the law in such a manner as would prejudice, the guarantees provided for in that Convention.

Article 9

The States parties to the present Covenant recognize the right of everyone to social security, including social insurance.

Article 10

The States parties to the present Covenant recognize that:

1. The widest possible protection and assistance should be accorded to the family, which is the natural and fundamental group unit of society, particularly for its establishment and while it is responsible for the care and education of dependent children. Marriage must be entered into with the free consent of the intending spouses.

2. Special protection should be accorded to mothers during a reasonable period before and after childbirth. During such period working mothers should be accorded paid leave or leave with adequate social security benefits.

3. Special measures of protection and assistance should be taken on behalf of all children and young persons without any discrimination for reasons of parentage or other conditions. Children and young persons should be protected from economic and social exploitation. Their employment in work harmful to their morals or health or dangerous to life or likely to hamper their normal development should be punishable by law. States should also set age limits below which the paid employment of child labour should be prohibited and punishable by law.

Article 11

1. The States parties to the present Covenant recognize the right of everyone to an adequate standard of living for himself and his family, including adequate food, clothing and housing, and to the continuous improvement of living conditions. The States parties will take appropriate steps to ensure the realization of this right, recognizing to this effect the essential importance of international co-operation based on free consent.

2. The States parties to the present Covenant, recognizing the fundamental right of everyone to be free from hunger, shall take, individually and through international co-operation, the measures, including specific programmes, which are needed:

(a) To improve methods of production, conservation and distribution of food by making full use of technical and scientific knowledge, by disseminating knowledge of the principles of nutrition and by developing or reforming agrarian systems in such a way as to achieve the most efficient development and utilization of natural resources;

(b) Taking into account the problems of both food-importing and food-exporting countries, to ensure an equitable distribution of world food supplies in relation to need.

Article 12

1. The States parties to the present Covenant recognize the right of everyone to the enjoyment of the highest attainable standard of physical and mental health.

2. The steps to be taken by the States parties to the present Covenant to achieve the full realization of this right shall include those necessary for:

(a) The provision for the reduction of the stillbirth-rate and of infant mortality and for the healthy development of the child;

(b) The improvement of all aspects of environmental and industrial hygiene;

(c) The prevention, treatment and control of epidemic, endemic,

occupational and other diseases;

(d) The creation of conditions which would assure to all medical service and medical attention in the event of sickness.

Article 13

1. The States parties to the present Covenant recognize the right of everyone to education. They agree that education shall be directed to the full development of the human personality and the sense of its dignity, and shall strengthen the respect for human rights and fundamental freedoms. They further agree that education shall enable all persons to participate effectively in a free society, promote understanding, tolerance and friendship among all nations and all racial, ethnic or religious groups, and further the activities of the United Nations for the maintenance of peace.

2. The States parties to the present Covenant recognize that, with a view to achieving the full realization of this right:

(a) Primary education shall be compulsory and available free to all;

(b) Secondary education in its different forms, including technical and vocational secondary education, shall be made generally available and accessible to all by every appropriate means, and in particular by the progressive introduction of free education;

(c) Higher education shall be made equally accessible to all, on the basis of capacity, by every appropriate means, and in particular by the progressive introduction of free education;

(d) Fundamental education shall be encouraged or intensified as far as possible for those persons who have not received or completed the whole period of their primary education;

(e) The development of a system of schools at all levels shall be actively pursued, an adequate fellowship system shall be established, and the material conditions of teaching staff shall be continuously improved.

3. The States parties to the present Covenant undertake to have respect for the liberty of parents and, when applicable, legal guardians to choose for their children schools, other than those established by the public authorities, which conform to such minimum educational standards as may be laid down or approved by the State and to ensure the religious and moral education of their children in conformity with their own convictions.

4. No part of this article shall be construed so as to interfere with the liberty of individuals and bodies to establish and direct educational institutions, subject always to the observance of the principles set forth in paragraph 1 of this article and to the requirement that the education given in such institutions shall conform to such minimum standards as may be laid down by the State.

Article 14

Each State Party to the present Covenant which, at the time of becoming a Party, has not been able to secure in its metropolitan territory or other territories under its jurisdiction compulsory primary education, free of charge, undertakes, within two years, to work out and adopt a detailed plan of action for the progressive implementation, within a reasonable number of years, to be fixed in the plan, of the principle of compulsory education free of charge for all.

Article 15

1. The States parties to the present Covenant recognize the right of everyone:

(a) To take part in cultural life;

(b) To enjoy the benefits of scientific progress and its applications;

(c) To benefit from the protection of the moral and material interests resulting from any scientific, literary or artistic production of which he is the author.

2. The steps to be taken by the States parties to the present Covenant to achieve the full realization of this right shall include those necessary for the conservation, the development and the diffusion of science and culture.

3. The States parties to the present Covenant undertake to respect the freedom indispensable for scientific research and creative activity.

4. The States parties to the present Covenant recognize the benefits to be derived from the encouragement and development of international contacts and co-operation in the scientific and cultural fields.

PART IV

Article 16

1. The States parties to the present Covenant undertake to submit in conformity with this part of the Covenant reports on the measures which they have adopted and the progress made in achieving the observance of the rights recognized herein.

2. (a) All reports shall be submitted to the Secretary-General of the United Nations, who shall transmit copies to the Economic and Social Council for consideration in accordance with the provisions of the present Covenant;

(b) The Secretary-General of the United Nations shall also transmit to the specialized agencies copies of the reports, or any relevant parts therefrom, from States parties to the present Covenant which are also members of these specialized agencies in so far as these reports, or parts therefrom, relate to any matters which fall within the responsibilities of the said agencies in accordance with their constitutional instruments.

Article 17

1. The States parties to the present Covenant shall furnish their reports in stages, in accordance with a programme to be established by the Economic and Social Council within one year of the entry into force of the present Covenant after consultation with the States parties and the specialized agencies concerned.

2. Reports may indicate factors and difficulties affecting the degree of fulfilment of obligations under the present Covenant.

3. Where relevant information has previously been furnished to the United Nations or to any specialized agency by any State Party to the present Covenant, it

will not be necessary to reproduce that information, but a precise reference to the information so furnished will suffice.

Article 18

Pursuant to its responsibilities under the Charter of the United Nations in the field of human rights and fundamental freedoms, the Economic and Social Council may make arrangements with the specialized agencies in respect of their reporting to it on the progress made in achieving the observance of the provisions of the present Covenant falling within the scope of their activities. These reports may include particulars of decisions and recommendations on such implementation adopted by their competent organs.

Article 19

The Economic and Social Council may transmit to the Commission on Human Rights for study and general recommendation or, as appropriate, for information the reports concerning human rights submitted by States in accordance with articles 16 and 17, and those concerning human rights submitted by the specialized agencies in accordance with article 18.

Article 20

The States parties to the present Covenant and the specialized agencies concerned may submit comments to the Economic and Social Council on any general recommendation under article 19 or reference to such general recommendation in any report of the Commission on Human Rights or any documentation referred to therein.

Article 21

The Economic and Social Council may submit from time to time to the General Assembly reports with recommendations of a general nature and a summary of the information received from the States parties to the present Covenant and the specialized agencies on the measures taken and the progress made in achieving general observance of the rights recognized in the present Covenant.

Article 22

The Economic and Social Council may bring to the attention of other organs of the United Nations, their subsidiary organs and specialized agencies concerned with furnishing technical assistance any matters arising out of the reports referred to in this part of the present Covenant which may assist such bodies in deciding, each within its field of competence, on the advisability of international measures likely to contribute to the effective progressive implementation of the present Covenant.

Article 23

The States parties to the present Covenant agree that international action for the achievement of the rights recognized in the present Covenant includes such methods as the conclusion of conventions, the adoption of recommendations, the furnishing of technical assistance and the holding of regional meetings and technical meetings for the purpose of consultation and study organized in conjunction with the Governments concerned.

Article 24

Nothing in the present Covenant shall be interpreted as impairing the provisions of the Charter of the United Nations and of the constitutions of the specialized agencies which define the respective responsibilities of the various organs of the United Nations and of the specialized agencies in regard to the matters dealt with in the present Covenant.

Article 25

Nothing in the present Covenant shall be interpreted as impairing the inherent right of all peoples to enjoy and utilize fully and freely their natural wealth and resources.

PART V

Article 26

1. The present Covenant is open for signature by any State Member of the United Nations or member of any of its specialized agencies, by any State Party to the Statute of the International Court of Justice, and by any other State which has been invited by the General Assembly of the United Nations to become a party to the present Covenant.

2. The present Covenant is subject to ratification. Instruments of ratification shall be deposited with the Secretary-General of the United Nations.

3. The present Covenant shall be open to accession by any State referred to in paragraph 1 of this article.

4. Accession shall be effected by the deposit of an instrument of accession with the Secretary-General of the United Nations.

5. The Secretary-General of the United Nations shall inform all States which have signed the present Covenant or acceded to it of the deposit of each instrument of ratification or accession.

Article 27

1. The present Covenant shall enter into force three months after the date of the deposit with the Secretary-General of the United Nations of the thirty-fifth instrument of ratification or instrument of accession.

2. For each State ratifying the present Covenant or acceding to it after the deposit of the thirty-fifth instrument of ratification or instrument of accession, the present Covenant shall enter into force three months after the date of the deposit of its own instrument of ratification or instrument of accession.

Article 28

The provisions of the present Covenant shall extend to all parts of federal States without any limitations or exceptions.

Article 29

1. Any State Party to the present Covenant may propose an amendment and file it with the Secretary-General of the United Nations. The Secretary-General shall thereupon communicate any proposed amendments to the States parties to the present Covenant with a request that they notify him whether they favour a Conference of States parties for the purpose of considering and voting upon the proposals. In the event that at least one third of the States parties favours such a conference, the Secretary-General shall convene the conference under the auspices of the United Nations. Any amendment adopted by a majority of the States parties present and voting at the conference shall be submitted to the General Assembly of the United Nations for approval.

2. Amendments shall come into force when they have been approved by the General Assembly of the United Nations and accepted by a two-thirds majority of the States parties to the present Covenant in accordance with their respective constitutional processes.

3. When amendments come into force they shall be binding on those States parties which have accepted them, other States parties still being bound by the provisions of the present Covenant and any earlier amendment which they have accepted.

Article 30

Irrespective of the notifications made under article 26, paragraph 5, the Secretary-General of the United Nations shall inform all States referred to in paragraph 1 of the same article of the following particulars:

(a) Signatures, ratifications and accessions under article 26;

(b) The date of the entry into force of the present Covenant under article 27 and the date of the entry into force of any amendments under article 29.

Article 31

1. The present Covenant, of which the Chinese, English, French, Russian and Spanish texts are equally authentic, shall be deposited in the archives of the United Nations.

2. The Secretary-General of the United Nations shall transmit certified copies of the present Covenant to all States referred to in article 26.

Index

Y

Z

About the Author

Dr. Curtis F.J. Doebbler is an international human rights lawyer with almost two decades of experience representing individuals before international human rights bodies in the United Nations, European, African and Inter-American systems for the protection of human rights. He has advised governments and non-government organizations on international human rights law and he has taught international human rights law at universities in Africa, Europe, Asia and the Middle East and lectured at law schools in the United States and South America. His articles on diverse subjects of politics and law are regularly published in both scholarly journals and national newspapers.

Dr. Doebbler can be contacted by email at:
Curtis@Doebbler.net

Dr. Doebbler's personal web page can be accessed at:
http://international-lawyers.org

CDPublishing™ can be contacted by email at:

Sales@cdpublishing.org

To purchase books from CD Publishing go to:

cdpublishing.org

Other Publications by
Curtis F.J. Doebbler

Doebbler, C.F.J., *Introduction to International Humanitarian Law* (pp. x/212"X7") (2005). Paperback: US$16.99, ISBN 978-0-9743570-6-5.

Doebbler, C.F.J., *International Human Rights Law: Cases and Materials* (pp. xxxiv/974, 2004) Paperback: US$49.95, ISBN 978-0-9743570-0-3 (also available in two volumes).

Doebbler, C.F.J., (Добблер, К.Ф.Д.), *Изучение Международного Права Прав Человека* (Russian) (2004). Paperback: US$15.00, ISBN 978-0-9743570-1-0.

International Study Team, (containing contributions by C.F.J. Doebbler), *Our Common Responsibility: The Impact of a New War on Iraqi Children* (2003). Paperback: US$15.00 and electronic book format: US$6.50.

Doebbler, C.F.J., (compiled by), *Selected Human Rights Treaties in Arabic and English* (2002). Paperback: US$12.50 and electronic book format: US$5.

Doebbler, C.F.J., (with the collaboration of Ahmed, J., and Dabhoiwala, M.), *Handbook for Using the Internet for Teaching and Research in Political Science* (2002). Paperback (spiral bound): US$10.00 and electronic book format: US$4.

Doebbler, C.F.J., *Handbook on the Human Rights Approach to Health* (2002). Paperback: US$10.00 and electronic book format: US$4.50.

[Postage charges are additional.]

All of these publications can be purchased
in printed or electronic form from:

CD Publishing
http://cdpublishing.filetap.com
email: cdpublishing@publicist.com

9 780974 357027